MW00784052

Compliments of...

wesleyan publishing house

P.O. Box 50434

Indianapolis, IN 46250-0434

Call: 800.493.7539 • Fax: 800.788.3535

E-mail: wph@wesleyan.org • Online: www.wesleyan.org/wph

Please send copies of any review or mention.

GALATIANS, PHILIPPIANS, COLOSSIANS

GALATIANS, PHILIPPIANS, COLOSSIANS

A Commentary for Bible Students

EARLE L. WILSON, ALEX R. G. DEASLEY, AND BARRY L. CALLEN

WESLEYAN BIBLE COMMENTARY SERIES

GENERAL PUBLISHER
Donald D. Cady

EXECUTIVE EDITOR
David W. Holdren, D.D., S.T.D.

EDITORIAL ADVISORY COMMITTEE

Joseph D. Allison, M.Div.
Coordinator of Communications and
Publishing
Church of God Ministries

Ray E. Barnwell, D.D.
District Superintendent, Illinois
The Wesleyan Church

Barry L. Callen, M.Div., M.Th., D.Rel., Ed.D.
University Professor of Christian Studies
Emeritus, Anderson University
Special Assistant to General Director, Church
of God Ministries

Ray Easley, M.Div., Ed.D.
Vice President of Academic Affairs
Wesley Biblical Seminary

Maj. Dorothy Hitzka
National Consultant for Christian Education
The Salvation Army

Arthur Kelly
Coordinator of Christian Education
and Congregational Life
Church of God Ministries

Stephen J. Lennox, Ph.D.
Professor of Bible and Chair, Division
of Religion and Philosophy
Indiana Wesleyan University

Bonnie J. Perry
Director
Beacon Hill Press of Kansas City

Dan Tipton, D.Min.
General Superintendent (retired)
Churches of Christ in Christian Union

John Van Valin
Free Methodist Pastor
Indianapolis, Indiana

EDITORS
Lawrence W. Wilson, M.Div.
Managing Editor

Stephen J. Lennox, Ph.D.
Theological Editor

Darlene Teague, M.Div.
Senior Editor

CONTENTS

EXECUTIVE EDITOR'S PREFACE

Life change. That, we believe, is the goal of God's written revelation. God has given His written Word so that we might know Him and become like Him—holy, as He is holy.

Life change is also the goal of this book, a volume in the Wesleyan Bible Commentary Series. This series has been created with the primary aim of promoting life change in believers by applying God's authoritative truth in relevant, practical ways. This commentary will impact Bible students with fresh insight into God's unchanging Word. Read it with your Bible in hand.

A second purpose of this series is to assist laypersons and pastors in their teaching ministries. Anyone called to assist others in Christian growth and service will appreciate the practical nature of these commentaries. Writers were selected based on their ability to soundly interpret God's Word and apply that unchanging truth in fresh, practical ways. Each biblical book is explained paragraph by paragraph, giving the reader both the big picture and sufficient detail to understand the meaning of significant words and phrases. Their results of scholarly research are presented in enough detail to clarify, for example, the meaning of important Greek or Hebrew words, but not in such a way that readers are overwhelmed. This series will be an invaluable tool for preaching, lesson preparation, and personal or group Bible study.

The third aim of this series is to present a Wesleyan-Arminian interpretation of Scripture in a clear and compelling fashion. Toward that end, the series has been developed with the cooperative effort of scholars, pastors, and church leaders in the Wesleyan, Nazarene, Free Methodist, Salvation Army, Church of God (Anderson), Churches of Christ in Christian Union, Brethren in Christ, and United Methodist denominations. These volumes present reliable interpretation of biblical texts in the tradition of John Wesley, Adam Clarke, and other renowned interpreters.

Throughout the production of this series, authors and editors have approached each Bible passage with this question in mind: How will my life change when I fully understand and apply this scripture?

Let that question be foremost in your mind also, as God speaks again through His Word.

DAVID W. HOLDREN

GALATIANS

EARLE L. WILSON

INTRODUCTION TO GALATIANS

When we read Philippians, we feel the warm breezes of pastoral love and apostolic joy. When reading Ephesians, we are uplifted in spirit by reflecting on the body of Christ. In Romans we sense immediately that we are in the presence of a master theologian rejoicing in the doctrines of grace.

Galatians is different. In this epistle we hear the thunder roll. From beginning to end, in all six chapters, many of the 149 verses abound with sarcasm and some with anger. Whatever tenderness there is in Galatians, it is limited to a one-time reference by Paul to the Galatians as "dear children" (4:19). The context reminds us of a mother disturbed by the anticipation of pain that she might have to endure because her children, who should have known better, are in danger of committing spiritual suicide. The general tone of the letter reflects Paul's astonishment that these people were departing so quickly from the truth of the gospel. He actually feared that they had been "bewitched" and deceived. He is obviously frustrated by this and, as J. B. Phillips translates it, calls them "my dear idiots" (3:1).

When you read Paul's letter to the Galatians you will ask the following questions: Who were the opponents to the gospel in Galatia with whom Paul was so angry? What was the reaction of the Galatians to Paul's message? What is the message for believers today who, like the Galatians, have been called to salvation in "this present evil age" (1:4)? As you study the letter to the Galatians by using this commentary, you will find a sincere attempt to answer these and other such questions, which were critical to them and now to us.

AUTHOR

That the epistle was written by Paul has never been seriously challenged. In fact, his authorship is upheld by the unanimous testimony of the ancient church. The apostolic fathers—Clement, Ignatius, Polycarp, and Justin Martyr—make indirect citations to this fact in their writings. Added to the external evidence, we have the internal evidence of Paul's authorship by allusions to his personal history and by his self-portrayal. The apostle's way of thinking and his personal characteristics are indelibly expressed in the letter.

Galatians contains an important autobiographical reference of Paul not found anywhere else in his writings. He spoke, in this letter, of a "previous way of life in Judaism," his ardor for the "traditions of [his] fathers," and his great zeal as a persecutor of the Christians (1:13–14). He is the founder of the Galatian churches (1:6–8); they are a product of his second missionary journey (Acts 16:6). During that journey he suffered bodily weakness (4:13) and was compelled to pause in Galatia. During his stay he planted Christianity there.

It will be helpful to know something of Paul's background. He was brought up in a Jewish family of the Diaspora, a term that refers to the scattering of an estimated 4.5 million Jews throughout the Roman Empire. It is likely that during this period there were more Jews in Rome than in Jerusalem. There is little doubt that some of these Jews scattered throughout the empire were removed both from the strict traditions of Judaism as well as from its cultic center and official headquarters in Judea. It is apparent, however, that Paul's family maintained strong personal ties with Palestinian Judaism. Jerome, writing in Bethlehem in A.D. 492, recorded an ancient tradition that Paul's hometown was the Palestinian village of Giscalis. If this is the case, and we have no historical evidence that it was, it probably suggests that Paul's father was associated with this village and then, after the capture of Jerusalem by Pompey in 63 B.C., migrated to Tarsus. We do know that Paul had relatives, including a nephew and a sister, who were residents of Jerusalem during the episode of the Jewish conspiracy against his life there (Acts 23:12–22).

Paul was trained as a tentmaker and, having completed his early education at the local synagogue in Tarsus, he went to Jerusalem to study under the great Rabbi Gamaliel in the Pharisaic school. From Gamaliel, Paul learned the intricacies of biblical interpretation that he would use in his writings, not only in Galatians but also in other letters.

Paul was a scholar in the finest sense of that word. This will commend him, after his conversion, to the early church and to the church of subsequent centuries and localities. Unlike some scholars, Paul was also an activist. Judaism spread throughout the Roman Empire as it did because of the fervent missionary spirit that guided Paul and other zealots of Judaism. The Pharisaic Judaism of Palestine, to which Paul was committed fully, was especially known for its aggressive proselytism. Jesus was aware of that himself when He rebuked the Pharisees: "You hypocrites!" (Matt. 23:15). Could it be that Paul was so anxious to advance in Judaism "beyond many Jews of my own age" (Gal. 1:14) that he had already committed himself as a full-time missionary, perhaps with a special orientation to the Gentile world, prior to his encounter with the risen Lord on the Damascus Road? Of course, then he was a missionary intent on winning converts to Judaism and obedience to the law, including the requirement of circumcision.

What wonderful providence that God would have chosen one like Paul to be His messenger in introducing Christianity and the cross to the Gentile world. Little wonder that Paul's letter to the Galatians attracted so much attention and caused so much concern among those who struggled to loosen their grip on the requirements of the law as an addendum to the gospel. Paul understood both Gentile and Jewish worlds.

He was also acquainted with the mystery religions of the East. He knew that his message about the resurrection of Christ from the dead was not the introduction of a new deity, as some suggested. Two crucial aspects of the Christian message that Paul proclaimed stood in irreconcilable contrast to the ancient mystery religions: its historicity and its exclusivity. Unlike the gospels of the mystery gods, he was fully convinced that the death and resurrection of Jesus were not timeless events, but were attached to a definite historical period. As the Apostles' Creed confesses, Jesus was crucified "under Pontius Pilate" and raised from the dead "on the third day." Paul knew that Christianity required undivided loyalty to one Lord; for just as there is only one God, so also there is only mediator between God and us, "the man Christ Jesus" (1 Tim. 2:5).

This was the person, Paul the great apostle, who was chosen by God to deliver God's message of salvation apart from the law to the world of his day and through his letters, to the world of our day.

DATE OF WRITING

There is nothing in the letter itself to indicate definitely either the time or the place of the writing. From Acts 14 and 16, we gather that Paul was in Galatia at least twice; the epistle may have been written subsequent to the journey he took across Asia Minor on his third missionary tour (Acts 18:22–19:1). The truth is, the date of Galatians has been and continues to be a rather difficult problem. Some place the date of writing after Paul's second missionary journey; others argue for a date near the end of the third missionary journey, when Paul was resident in Corinth.

Depending on one's point of view as to the destination of the letter, whether to the churches located in north central Asia Minor (Pessinus, Ancyra, and Tavium) or to the churches in the southern area of the Roman province (Antioch, Iconium, Lystra, and Derbe), the date will range from as early as A.D. 51 to A.D. 57. Most Bible scholars agree that it belongs to the period of the legalist controversy and, therefore, to the second group of Paul's epistles. That would place the date of the writing in the later, rather than an earlier, period of the third missionary journey.[1]

PURPOSE AND ANALYSIS

Paul visited Galatia during all three of his missionary journeys. Galatia in Paul's day was central Asia Minor, which is modern-day Turkey and some surrounding territories. On his second visit to Galatia, Paul found that false teachers were at work among the churches and had, in fact, succeeded in troubling and confusing them. We learn from Paul himself (1:6–9) that this teaching was directly subversive to the gospel and, therefore, opposed to the fundamental truths of Christianity.

The epistle is intensely polemical. It becomes a controversial letter in two disputes: (1) Paul's apostleship, and (2) the nature of the gospel and the sufficiency of faith in Christ for full salvation. These disputes are treated in the first two main parts of the epistle. The third section is of a moral and hortatory nature. Paul could not tolerate the Galatian apostasy. One imagines that Paul hopes rebuke will be convincing where reason has not. A great deal is at stake, not simply Paul's authority as an apostle (though that must in no way be minimized) but the truth of the gospel itself.

The people against whom Paul was defending himself and his gospel were the Judaizers, the teachers who sought to add certain strictures of the Jewish law, notably circumcision, as a requirement for inclusion in the Christian church. He wished to put them right and call them back from Judaism in order that they may preserve faith in Christ alone and receive from Christ the hope of salvation and of His promises, because no one is saved by the works of the law. So, in order to show that what they were adding was wrong, he wished to confirm the truth of his gospel.

It is interesting to note that both Luther and Calvin accepted this traditional view and forwarded it unaltered, except that they found a direct analogy between the opponents Paul faced in Galatia and those they faced who refused to embrace the gospel of grace in their day. Calvin called them "the false apostles, who had deceived the Galatians to advance their own claims, pretending that they had received a commission from the apostles. Their method of infiltration was to convince people that they represented the apostles and delivered a message from them. But they took away from Paul the name and authority of the apostle . . . in attacking Paul they were really attacking the truth of the gospel."[2]

So we have in this epistle the teaching of those who denied the doctrine of justification through the atoning death of Christ and faith in Him. These false teachers were teaching that the only way by which anyone, whether Jew or Gentile, could obtain life was by keeping the Law of Moses and establishing his own righteousness. This legalism was brought to Galatia; they demanded circumcision and observation of other features of the law. They fully intended to upset the teaching of Paul by maintaining that he was not one of the primary Twelve, that he could be invested with only a secondary and subordinate rank and authority, and that his teaching of a gospel free from conformity to the Law of Moses might be set aside. They tried to prove that Paul himself was inconsistent since he preached circumcision at some points in time and for some men, but at other times he was willing to accommodate his message to the prejudices of his converts. They did what they could to turn the affections of the Galatian people from Paul. To a great degree, they succeeded.

No wonder Paul so vehemently defends his authority as an apostle. He intends to prove the validity of his commission and, at the same time, to set forth again the doctrine of justification by faith. He reminds the Galatian Christians of genuine spiritual religion in contrast to the Mosaic Law and a religion of externals.

ENDNOTES

1. For a more detailed account of the date and recipients of the letter see Timothy George, *Galatians,* The New American Commentary (Nashville, Tenn.: Broadman and Holman, 1994), pp. 38–56.

2. John Calvin, *The Epistles of Paul to the Galatians, Ephesians, Philippians, and Colossians,* Calvin's New Testament Commentary, vol. 11, trans. T. H. L. Parker (Grand Rapids, Mich.: William B. Eerdmans, 1965), p. 114.

OUTLINE OF GALATIANS

I. Historical and personal (1:1–2:21)
- A. Apostolic salutation (1:1–5)
- B. Apostolic denunciation (1:6–9)
- C. Apostolic authentication (1:10–2:21)
  1. Calling (1:11–12)
  2. Conversion (1:13–17)
  3. First visit to Jerusalem (1:18–24)
  4. Second visit to Jerusalem (2:1–10)
     - a. The case of Titus and circumcision (2:1–3)
     - b. False brothers (2:4–5)
  5. Incident at Antioch (2:11–13)
  6. Protest with Peter (2:14)
  7. The principle (2:15–21)

II. Doctrinal: liberty and faith (3:1–4:31)
- A. The Galatians' experience (3:1–5)
- B. The case of Abraham (3:6–9)
- C. Christ and the curse (3:10–12)
- D. The promised redemption (3:13–14)
- E. The law and the promise (3:15–18)
- F. The purpose of the law (3:19–25)
- G. Sons and servants (3:26–4:11)
- H. Paul's personal appeal (4:12–20)
- I. The analogy of Hagar and Sarah (4:21–31)

III. Practical and ethical (5:1–6:10)
- A. Freedom in Christ (5:1–12)
- B. Flesh and Spirit (5:13–26)
  1. Life in the Spirit (5:16–18)
  2. Works of the flesh (5:19–21)
  3. Fruit of the Spirit (5:22–26)
- C. Freedom in service (6:1–10)

IV. Conclusion and benediction (6:11–18)
- A. The apostolic seal (6:11–16)
- B. The brand marks of Christ (6:17)
- C. The benediction (6:18)

Part One

A Historical and Personal Defense

GALATIANS 1:1–2:21

A SALUTATION AND A DENUNCIATION

Galatians 1:1–9

Because Paul faced special and difficult problems with the church in Galatia, his salutation is particularly important. He needed to provide a clear and concise statement regarding his apostolic calling and work. He also knew it was necessary for him, at the beginning of the letter, to include a detailed declaration of the saving work of Jesus Christ. Therefore, even in the salutation we are confronted with the two major themes that will dominate Paul's letter to the Galatians: the vindication of his own apostolic authority and the divine initiative God has taken to redeem men and women through His Son, Jesus Christ, and Him alone.

1. APOSTOLIC SALUTATION 1:1–5

In the first century it was a common practice, both in the Jewish and Greek traditions, to begin a letter with a salutation that included the name of the sender, that of the recipient, and some formula of greeting. The greeting usually used was *chairein,* which literally means "rejoice" but was so commonly used that it came to mean welcome or hello.[1]

The apostle Paul began each of his letters with a salutation. Rather than using the everyday word for greetings, he gave the Christian world a new and distinctive Christian expression: "Grace and peace." Having said hello, usually he added a word of blessing or prayer of thanksgiving for the person or people to whom he was writing. And, as we often do today in writing letters, Paul adapted his salutations to fit the unique circumstances of a particular person or place.

The Galatian salutation is interesting in what it does not contain. There is not the traditional prayer of thanksgiving that Paul usually employed as he began his other letters. (See Rom. 1:8–10; 1 Cor. 1:4–9; 1 Thess. 1:2–3.) Rather, he lashed out at the Galatians with his statement of astonishment that they had become apostate so soon after they had received his word of truth: **I am astonished that you are so quickly deserting** (1:6). Since the words of blessing and affirmation are missing from this salutation and the word of rebuke given instead, we can expect to hear strong, emotional, and intense language in the letter that follows. We are not disappointed.

A great deal was at stake, including the heart of the gospel as Paul had proclaimed it to the Galatians. Paul was drawing a theological line in the sand against the false teachers who had done so much damage to the Galatian church by undermining the gospel and his apostolic authority in the process: **Paul . . . sent not from men nor by man** (1:1).[2] One can only imagine how painful it must have been to Paul when he first became aware that spurious teachers were questioning the validity of his apostolic call. Even more painful for him was to discover that the Galatians, his own converts, were so readily giving credence to those who were maligning him. The primary concern was not for him personally (though that concern was enormous) but more serious was the devastating injury to the spiritual life of the Galatians themselves. It was one thing to entertain suspicions regarding the reputation of Paul as an apostle; it was quite another to cherish suspicions as to the divine character of the truth they had been taught by him. He had no choice but to deal with this immediately. Paul declared boldly and emphatically that his commission was direct from God, and he bore the same stamp as that of the other apostles, whose authority the false teachers had not the courage to deny.

It is important to understand the meaning of the word *apostle*.[3] An apostle is one who is dispatched or sent forth. Applied to a person, the apostle is not only a messenger but also the delegate of the person who sends him. He is entrusted with a mission and has powers conferred upon him. Paul called himself **an apostle**. Without question this was his

24

favorite term of self-designation and occurs in eight of the twelve letters in the New Testament that bear his name. The word *apostle* was known across the Jewish world since the term was in common use. It was the title borne by those who were dispatched from Jerusalem by the rulers of the Jews on any mission throughout Judea, particularly those who had the responsibility of collecting tribute to be paid for Temple service. After the destruction of Jerusalem in A.D. 70, these Jewish apostles formed a council of sorts to assist the Jewish patriarch in his deliberations at home and in executing his orders abroad. Therefore, when Jesus designated His immediate and most favored disciples "apostles," our Lord was not introducing a new term, but adopting one that already carried the idea of a highly responsible envoy. When first instituted as an office in the Christian community, the apostles were twelve in number, but there is no indication in Scripture that the number was intended to be limited to twelve any more than that the number of deacons was to be limited to seven. In establishing himself as an apostle, Paul was reminding the church of the high honor Christ bestows on His chosen servants.

Paul was called **by Jesus Christ and God the Father, who raised him from the dead** (1:1). This is strong, positive language. Negatively Paul qualified his calling by saying it was neither from men, that is, from a human source, nor by men, that is, mediated through any particular person, whether Peter, James, Ananias, or whomever. Then comes the strong positive: **but by Jesus Christ and God the Father, who raised him from the dead**. Paul separated Jesus Christ from all other humans and placed Him on the side of God. This was not a denial of the humanity of Jesus, but it was a witness to the fact that Jesus was more than a mere man. He is qualitatively different from every other human being both in respect to His unique relationship to the Father and to His sinless life. One cannot overstate how critical this was to Paul; if Jesus Christ were not fully divine, He could never have redeemed us from the curse of the law or freed us from the power of sin by His death on the cross.

And all the brothers with me . . . (1:2). Paul was not only concerned about his own reputation under attack, but also he wanted to make it clear that he and other believers were one with them in Christ, in the belief of and fidelity to the truth, in the arduous task of pioneer Christian work, and in building up and consolidating the church. This is a not-so-subtle means by Paul of promoting fellowship of believers and affirming the unifying force of redemption. It may be necessary, in ecclesiastical structures, to have ministerial ranks for maintaining order and discipline, but Christ, the Head of the church, teaches the law of religious equality: "you have only one Master and you are all brothers" (Matt. 23:8).

Grace and peace to you from God (1:3). Each of Paul's letters begins with a reference to **grace and peace**. Grace (*charis*) is closely related to the common Greek word for hello (*chaire*). In Paul's view, grace is synonymous with Jesus Christ; Paul never speaks of it as something impersonal. Rather, grace is God's unmerited goodwill given freely and effectively in the saving work of Jesus Christ. Peace results from a state of wholeness and freedom that the grace of God brings. It is a peace of conscience, a quietness and tranquility of mind because one has been reconciled to God. It is peace with God's creatures, with angels, with the godly, in our hearts, and with our enemies. Grace releases us from sin; peace makes the conscience quiet. We are tormented by sin and guilt, but Christ triumphs over both through grace and peace. It is important to note that Paul distinguishes grace and peace in the Christian context from all other grace and peace. He wishes for the Galatians grace and peace not from some earthly monarch, but from God our Father. This is God's grace and heavenly peace. This double blessing comes from a single source—the one God who knows himself as Father, Son, and Holy Spirit.

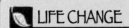

LIFE CHANGE

WORSHIPING GOD

Such a great God is worthy of our highest praise. To contemplate who God is and what He has done in Jesus Christ is to fall on our knees in worship and praise. We study the great doctrines of the Christian faith not simply out of curiosity, but that we might come more fully to love and enjoy the gracious God who delights in our praise.

Gave himself (1:4). Paul had already referred to the resurrection in verse 1, but in verse 4 he brought into consideration the suffering and death of Christ on the cross. Christ himself gave us His own description of His mission in Mark 10:45: "to serve, and to give his life." Paul further developed this wonderful theme in the kenotic hymn in Philippians 2:5–11: Jesus became "obedient to death—even death on a cross." Do not say that Christ's death was an accident or that He was forced to die. He willingly submitted himself to fulfill the divine purpose of His Father. His death was voluntary—**gave himself for our sins** (1:4). His death was vicarious; the death of God's Son can reconcile us to the Father.

The purpose for Christ's giving himself is clear—**to rescue us** (1:4). The presence of evil in society is obvious, and it manifests itself through desires and principles that are contrary to God's nature and will for humanity. Salvation is both personal and cosmic. Paul was concerned for his readers' personal salvation to be sure, but he also was thinking of God's redemptive purpose in the wider cosmic arena. Martin Luther and other Reformation theologians stressed the point that Galatians is about individual salvation and justification by faith. Such a limited interpretation is understandable against the backdrop of the world of their day. However, the language **present evil age** suggests historic, cosmic, and eschatological implications in Jesus' rescuing us. All of this unfolds **according to the will of our God and Father** (1:4). It was the will of God that we should be saved. Christ was the appointed agent of that salvation. The sacrifice of Christ was voluntary.

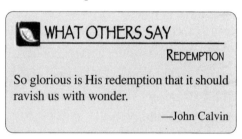

WHAT OTHERS SAY

REDEMPTION

So glorious is His redemption that it should ravish us with wonder.

—John Calvin

2. APOSTOLIC DENUNCIATION 1:6–9

How quickly Paul moved from the salutation into the body of the letter itself. The thanksgiving section that usually comes at this point of Paul's letters is omitted in Galatians. Rather than giving thanks for the Galatians and their advance of the gospel, Paul expressed astonishment at their apostasy. He charged them with **deserting** and **turning to a different gospel** (1:6). There is an expression of irritation, irony, and surprise in the use of Paul's word *astonished*. God had blessed the efforts of Paul and Barnabas in their ministry in Galatia in spite of strong opposition. Many were won to Christ, churches were planted, elders appointed, and miracles witnessed.

One can only imagine Paul's disappointment and spiritual pain that the people who had begun the race so well were "so quickly" turning to a false gospel. How could people so soundly converted become ship-wrecked so soon?

It is encouraging to note that while Paul was frustrated with the Galatians, and perhaps even angry, he did not give up on them. Instead he wrote this letter in hopes of winning them back from the verge of spiritual collapse and ruin.

Young believers are fragile. We need to remember that in our efforts to disciple people. We can be sure that whenever there is a genuine moving of the Spirit of God and the work of God's kingdom is advanced, Satan will be at work casting doubt, sowing discord, and wreaking havoc. Our service for Christ is shoddy when we lead men and women to profess faith in Christ, leave them vulnerable to Satan's worst, and fail to nurture them as babies in Christ.

A different gospel (1:6). Actually, the Galatians were following a perverted gospel, not another gospel. There is one way of salvation by Christ whereby all are to be saved; the false teachers disrupting the believers were subverting that one gospel. It seems there were several spurious gospels in circulation in the early Christian church. How disturbing to Paul that not only were these Galatians defecting from him, but they were switching their allegiance from the true gospel to a perverted one. In truth they were deserting God. Paul used a present tense verb to describe what they were doing: **you are . . . deserting** or "you are in process of leaving," which indicates that their apostasy was not yet complete. Paul had great faith in God's ability to bring them back, for he declares that "we will reap a harvest if we do not give up" (6:9).

It is interesting to note that Paul did not identify the false teachers who were leading the Galatian believers away from the true gospel. He merely stated that **some people are throwing you into confusion** (1:7). The confusion came from their creating divisions and tampering with the gospel. When you tamper with the gospel, you trouble the church. The greatest troublemakers are not those outside the church who oppose and persecute, but those inside the church who try to change the gospel in some way. In this case they were professing to maintain the gospel but were adding to it something of their own out of the law—a salvation by works. In this way they perverted and turned the gospel of Christ upside down. Any teaching that maintains that justification is partly by Christ and partly by the merit of good works is a perverting of the gospel; it contradicts the primary premise of the gospel, which is to exalt Christ as our one and only Savior.

KEY IDEAS

FROM THE LAW TO THE GOSPEL

The Law	Judaism	The Gospel
Ceremonial	Gospel + Law	Grace
Sacrifices	Circumcision	Cross and Resurrection

It is critical that we have it settled in our minds forever that there is only one, true gospel, and it is the gospel that Paul himself preached. Because this is so important, Paul proclaimed a solemn curse on anyone who proclaimed a counterfeit gospel. Paul could not have used stronger words to denounce false teachers and, in fact, actually repeated them for emphasis. There may not be a stronger word of denunciation in all of Scripture. How strong is his word? Note that he brought himself and angels under the purview of his denunciation: **if we or an angel . . . preach [another] gospel . . . let him be eternally condemned!** (1:8). As Luther put it, "Here Paul is breathing fire. His zeal is so fervent that he almost begins to curse the angels themselves."[4]

ENDNOTES

1. Timothy George, *Galatians,* The New American Commentary (Nashville, Tenn.: Broadman and Holman, 1994), p. 76.

2. The name *Paul* in Greek literally means "small" or "little." The earliest physical description we have of Paul depicts him as "a man small of stature, with a bald head and crooked eyes" (E. Hennecke and W. Schneemelcher, eds. *New Testament Apocrypha* [Philadelphia: Westminster, 1964], p. 2:354).

3. See the discussion of *apostle* by Ernest DeWitt Burton in *A Critical and Exegetical Commentary on the Epistle to the Galatians*, International Critical Commentary (Edinburgh, Scotland: T. & T. Clark, 1921), pp. 363–84.

4. Martin Luther, *Luther's Works,* vol. 26 (St. Louis: Concordia, 1963–64), p. 55.

APOSTOLIC AUTHENTICATION

Galatians 1:10-24

In Galatians 1:10, Paul's emotions were running high, perhaps *seething* is the word. To this point in the epistle, he had mentioned himself only once: his self-introduction as an apostle of Christ in 1:1. At this point, however, he was aware of the fact that he must mention himself again, this time to vindicate his motive for ministry. After all, the charges leveled by his opponents were not only an attack on his message but on him as well.

Paul had been accused of duplicity when it came to the gospel, of turning like a weather-vane whichever way the wind blows. It was necessary for him to defend himself now. Hence he asked the question relative to pleasing God or pleasing people. There was a time when Paul did try to please people. Before his conversion to Christ he was seeking earnestly to please the highest echelons of the Jewish rabbinic establishment. His entire career in his preconversion days was designed to justify himself before God and to gain the favor of those in power to advance his own ambitions. But that kind of self-service was forever shattered when Saul of Tarsus and Jesus of Nazareth met dramatically outside Damascus. He learned then what each of us must

 WHAT OTHERS SAY

TO BE A FAITHFUL MINISTER

He that would be a faithful minister of the gospel must deny the pride of his heart and be emptied of ambition, and set himself wholly to seek the glory of God in his calling.

—William Perkins

learn: Serving Christ and pleasing humanity are, at times, mutually exclusive alternatives.

Paul's vindication of his ministry was not an angry outburst of an egotistical preacher. He was rejecting the charge of having unworthy motives for ministry.

1. PAUL'S CALLING 1:11–12

Verses 11 and 12 contain Paul's call to Christ. Paul's reception of the gospel was not only a revelation of Christ to him, but a revelation of Christ in him. Not only was the gospel different from any other so-called revelation from God, but he received it independent of anyone else. Paul declares that he did not make this up. This gospel does not belong to the purely human level of things, for the gospel did not come through human channels—it was mediated to Paul through Jesus Christ himself (1:12). And his preaching of the gospel was not guided by any human motives or ambitions.

The gospel we preach authenticates our ministries. If the word we give is a human word, then we speak without the authority of God. If, as Paul argued, the gospel is from God himself, then it comes to us and through us with a divine power and urgency. It is critical that all who would speak the Word of God be assured that the doctrine of the gospel and the Scripture is not of human origin but of God. It is also critical that all ministers of the gospel be assured that their calling and authority are from God.

2. PAUL'S CONVERSION 1:13–17

Nothing in Paul's religious background could account for his acceptance of the gospel (1:13–14). He adhered to the strictest traditions of Judaism. That is precisely why he took up arms against the Christians and did what he could to destroy the believers. The Galatians probably knew of Paul's past life, but he reminded them of his deeds against the church. His purpose was not to boast about his misdeeds when a pre-Christian, but to make clear the sovereign initiative of God in turning him from darkness to light. It is not becoming for converts to magnify their sinful past more than their rescue from that past. Paul always spoke of his past life with great sorrow and shame. He even said on one occasion that he was the "least of the apostles" (1 Cor. 15:9) because he had **persecuted the church of God** (Gal. 1:13).

PAUL'S ZEAL FOR RELIGION

Why did Paul seek to exterminate the Christians? He was a protégé of the famous Jewish theologian Gamaliel. It was apparent that he was considered to be a rising star in Pharisaic Judaism. He was advancing in Judaism beyond his contemporaries by being extremely zealous. We need to remember what A. D. Nock noted: "When Paul first learned of the body which was the germ cell of later Christianity, there was no title 'Christian': that came into being at Antioch, and perhaps as a nickname."[1] Paul encountered a sect within Judaism that, because of its devotion to Jesus as Messiah, was redefining the boundaries of the community of Israel in ways that were profoundly disturbing to such a strict Pharisaic leader as Paul.

At least two aspects of the early Christian message were particularly offensive to Paul. The first was the teaching that Jesus was the Messiah. With most of the Jews, Paul's conception of a Messiah would be one who would put down Roman authority and establish himself on the throne of David. A condemned and crucified Messiah was not what the Jews had in mind. Furthermore the idea that this Messiah was raised from the dead, exalted to heaven with the status of deity, and demanded the kind of worship reserved only for God amounted to blasphemy.

Paul's reference to **the traditions of my fathers** (1:14) suggests that he saw the gospel as a dangerous message because he thought that Jesus was displacing the law as the means for right standing before God. It was unthinkable to Paul that the Torah was not sufficient. Whether the early church was aware of the full implications of its message is an open question. It can be argued that Stephen's address to the Sanhedrin (Acts 7) constituted an early teaching of the inadequacy of the law and the Temple as a way of salvation. That address and that implication probably prompted Paul to play a major role in Stephen's execution.

It is significant that Paul uses **zealous** in describing his activity against the church. Maccabean literature prominently connected the word zeal to Jewish leaders who were quite willing to use force in order to defend their homeland, Temple, and law against foreign intruders. Old Testament prototypes such as Phinehas (Num. 25), Joshua (Josh. 7), and Elijah (1 Kings 18:19) sanctioned violence and death for those who violated the covenantal community. Paul obviously saw himself as standing in the tradition of these zealous leaders in his violent efforts against Christians, who he viewed as contravening the purposes of God by subverting His holy law.

PAUL'S FERVOR FOR CHRIST

The convictions found in Paul's love for Jewish tradition and his belief that the law and the Temple were instituted by God to bring people to rightness with God led him to persecute the Christians. Paul's convictions also drove and drew him across the Mediterranean basin following his conversion to promulgate the gospel. There is no evidence that he carried out his agenda against the Christians with a guilty conscience or burdened with self-doubts. He was a contented Jew, happy with his religious tradition, believing in it fully. He made that perfectly clear when he wrote to the Philippians reconstructing his credentials as a Jew—his circumcision, his roots in the tribe of Benjamin, his membership in the Pharisaic party, and his blameless devotion to the law. You will recall that he counted all of these as "profit" before he met Christ (Phil. 3:4–7). Of course he viewed those same credentials as "loss," refuse, trash-worthy, and only to be hurled onto the dung heap once he came to know Christ.

The initiative leading ultimately to Paul's conversion came from God himself (1:15). **But when God, who set me apart from birth and called me by his grace, was pleased to reveal his Son in me so that I might preach him among the Gentiles, I did not consult**

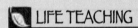 LIFE TEACHING

COMING TO SALVATION

If Paul would regard his credentials as refuse compared to knowing Christ, we should be willing to confess that our sins are an abomination to God. We cannot be saved until we know we are not saved. We do not become saved until we recognize how even our so-called virtues are worthless in their ability to make us acceptable to God.

any man (1:15–16). Paul uses "set apart" in Romans 1:1, where he described himself as being "set apart for the gospel of God." The word means to determine beforehand, to fix a boundary, a frontier, to cordon off for a special purpose. Although Paul was converted suddenly, God had had thoughts of mercy toward him from his birth. God did not begin to work with him when he was on the road to Damascus. There is a preceding work of grace. Perhaps Paul was thinking of the prophet Jeremiah (Jer. 1:4), who was set apart by God, or Isaiah (Isa. 49:1–6) when he expressed his own sense of being chosen by God and called into service by God's great grace.

The doctrine of election is a theological battleground where many scalps lie. To attempt to determine how to reconcile divine sovereignty with human free will is not an easy task. On the one hand we cannot deny the biblical basis for a doctrine of election when Scripture includes, "Therefore God has mercy on whom he wants to have mercy, and he hardens whom he wants to harden" (Rom. 9:18). Ephesians states, "In him we were also chosen, having been predestined according to the plan of him who works out everything in conformity with the purpose of his will" (Eph. 1:11). However we do not believe that one's standing before God is determined by religious activity, good works, or some other form of moral striving (see Eph. 2:8–9). The Judaizers of Galatia were close to this heresy by advocating their own gospel, which turned out to be a combination of the gospel of Christ plus law.

On the other hand, others have used a doctrine of election as a pretext for a do-nothing approach to evangelism and world missions. They argue that if God has chosen some to salvation before the foundation of the world, then why preach the gospel, send missionaries, or do anything? A hyper-Calvinism view implies that conversion takes place by God's sovereign will and faith follows. This teaching ignores the fact that the God who calls us to salvation also ordains the means—including the preaching of the gospel to all people everywhere—that will lead to repentance and faith. Any doctrine of election that automatically and arbitrarily consigns certain people to heaven and others to perdition cannot be justified. "The Lord is not slow in keeping his promise, as some understand slowness. He is patient with you, not wanting anyone to perish, but everyone to come to repentance" (2 Pet. 3:9).

The conversion of Paul was based on God's revelation to him (1:16). The dazzling appearance of Christ before his eyes and the summons of His voice formed the special mode in which it pleased God to call him to apostleship. There was also the inward revelation of Christ to his heart by the Holy Spirit. It was this which produced the great spiritual change in him and inspired him to be a witness for Christ among the Gentiles. His Judaic prejudices were taken away, and he became a champion of a universal gospel. While some refer to Christ's revelation to Paul as mystical and dismiss the idea that Jesus Christ appeared in person to Paul at a particular place in time, we accept Paul's testimony that Christ actually appeared to him.

So complete and convincing was Christ's revelation to him that Paul did **not consult any man** (1:16). Obviously the counsel of the wise is valuable and ordinarily should be sought diligently and considered thoroughly. However, the call of God reaches beyond human authority. Paul might confer with others as to the method of his work, but his call to Christian work was imposed on him by a higher power, a power to which human ecclesiastical leaders must submit themselves.

Paul did go **into Arabia** (1:17), which was contiguous to Damascus. It was during this period that Paul received special preparation for his life ministry. The Galatians' charge against him was that he received the gospel secondhand from those who were apostles before him. He is anxious to show that he was not only called and commissioned by Christ himself apart from any human mediation, but also that he was engaged in ministry prior to his first meeting with any of the Jerusalem authorities. Why Paul went to Arabia is an open question. There may well have been two reasons for his going there—for solitude, prayer, and reflection or on a preaching message. But even such a brilliant and well-trained thinker as Paul would require a period of intensive preparation for the life work to which he had been called.

3. PAUL'S FIRST VISIT TO JERUSALEM 1:18-24

After three years (1:18) undoubtedly refers back to the time of Paul's conversion rather than to the time of his return to Damascus from Arabia. Paul's primary concern, however, was refuting the false charges leveled against him, not chronological precision. It was necessary for him to show that his first trip to Jerusalem occurred after a considerable lapse of time from his conversion and early preaching ministry.

Paul indicated that he went to Jerusalem to **get acquainted with Peter** (1:18). What interesting conversation they must have had. Paul did not need Peter to teach him the gospel. He had already received the message of the gospel along with his commission directly from the risen Christ. Rather, he was interested in Peter's account of the earthly life of Jesus, His miracles and teachings, His death and resurrection. It would have been a wonderful experience to listen in on the conversations of these two great men. One can imagine that Peter told Paul about his own call and his confession of Christ at Caesarea Philippi (Matt. 16:13–20). Did he tell Paul about his threefold denial and subsequent restoration by Christ? Jerome put it rather humorously that Paul did not go to Jerusalem to "look at Peter." He did not seek authorization of his message or validation of his ministry. He did seek a close fellowship in the things of the Lord as well as a unique partnership in their common mission as apostles.

Paul indicated that he saw none of the other apostles except James, the brother of Jesus. James, it appears, was a person of some authority, a representative of the early Christian society, known as "James the Just." He was apparently not a follower of Christ during His earthly life. It appears that with the exception of Mary, His mother, none of Jesus' earthly relatives accepted His claim to be the Messiah prior to the resurrection (John 7:5). Jesus did make a special resurrection appearance to James, and thereafter he is listed as one of the witnesses of the resurrection. James became a member of the Jerusalem church and was among the 120 who witnessed the outpouring of the Holy Spirit on the Day of Pentecost (Acts 1:14–2:1). He rose early on to leadership within the church at Jerusalem taking the position of Peter after Peter's departure from the city. In all likelihood James wrote the epistle that bears his name. We will hear of him again in chapter 2 as one of the "pillars" Paul conferred with and then as the point of reference for "certain men" who instigated controversy in the church at Antioch (2:9, 12).

It is interesting that in verse 20 Paul states, **What I am writing you is no lie**. We have to conclude that because his adversaries had made so much of the idea that Paul preached a derived gospel and that he was a renegade

37

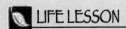

LIFE LESSON

TAKING OATHS

The choicest servants of Christ may be looked upon as liars and unworthy to be trusted, even by those to whom they are sent. Christians may take an oath providing it be with these conditions: (1) that the thing we swear to be the truth; (2) that there are weighty reasons for taking an oath; (3) that we swear only by the name of God, and not by the creatures, since none but God can bear witness to the secrets of the heart.

disciple of Peter and the other disciples, he makes a voluntary oath, common in the Roman legal system of his day. We know that Paul did not believe a Christian should take another Christian to court (1 Cor. 6:1–8), but he did not hesitate to draw an analogy to an actual legal proceeding. He was prepared to present his case with absolute confidence to the "jury" of Galatian believers who had heard only the other side of the story.

TO SYRIA AND CILICIA

Paul had intended to stay in Jerusalem for more than two weeks; he tried to join the other disciples there, but they rejected him (Acts 9:26). We know Barnabas befriended him and introduced him to the apostles (Acts 9:27). And we know Paul preached freely throughout the city, speaking boldly in the name of the Lord as he had done in Damascus (Acts 9:28). We know that his debates with the Hellenistic Jews led to their efforts to put him to death (Acts 9:29).

It is during this first visit to Jerusalem that Paul had a vision while praying in the Temple. In a trance, he saw Christ, who told him to leave Jerusalem immediately since his testimony would not be received there. Paul was reluctant to leave because he thought he should witness to those he had formerly persecuted. However, the Lord said He would send Paul to the Gentiles (Acts 22:17–21). When the Jerusalem Christians discovered the plot against Paul's life, they accompanied him to the port city of Caesarea and sent him off to Tarsus (in Cilicia). So begins Paul's journey **to Syria and Cilicia** (1:21). In a sense, this excursion was really Paul's first missionary journey.

We do not know the full extent of Paul's ministry in Syria and Cilicia, except that there were people who came to faith in Christ as a result of his ministry. Later on the Jerusalem Council addressed a letter "to the

Gentile believers in Antioch, Syria and Cilicia" (Acts 15:23). We also read of a later journey of Paul and Silas "through Syria and Cilicia, strengthening the churches" (Acts 15:23–41).

TO GOD'S GLORY

To further his argument that he was not a disciple of the other apostles, Paul states that he was **unknown to the churches of Judea** (1:22). This is the primary, if not the sole, object of the context. The churches in Jerusalem probably had seen Paul and heard him, but Judea was much larger than just Jerusalem. Apparently the churches throughout the province, the "country" churches, had not seen or heard Paul in person even though they had heard about him.

We are carried back in verse 24 to the worship of the early Judean Christians as they praised God for His stupendous work in the life of Paul. The chorus of praise here at the end of chapter 1 echoes the earlier doxology at the conclusion of the introduction (1:5). The first doxology is a hymn of praise for what God had done through the atoning death and triumphant resurrection of Jesus Christ. The second doxology celebrates that same victory as seen in the calling and apostolic ministry of Paul. Both doxologies celebrate the triumph of God. Against all odds, God reigns. He reigns despite the efforts of Satan, despite the insinuations and plots of the

LIFE TEACHING

GOD'S WILL

God's kingdom, His eternal will, and His purpose in grace will always prevail. We can trust the church to God's care.

false teachers, and despite persecution and hardship. Our God reigns!

As we leave chapter 1 of Galatians, we can develop Paul's argument as follows:

I received my gospel directly from Jesus Christ, not from any human sources. In fact I only visited Jerusalem sometime after my conversion for a short time to get acquainted with Peter. Rather than being a clone of the apostles, I was hardly known to most Christians there. However, when they did hear of what God was doing through me, they praised and glorified Him on that account. I was not an embarrassment to the church in Jerusalem nor to the believers in Judea. Through the grace of God, I was a cause of their rejoicing.[2]

ENDNOTES

What Others Say Sidebar: William Perkins, *A Commentary on Galatians*, ed. Gerald T. Sheppard (New York: Pilgrim, 1989), pp. 36–37.

1. A. D. Nock, *St. Paul* (New York: Harper, 1938), p. 35.
2. Timothy George, *Galatians,* The New American Commentary (Nashville, Tenn.: Broadman and Holman, 1994), p. 133.

THE APOSTLES INCLUDE PAUL

Galatians 2:1–10

As we begin the study of Galatians 2, it will be important to note that Paul continues the train of thought he had developed in chapter 1: the independence of his apostleship and the integrity of the gospel freed from the requirements of the law. There are two main sections in this chapter: 2:1–10 and 2:11–21. In the first ten verses Paul tells of the important meeting he had with the leaders of the Jerusalem church (2:1–10). In the second part, Paul has a second meeting with Peter in Antioch (2:11–21).

The issue of circumcision arises in 2:1–10, and it dominates Paul's thinking because of the appeal being made by the false teachers to his Galatian converts. This issue surfaced at an earlier meeting with reference to Titus, a Gentile believer whom Paul refused to have circumcised despite pressure from certain "false brothers."

Although this conflict runs through the passage, Paul manages to major on his solidarity with the Jerusalem leaders and their common objective in the work of the gospel. Paul declared that they did not add to his message and that they acknowledged the grace that had been given to him.

1. PAUL'S SECOND VISIT TO JERUSALEM 2:1–2

In the opening verses of chapter 2, Paul sets the stage for us in preparation for the drama that is about to unfold. The drama is the event; parties are involved; and there is a definite motive attached to Paul's action.

The first word in the Greek text of chapter 2 is *èpeita*, which is translated as "later" (NIV), "next" (NEB), or "after" (RSV). In chapter 1 Paul reminded the Galatians that his first visit to Jerusalem occurred sometime after his conversion and that it lasted for only a brief time—fifteen days. During that visit he became acquainted with Peter. Then, following this visit, his ministry carried him far from Jerusalem, so that the churches in that area only knew of his activities by hearsay. It was fourteen years before he visited Jerusalem for a second time after his conversion.

There is little doubt that the meeting he described in chapter 2 occurred during the course of his second post-conversion visit to Jerusalem. Paul was not running back and forth to Jerusalem so frequently that he could have confused the sequence of his visits, especially when such a momentous issue for his own apostolic work was at stake. Furthermore, he had already taken an oath before the bar of God to verify the unerring accuracy of his narration (1:20).

THE CONFERENCE IN JERUSALEM

There are different interpretations concerning the conference in Jerusalem and where it should be placed in the life of Paul. It can be argued that this is the most complicated historical problem in the whole epistle. There are three issues that bear on a reconstruction of this event.

First, there is the question of what did Paul mean by the expression **fourteen years later**? Often, in the New Testament era, an inclusive method of reckoning periods of time was used. This means that any portion of a given year could be counted as a whole year. Therefore in 1:18 the "three years" could have been slightly more than one, and the "fourteen years" of 2:1 possibly could have covered only twelve.

Second, what was the chronological benchmark from which Paul was determining the time of his second visit to Jerusalem? Was it fourteen years after his first visit (1:18) or, as seems more likely, his conversion encounter with Christ? If we assume the latter and then factor in the inclusive counting of years, we can place the date for Paul's second visit to Jerusalem around A.D. 44–46. This would mean that the events of

Galatians 2:1–10 parallel the "famine visit" Paul and Barnabas made to Jerusalem as recorded in Acts 11:25–30.

F. F. Bruce in his commentary on Galatians argues for this date, but Adam Clarke and the majority of other scholars equate Galatians 2:1–10 with Acts 15:1–21, the council at Jerusalem that produced an agreement endorsed by Paul and the Jerusalem leaders concerning the admission of Gentile converts into the Christian community.[1] There are, indeed, marked similarities between the two passages. In both, Paul and Barnabas are on one side with Peter and James on the other. Both messages deal with the issue of circumcision and both reflect a similar outcome, one that was essentially favorable to Paul.

An even more striking study is to examine the differences. In Acts 15, Paul and Barnabas are sent as part of an official delegation from the church at Antioch to resolve a dispute introduced into their congregation by intruders from Judea. In Galatians 2, Paul himself, prompted by a divine revelation, takes the initiative for the meeting. The council of Acts 15 was a public meeting involving lengthy discussion and presentations addressed to the whole assembly by Peter, Paul, Barnabas, and James. By contrast, the conference of Galatians 2 was carried on in private conversation among the principal leaders.

The greatest and most obvious difference, however, is the fact that nowhere in Galatians does Paul refer to the outcome of the Jerusalem Council or to the apostolic decree which, according to Acts, he and Barnabas later distributed among the churches of Syria, Cilicia, and also Galatia (Acts 16:1–6). As Bruce has observed, "After the publication of the apostolic decree of Acts 15:20–29, it would have been difficult for Judaizing preachers invoking the authority of the leaders of the Jerusalem church to impose circumcision on Gentile Christians."[2]

There are three parties involved in Paul's second visit to Jerusalem. First, there is the Pauline party consisting of Barnabas, Titus, and Paul. Second, there are the "false brothers" who agitated for Titus to be circumcised and later attempted to import their Judaistic tendencies to Antioch. This group would have to be considered as an extreme wing of the Jewish-Christian movement. They had strong attachments to the Jerusalem church, particularly to James. They viewed Paul's law-free gospel as a serious threat to the Christian faith as they understood it. We understand rather clearly their position when we read in Acts 15 that there were men from Judea teaching that one must be circumcised to be saved (Acts 15:1–2). It could be that some of these were the same people who created the stir in Antioch that led to the breach between Paul and Peter. Here were people who had penetrated the churches of Galatia, "spying on" the Christian freedom of the new believers there just as they had done at Antioch and elsewhere.

The third party that played a prominent role in the Jerusalem meeting were the leaders of the Jerusalem church, James, Peter, and John, who were thought of as "pillars" in the church. Paul's negotiations on this second visit to Jerusalem were with these men, not with the Judaizing detractors referred to earlier. It is likely, however, that some of the more zealous disciples contributed to some of the tension involved in this discussion.

REASONS FOR THE VISIT TO JERUSALEM

There were three reasons why Paul, with Barnabas and Titus, made this visit to Jerusalem. The first was because he was prompted by **revelation** (2:2). The Amplified Bible captures the meaning of Paul's sentiment: "it was specially and divinely revealed to me." This could mean that Paul felt it was his duty to go. It could also mean that since Paul received God's revelation to preach the gospel of Christ among the Gentiles, he went up to Jerusalem. The context seems to indicate that Paul had a specific word from the Lord. That word related to the growing rift and controversy concerning Paul's message and its reception throughout the

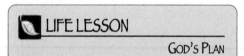

LIFE LESSON

GOD'S PLAN

In the life of every servant of the Lord there are special times when God reveals His plan in reference to that servant.

church at large. Paul was not summoned by the apostles; he was sent by the Spirit of God. Paul was not a stranger to these revelations (Eph. 3:3). He had them at every crisis in his career; they came through inner promptings and prohibitions (Acts 16:6–7), through dreams and visions (Acts 16:9–10), and through inspired men (Acts 13:3; 21:10–11).

The second reason Paul went to Jerusalem to convene the conference was to **set before them the gospel** (2:2). The phrase translated "set before them" means "to declare, communicate, advocate, or propound." We know there were those who were maligning Paul and his message. They probably had higher hopes for him since he was trained so well in God's Torah. Now they felt he was departing from the faith of Jesus and the apostles. Paul appeared to be carrying out a negative campaign against the law, totally divorcing the Messiah from the nation Israel. Some thought of him as a dangerous radical who must be stopped before he overturned the Jewish character of the faith by bringing those Gentiles into the church, Gentiles who shunned the basic requirement of the law—circumcision.

One can see how necessary it was for Paul to set forth the true gospel he was proclaiming among the Gentiles. His gospel was the same gospel the Jerusalem apostles also believed and preached. The problem was that everyone did not grasp the full implications of this message in a new missionary situation. We have, therefore in Galatians 2, the early church wrestling with the problems of law and gospel, faith and freedom, historical exclusivism and evangelical inclusiveness.

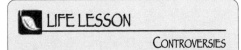

LIFE LESSON

CONTROVERSIES

It is never right to provoke controversy in an unchristlike manner. We must always make every effort to do what leads to peace and to mutual edification. There are occasions, however, when in order to be faithful to the gospel we must speak out publicly and even bluntly on matters that cannot be compromised.

The third reason for the conference relates to an issue that flows just beneath the surface of the text. Paul made it clear that the conference was called at his initiative, not that of the Jerusalem leaders. Neither his teaching nor his office was called into question. Nor did he fear the most searching inquiry into his commission. He himself sought the meeting in order to resolve a crisis that could have led to a major division within the body of Christ. This is why Paul called for a private meeting, not a public hearing.

2. THE CASE OF TITUS 2:3-5

The issue of the circumcision of Titus was likely an interruption in Paul's private conference with the Jerusalem church leaders. We seem to have a digression in Paul's narration of his second visit to Jerusalem. One wonders how distraught Paul must have been by the Titus incident since the writing was so unlike Paul. J. B. Lightfoot describes it as a "ship-wreck of grammar."[3] For example, in the Greek text, verse 4 lacks both a proper subject and verb. These are supplied by the translators in order to make sense of Paul's broken syntax. Paul was under emotional stress. Beyond the grammatical difficulties, we must keep in mind that there was a serious theological crisis in the churches of Galatia.

Titus was a Gentile convert whom Paul addresses as his "true son in our common faith" (Titus 1:4). It appears Titus was won to Christ through the ministry of Paul and, therefore, became one of his most trusted coworkers (2 Cor. 8:23). While Titus is not mentioned in Acts, he does appear frequently in Paul's letters as serving as an agent for Paul, especially in the gathering and administration of the love offering the Gentile churches were collecting for the poor saints in Jerusalem (2 Cor. 8:16–20; 12:17–18). Titus was a man of unquestioned integrity who apparently possessed significant people skills.

Did Paul take Titus with him to Jerusalem because of his gifts or as a living example of a Gentile convert whom he could introduce to the leaders there? We cannot be certain, but Paul surely knew Titus was uncircumcised and may have reasoned that, in the midst of the controversy over this issue, it would be helpful to have a person present who represented his argument in flesh and blood. We have in Titus a test case for the principle of Christian freedom that Paul intended to make to the leaders of the Jerusalem church.

CIRCUMCISION

We face the issue of circumcision here for the first time in Galatians. In some references, the Greek word for *circumcised* is translated "Jews"; *uncircumcised* is "Gentiles." Circumcision will be mentioned again in this same chapter and again in the closing section of the book (2:7–9, 12; 5:1–12; 6:12–15). What an enormous issue this was for the early church. Paul faced it in Rome (Rom. 2:25–29; 3:1–20; 4:9–12; 15:8), in Philippi (Phil. 3:3–5), in Corinth (1 Cor. 7:18–20), and in Colosse (Col. 2:9–15; 3:10–11). Paul referred to these people as the circumcision group, people who oppose sound doctrine, and mere talkers and deceivers. What was so significant with regard to the circumcision issue?

Circumcision is the act of removing the foreskin of the male genitalia, a rite practiced among various people of the ancient world as a sign of initiation at puberty or marriage.

To understand circumcision as it related to God's people, we must go back to the special covenant God made with Abraham (Gen. 17:1–27) that required every male child, whether a freeborn Israelite or a household slave, to be circumcised on the eighth day after his birth as a sign of participation in the chosen people of God. The prophets spoke metaphorically when they referred to circumcision as an act of repentance and total consecration demanded by God. Jeremiah, for example, had this word for the people: "Circumcise yourselves to the LORD, and take away the foreskins of your heart" (Jer. 4:4 KJV). As time passed, the people of Israel became too reliant on the external rite of circumcision and the whole system of sacrifice; they neglected what Jesus called "the more important matters of the law—justice, mercy, and faithfulness" (Matt. 23:23).

During the Roman period, influenced by Greek culture, circumcision became so totally identified with the people of Israel that it became the focal point of hostility. According to the Maccabean literature, there was a terrible reign of terror unleashed on the people of Israel that included the prohibition of circumcision. It also included a policy requiring that all babies who had been circumcised be put to death along with the mothers who had submitted them to this sign of the covenant. The effect of this policy raised circumcision to a higher status as a sign of the election and purity of the national Israel. So the sign of God's covenant with His people became a sign of special election to the Jews and a reason for intensified hatred to the Romans.

The Jews saw the Messiah coming to the Holy Land when it had been purified of all uncircumcised Gentiles. Therefore, during the period of the

New Testament, the Jews regarded circumcision as absolutely essential in any consideration of anyone's participation in God's covenant community. The strictest Jews demanded that even proselytes be circumcised as a rite of initiation into the special people of God. The reader will remember that Paul, when boasting of his preconversion credits, pointed to the fact that he had been "circumcised on the eighth day" (Phil. 3:5). In doing so he was witnessing to the most powerful ideological and emotional force this ancient rite conveyed to Jewish people in the world.

Against all of this we can understand why the Jewish leaders in Jerusalem had suspicions regarding the mission and message of Paul. Since they interpreted the Christian faith in terms of some kind of a continuity with the Old Testament law, worship in the Temple, and observance of the ancient rite of circumcision, Paul was too far to the left for these ultra-right-wing Jewish Christians. The fact is, Paul honored circumcision as a sign of Jewish identity, and he encouraged Jewish Christians to continue to circumcise their male offspring. He wrote to the Corinthians, "This is the rule I lay down in all the churches. Was a man already circumcised when he was called? He should not become uncircumcised. Was a man uncircumcised when he was called? He should not be circumcised. Circumcision is nothing and uncircumcision is nothing. Keeping God's commands is what counts" (1 Cor. 7:17–19).[4]

THE CASE OF TITUS

Going back to the issue over Titus, one may ask the question, "Why not submit Titus to this harmless ritual?" The answer rests on the claims for circumcision advanced by the Judaizing party who declared men had to be circumcised to be saved (Acts 15:1). Paul knew that if he accepted that position, it would be tantamount to renouncing the truth of the gospel. He knew that salvation is by divine grace in the completed work of Christ on the cross and is received through personal faith in the Redeemer alone, apart from the works of the law. That is why he said that for Gentile believers to be required to submit to circumcision was to make Christ of no value to them (Gal. 5:2). If Christ is of no value to a person, that person is still under the curse of the law, without God and without hope in this world and the next.

So the dispute over Titus outlined the parameters of the crisis in Galatia in a person in their presence. This is precisely the issue that would appear again at the Jerusalem Council (Acts 15), the outcome of which was absolutely essential for the integrity of the gospel and ultimately the unity of the church. A. G. Ebeling stated it well:

> The treatment of circumcision had become a test of the Christian faith. In historical terms, it must be decided whether Christianity is something other than a new Jewish sect. In theological terms, the decision is whether one's relationship with Christ is dependent on being under the law, or the relationship to the law is dependent on being in Christ.[5]

3. FALSE BROTHERS 2:4–5

The church, even when at its best, has wicked people and hypocrites in it. In Adam's family there was Cain, in Christ's family there was Judas, and in the early church there were false brothers. A perfect church is an impossible dream; there are wolves within. Christ is the door of the church, and His true sheep enter by Him. False brothers creep in some other way. Hence Paul states that they **had infiltrated our ranks** (2:4). These people slandered Paul's doctrine and distracted from his authority because he withstood their demands by insisting on the circumcision of Titus. Paul was incensed by these **false brothers**; he uses colorful, powerful, even combative language to describe them. These people are dangerous. In appearance they seem to follow Christ, but they attempt to add something to Him and, as a result, do not present the true gospel.

These false brothers were secretive in their work of disruption. They were not what they seemed to be; they had a plan to carry out their destructive mission. Their mission was to restrict Christian liberty and to gain spiritual ascendancy over the believers' conscience.[6]

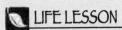 LIFE LESSON

DANGERS OF FALSE "BROTHERS"

False "brothers" may creep in to the church. They are the most dangerous to true Christian liberty. Weak brothers may disturb the church, but false brothers undermine and destroy it. The first duty of Christians should be to preserve the truth.

Paul would not give in to these false brothers **for a moment** (2:5). It is appropriate to reconcile church differences in a spirit of meekness. When it comes to truth, however, we dare not submit to the cause of our adversaries whether outside of the church or within.

Two concepts will dominate the remainder of Galatians: freedom and truth. Galatians has been called "the Magna Carta of Christian Liberty." The false brothers attempted to subvert **the freedom we have in Christ Jesus** (2:4). Paul will not submit to their demands, for to do so would result in the abrogation of the gospel. Christian liberty, as defined by Paul, did not permit such individualism as to allow for doctrinal license or moral laxity. The freedom for which Christ has set us free is a liberty grounded in **the truth of the gospel** (2:5).

4. THE MEN OF REPUTATION 2:6–10

After writing of the false brothers and the Titus case, Paul returns to his account of the Jerusalem meeting. In 2:6–10 we have one of those famous runaway Greek sentences of Paul. This sentence contains a number of important ideas. Beginning negatively Paul makes a sharp distinction between the false brothers, whom he described as sneaks and spies, and the church leaders with whom he had come to Jerusalem to confer. The former were spies of Satan; the latter were partners with Paul and pillars in the church.

There has been debate by scholars with regard to Paul's use of the word **seemed** (2:6). In verse 2 he referred to **those who seemed** or appeared **to be leaders**. In verse 6 these same persons are identified as **those who seemed to be important**. In verse 9 Paul identifies these persons as James, Peter, and John, who are also described as **those reputed to be pillars**. The debate over Paul's use of the word *seem* or *appear* (*dokein* in Greek) is whether there is some derogatory connotation. The context would argue against that, since Paul is not placing himself in any way in opposition to these leaders but rather making the point that there is unity and reciprocity in their mutual tasks of promoting the gospel.

God does not judge by external appearance (2:6). A literal translation reads, "God does not accept the face of a man." Tradition has it that Paul was not very impressive physically. We know that he was criticized by some of his enemies in Corinth for lacking speaking ability and platform appearance (2 Cor. 10:10). While it is debatable whether or not these personal attacks played into Paul's words in Galatians 2, it is not debatable that God looks on the heart and not on the outward appearance.

The result of the meeting of Paul with the Jerusalem leaders was that **those men added nothing** to Paul's message (2:6). The gospel is of supernatural origin. Trust in Christ alone, not the requirements of the law, provides salvation and forgiveness of one's sins. Paul would never have agreed to anything being added to the gospel of grace as a requirement for salvation. The message is simple and clear: "Believe in the Lord Jesus, and you will be saved" (Acts 16:31).

At the Jerusalem conference, the church leaders gave Paul and Barnabas **the right hand of fellowship** (2:9). Giving the right hand of fellowship is an indication of confidence, friendship, and fellowship. Fellowship (*koinonia*) symbolizes the common life of the Holy Spirit. Obviously the Jerusalem leaders noted the grace that was given to Paul. The significant outcomes of the conference were recognition of the doctrine of grace that Paul preached and recognition of that grace in his own life and ministry.

Remember the poor (2:10) is added as a postscript to the Jerusalem agreement. We need to remember that concern for the poor has been a priority from the earliest days of the Christian church.

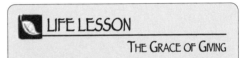

LIFE LESSON

THE GRACE OF GIVING

A measure of our devotion to Christ is the generosity we display in ministering to the needs of society. Christianity is one of the most significant sources of philanthropy; the hope of the poor and needy.

Often the acceptance of Christ means the loss of friends and fortune. This was true in the world of Paul's day and it continues to be true today. Judea was devastated during the reign of Claudius Caesar, so the apostles organized relief for the people suffering in the Judean churches (Acts 11:27–30). Paul's first concern was for the Jewish poor, though many of them impugned his apostolic authority and sought to ruin his influence. He encouraged Gentile converts to use their wealth to meet the needs of poor Jewish brothers. Paul's mission and ours must include both evangelistic responsibility and social concern.

ENDNOTES

1. See F. F. Bruce, *Galatians* (Grand Rapids, Mich.: William B. Eerdmans, 1982), pp. 43–56 and "Further Thoughts in Paul's Biography," pp. 21–29 of the same book.

2. Bruce, *Galatians*, p. 52.

3. J. B. Lightfoot, *St. Paul's Epistle to the Galatians* (London: Macmillan, 1986), p. 104.

4. See also the treatment of circumcision by J. S. Gunther, *Saint Paul's Opponents and Their Background* (London: Brill, 1973), pp. 82–89.

5. A. G. Ebeling, *Truth of the Gospel: An Exposition of Galatians* (Philadelphia: Fortress, 1985), p. 97.

6. Paul used the term "false brothers" in 2 Corinthians 11:26, where they appear as one of the items in his catalogs of sufferings. In the same chapter (verse 13) he spoke of "false apostles, deceitful workmen, masquerading as apostles of Christ."

4

FAITH IN JESUS CHRIST ALONE

Galatians 2:11-21

This second passage of Galatians 2 centers on a meeting between Paul and Peter in Antioch, where once again the issue of legalism threatened to disrupt the unity of the church. Paul confronted Peter because he yielded to pressures from a group of Judaizing intruders and withdrew from fellowship at the table with uncircumcised believers. This incident at Antioch provided an occasion for Paul to state clearly the principle of justification by faith. The closing verses of chapter 2 are transitional, leading to the major theological center of the book in Galatians 3 and 4.

1. THE INCIDENT AT ANTIOCH 2:11-13

As a result of Stephen's death, Christians were forced to scatter to other city-states. Because of the believers' relocating, these cities, including Antioch, were evangelized. Both Jewish and Gentile converts were included in the church in Antioch (Acts 11:19–21). The church grew numerically and materially; they were able to send gifts to other Christian communities in Judea. When Paul and Barnabas returned from Jerusalem, the church at Antioch sent them on their first missionary journey (Acts 12:25–14:28), on which they established churches in Asia Minor and Galatia.

Upon the completion of that missionary journey, Paul and Barnabas returned to Antioch and ministered in that city for a long period of time.

It was during this time of ministry that the issue arose concerning table fellowship and the public conflict between Paul and Peter (Acts 14:26–28; Gal. 2:11–14). When Christians from churches in Judea arrived at Antioch, Peter pulled away from fellowship with the Gentile Christians. Because of fear of **the circumcision group** (2:12), circumcision and fellowship at the communion table became issues once again. Paul had earlier dealt with the circumcision question, and he would not bow to Judaizers on that issue. However, Peter began withdrawing himself from such table fellowship with Gentile believers because **he was afraid of . . . the circumcision group** (2:12). Other Jews sided with Peter in this practice, and **even Barnabas was led astray** (2:13). These two points of conflict caused the church at Antioch to send Paul and Barnabas to Jerusalem to confer with the apostles and elders there (Acts 15).

To understand the problem it is helpful to know something of the city of Antioch. Today the town of Antakiya occupies the site of ancient Antioch. While the town is not impressive now, Antioch was impressive in Paul's time. It was the third largest city in the Roman Empire, with a population of more than a half a million. It was known for its architectural beauty and had political significance because it served as the capital city of the Roman province of Syria. Emperors such as Julius Caesar gave a great deal of attention and wealth to Antioch, even calling it "Rome of the East."

A great many Jews lived in Antioch, and it became the base for the first major expansion of Christianity outside of Palestine. Persecution fanned a flame of missionary zeal and evangelism that caused the church to multiply its witness. "Those who had been scattered preached the word wherever they went" (Acts 8:4). Among those who heard the gospel in Antioch were the Jews first and then the Gentiles. When the Jerusalem church leaders learned of the Christian wakening in Antioch, they sent Barnabas (Acts 11:22) to work with the new believers there. Barnabas then journeyed to Tarsus to recruit Paul to assist him in the work. Becoming a human bridge, Barnabas reached out to Paul and the Gentile believers with one hand and to Peter, James, and the other leaders of the Jerusalem church with the other.

Table fellowship was terribly significant in Judaism because it literally meant fellowship before God. To break bread together at the table indicated that all participants shared in the blessing of the master of the house. This became important in the life of the early believers. They had all come to Christ and were members of His body. A sign of that oneness was the table fellowship. When Peter came to Antioch, he found Jewish and Gentile believers eating together at the same table, and he joined them in this practice. We do not know exactly what these meals were, but in all likelihood they included the *agape* or Christian love feast, of which the celebration of the Lord's Supper was a primary part (1 Cor. 11:20–21).

The confrontation between Paul and Peter took place after the Jerusalem delegation arrived at Antioch. Peter withdrew from the common table fellowship; then followed the wholesale defection by Barnabas and other Jewish Christians. We do not know who these **men . . . from James** (2:12) who came to Antioch were. They may have been the false brothers who had clamored for Titus to be circumcised (2:3–4). We do know these men had some attachment to James, respected his leadership in Jerusalem, and perhaps even carried letters of recommendation from him, a common practice of that day. They were certainly zealous members of the ultra-right wing party within the Palestinian movement.

The **men . . . from James** were shocked when they saw how freely Peter was sharing table fellowship with the uncircumcised believers. This was not the usual practice of Jewish Christians back in Jerusalem. We do not know whether they said anything to Peter or not. Perhaps just their presence was enough to cause Peter to **draw back**. In the Greek tense the verbs in the phrases "began to draw back" and "separate himself" are in the imperfect tense, indicating that Peter's action may have happened gradually. Little by little, he reacted to the increasing pressures of the Jerusalem visitors until finally, "he drew back and began to hold aloof" (NEB). Even more shameful, not only did Peter draw back, but all of the other Jewish Christians at Antioch were swept along with him in this playacting.

It is at this point that Paul gives us one of the most poignant statements in the entire epistle: **by their hypocrisy even Barnabas was led astray** (2:13). What a painful thing this must have been to Paul and even to Barnabas. It was Barnabas who had introduced Paul to the Jerusalem believers when others in the city thought he was still a persecutor. It was Barnabas who had sought out Paul in Tarsus and persuaded him to become a part of the ministry team at Antioch. It was Barnabas who had stood with Paul in Jerusalem when he defended the liberty of the gospel against the false brothers. It was Barnabas who accompanied Paul on the first missionary journey when many Gentile believers were won to Christ and the churches in Galatia were established. It is hard to imagine a more severe blow than for **even Barnabas** to be carried away.

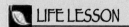

LIFE LESSON

STAND FIRM

There are times when we must stand alone when a Christian principle is at stake. Even the most devout and loyal friends do not always evaluate events and truths on the same level of importance.

There are those who relate Barnabas's defection at Antioch to the sharp disagreement Paul and Barnabas had over John Mark at the beginning of the second missionary journey (see Acts 15:36–41). It seems highly unlikely because we have evidence that this break was not permanent. Barnabas again stood with Paul at the Jerusalem Council, and Paul later associated himself with Barnabas in a positive manner (Acts 15:2; 1 Cor. 9:5–6). But the fact that even Barnabas could be pressured to yield over the issue of table fellowship indicates both the strong influence exerted by the legalistic Jewish Christians and the loneliness of Paul's resistance to their demands.

2. PROTEST WITH PETER 2:14

Peter was in the wrong and Paul confronted him. Peter was not acting **in line with the truth of the gospel**. We are not certain why Peter acted like he did in withdrawing from the table fellowship. Paul said Peter was afraid of the circumcision group. Perhaps the nature of his fear was that he was afraid he would not be able to fulfill his role as the apostle to the Jews if he were seen treating the obligations of the Torah so loosely. Perhaps the men who came from James brought word of an insurgent Jewish nationalism, a Zealot movement that was pressuring Jewish Christians to follow the rules of Judaism more strictly. If any of these factors were true, it is easy to understand how Peter's consorting with the Gentiles could have threatened to precipitate an act of reprisal against him personally or against the Jewish Christian communities.

As far as Paul was concerned, Peter was without excuse. Perhaps John Calvin said it best, "It is foolish to defend what the Holy Spirit has condemned by the mouth of Paul. This was no human business matter but involved the purity of the gospel."[1] Paul used two strong words in his public condemnation of Peter and the other Jewish Christians at Antioch who had separated from their Gentiles brothers and sisters. **Hypocrisy** (2:13) comes from the world of the theater and refers to wearing a mask, playacting, a pretense, insincerity, or acting in a way that belies one's true convictions. The other phrase is "crooked walking" (2:14, translated as "not acting in line" in the NIV); they did not walk with a straight step—they did not maintain firm footing. **You are a Jew, yet you live like a Gentile and not like a Jew.** In other words, you should have known better; Peter was not guilty of an honest mistake. There is no evidence that he changed his mind about including the Gentiles in the plan of salvation; after all, this truth was revealed to him by a special revelation. Peter had put on a mask; he was shamefully acting a part totally contrary to his own true convictions. He was not walking a straight line of gospel truth, and he knew it. Paul had to rebuke him for such inconsistency of conduct—and he did.

How disappointing this action of Peter was to Paul. Did Paul think of earlier days when Peter vacillated and denied his Lord three times? Was Paul remembering the incident when Peter took his eyes off Christ during the storm on the sea and began to sink? Peter became known as a rock of a man, but was there another situation when Peter became obsessed with external circumstances or his own personal position and did not act **in line with the truth of the gospel**?

Paul's rebuke was cutting indeed. Peter was a Jew and had scrupulously observed the law. It required a miracle to convince him that the Gentiles were accepted in Christ just as Jews were. They were admitted by believing in Christ and became members of the same church, fellow heirs of the hope of eternal life. The result of that miracle was that he went in with the Gentiles and ate with them (associated with them) as he would with the Jews. But now, fearing them of the circumcision, he withdrew from this fellowship. Paul would not, could not, tolerate such behavior. He virtually exploded with indignation, calling Peter to account in front of the whole assembly. Paul had probably confronted Peter first in private, an appeal which did not produce the desired results. The rebuke must be a public one because this was not just an issue between two apostles; the truth of the gospel and unity of the church were at stake. Peter, not Paul, lacked the courage of his convictions.

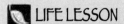

LIFE LESSON

FALLEN LEADERS

Great leaders can fall. Over the years the church has witnessed the failure of many greatly gifted and highly visible leaders. Their fall is not only a matter of personal tragedy but also blight on the body of Christ. May God help us to test every one and each message we hear by the touchstone of His Word and save us from exalting any human leader above measure.

The real issue at Antioch was not what one ate and with whom one ate; the basis of the Christian life, the doctrine of salvation by grace alone, was the issue. If the Gentiles were really included in the gospel of grace, they were also included in the church, the body of believers. As such, to withdraw from them in something as important as the communion table, or any other table of fellowship, was to reduce them to the bondage from which Christ died to make them free. Jews and Gentiles alike had been redeemed by the same Christ, regenerated by the same Holy Spirit, and made partakers of the same fellowship. Who dared say they could not come to the same table to partake of the same Lord's Supper? "Who will separate us from the love of Christ" or from one another? "It is God who justifies . . . it is Christ Jesus who died" (Rom. 8:33–35).

3. THE PRINCIPLE 2:15–21

The Antioch incident was not a personality clash between two great leaders. This was no power struggle between Paul and Peter. The issue was a theological one. It is fair to say that, notwithstanding the personal rebuke of Peter, Paul handled the conflict as both historical and theological. Paul's historical narrative flows so smoothly into his theological exposition that it is obvious that the two, history and theology, were inextricably bound together in Paul's defense of the gospel.

In the final verses of chapter 2 Paul brings to a conclusion the historical argument he has been pursuing. He actually moves into a theological exposition that will maintain his attention in the next two chapters. The NIV includes the entire section (2:15–21) in quotations, indicating that we have here a summary, if not a transcript, of Paul's address to Peter at Antioch. In these seven verses Paul uses compressed language to set forth his central thesis that acceptance with God is effected through a simple act of trust in Jesus Christ and not through anything else.

Paul uses terms that need explanation: justification, works of the law, and faith. What did he mean when he spoke of having **died to the law** (2:19) or having been **crucified with Christ** (2:20)? How does he relate the acceptance with God and the life of faith that follows that acceptance? Paul will answer these questions in the final four chapters. He introduces them in this closing section of chapter 2.

Paul's central theme is justification by faith. That was the principle introduced by the problem of table fellowship at Antioch and brought to the fore in his protest against Peter. The Galatians had to move beyond the personal clash between Paul and Peter and move to the real issue: the basis of salvation for all people everywhere. Paul drew his argument to a conclusion by saying, **If righteousness could be gained through the law, Christ died for nothing!** (2:21).

In 2:15–16, Paul began his definition of justification by identifying himself with his fellow Jewish Christians and Peter. He made it clear that those who were Jews by heritage and birth had a great advantage over those who were "Gentile sinners." The Jews regarded the Gentiles as sinners simply by virtue of the fact they were Gentiles. Obviously the Jews had benefits that the Gentiles did not. They had received the Law of God and circumcision, which was a sign of the covenant. They had the Old Testament Scriptures. However, even the Jews, who could claim so many privileges as the chosen people, had to realize that no one could be justified by observing the Law. Therefore, the Gentiles, who did not have the privileges of the Jews, would also be accepted through faith in Jesus Christ rather than by observing the Law. Neither the works of the Jewish Law or any other law could justify a person. Justification by faith in the boundless mercy of God is as reasonable as it is scriptural and necessary. Paul quotes Psalm

143:2: "Do not bring your servant into judgment," the psalmist had prayed, "for no one living is righteous before you." Paul changed the quotation to read **by observing the law no one will be justified**.

When Paul wrote **no one will be justified**, he was contrasting the acts of the sinful nature to the fruit of the Spirit. For Paul, flesh was that realm of human experience that was most vulnerable to the ravages of sin. Flesh was not evil in itself since it was created by a good God, but in its fallen state, it was subject to the debilitating forces of desire, decay, and death. So in Galatians 2:16, Paul is careful to say that humanity, because of its weakness and susceptibility to sin, cannot keep the law. He spelled this out more fully in Romans 8:3 (NASB): "For what the Law could not do, weak as it was through the flesh, God did: sending His own Son in the likeness of sinful flesh and as an offering for sin, He condemned sin in the flesh." The point is that no one could find salvation by keeping the law because no one can keep the law.

JUSTIFICATION

Justification is the "judicial or declarative act of God, by which He pronounces those who believingly accept the propitiatory offering of Christ, as absolved from their sins, released from their penalty, and accepted as righteous before Him."[2] The classical Protestant understanding of justification is set forth in Question 60 of the Heidelberg Catechism: "How are you righteous before God?" The following answer is given:

Only by true faith in Jesus Christ. In spite of the fact that my conscience accuses me that I have grievously sinned against all the commandments of God, and have not kept any one of them, and that I am still prone to all that is evil, nevertheless, God, without any merit of my own, out of pure grace, grants me the benefits of the perfect expiation of Christ, imputing to me his righteousness and holiness as if I had never committed a single sin or had ever been sinful, having fulfilled myself all the obedience which Christ has carried out for me, if only I accept such favor with a trusting heart.[3]

THE WORKS OF THE LAW

Paraphrasing Paul's explanation, "We Jewish Christians know that a person is not justified by observing the law . . . for this reason even we have trusted in Christ in order that we could be justified by faith rather than by the works of the law . . . since (as the psalmist said) no human being can be justified by the works of the law." The law, to Paul, refers to the divine requirements given to Israel through Moses. While the law itself is holy, it cannot produce a right standing before God. The "works of the law" refers to the commandments given by God in the Mosaic legislation in both its ceremonial and moral aspects, holy and good in themselves. Because of the fallen nature of human beings, "no flesh" could ever be justified by observing the law. Since God knew this was the case, why did He give the law? Paul answers that question in chapters 3 and 4.

FAITH IN CHRIST

Saving faith is a gift of God not a mere human hope (Eph. 2:8–9). We must never consider faith as one of the works of the law. Faith is not an achievement that earns salvation any more than circumcision is. Faith is the evidence of saving grace that is seen in the renewal of the heart by the Holy Spirit. There is nothing within us that is a cause of our justification but faith, and nothing grasps Christ's obedience for our justification but faith.

In verses 17 and 18, Paul addresses the question of false methods of salvation. In verse 17 Paul had in mind the earlier phase of the Antioch situation when Jewish and Gentile believers enjoyed a shared fellowship around a common table. Verse 18 recalls the later development that shattered the unity and brought the two great apostles into open conflict. **If, while we seek to be justified in Christ, it becomes evident that we ourselves are sinners, does that mean that Christ promotes sin? Absolutely not!** Or, if while we acknowledge that we must be justified by faith in Christ, we ourselves are found sinners, we can never be justified by observing the rites and ceremonies of the law, which never could and never can justify. Therefore, by submitting to circumcision, we lay ourselves under the necessity of fulfilling the law, which is impossible.

Paul makes the case that having an open table with the Gentiles is itself a repudiation of the law. By seeking to reinstate the requirements of the law as a test of fellowship, Peter, Barnabas, and the other Jewish Christians who withdrew from the table fellowship had dishonored Christ and had actually transgressed His command. Paul's point is that to go back on this fundamental commitment and build again the old structures of the slavery of the law would be tantamount to destroying the work Christ did on Calvary. The result would be to make Christ an agent of sin. Paul has a strong expression for that: "God forbid."

In verses 19 and 20, Paul addresses another question of his doctrine of justification by faith. Does Paul undermine the basis for living a righteous life by refuting the law as a means of one having a right relationship or standing before God? Did not Moses command the children of Israel to walk in God's ways and to "keep his commandments, decrees and laws" (Deut. 30:16) in order to live? Is justification simply a wonderful doctrine to die by but not a good one to live by?

I died to the law (2:19). Paul did not mean he died to the moral law of God. Every rational creature is under its dominion. He meant he died to it as a covenant between God and himself. The law still stands in all its pristine authority, purity, and majesty; he honors it and strives to obey it. But its life-giving and death-bringing powers are at an end. He is dead to all hope and expectation of heaven or salvation from the law. The connection between Paul and the law is over, and so are all the slavish, painful feelings arising out of it. Paul takes refuge in Christ rather than in the law. When Paul said he was dead to the law, he did not mean the law had lost all relevance for him or that it does for the believer. That is the error of antinomianism. There is an ethical imperative in the Christian life that flows from a proper understanding of justification. For example, we are to carry one another's burdens and so "fulfill the law of Christ" (6:2).

Paul used the expression "to die to" in other references to the self, to sin, and to the world. He meant that his relationship to these had been so completely altered by his union with Christ that they no longer controlled, dominated, or defined his existence. In that sense he is dead to them. In the same way, he is dead to the law.

Paul speaks for us all when he says, **I have been crucified with Christ** (2:20). The death of Christ on the cross has made it clear that there is no hope of salvation by the law. We are dead, therefore, to all expectations of justification by the law, as Christ was dead when He gave up His spirit on the cross. Through Him alone we live, enjoy a present life, and have the prospect of future glory. Obviously Paul did not mean that the death of Christ is repeatable and not unique. Christ stands alone in His substitutionary suffering and vicarious death, but the benefits of Christ's atoning death—including justification—are without effect unless we are identified with Christ in His death and resurrection. **I no longer live, but Christ lives in me** (2:20). God made human beings to be a habitation of His own Spirit. The law cannot live within us to give us a divine life. The law does not animate but kills. Christ lives in us; He is the soul of our soul so that we live to God. Not only are we justified by faith, but we live by faith. Saving faith is a living, dynamic reality that permeates every aspect of the believer's life. By believing on Christ as a sacrifice for sin, knowing that He loved us and gave himself for us, we are saved from the pains of eternal death and saved to a life of faith.

In verse 21 we have a word of warning. We must not set aside the grace of God or render it useless. Paul had defended himself against the charge that by displacing the law as a means of salvation he himself had thwarted God's grace. Actually the reverse is true. If it were possible to obtain a right standing by God through the works of the law, then Christ died in vain. Everything about the gospel is at stake here. Are we going to say Christ was a false messiah, a common criminal whose death was a trivial footnote in history? Of course not! But if we persist in rebuilding the wall that Christ tore down,

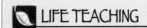

LIFE TEACHING

THE GIFT OF GOD

Justification by works makes void the grace of God. God's grace cannot stand with human merit. Grace is not grace unless it is freely given. The joining of faith and works in the matter of justification is a total excluding of God's free grace. Grace admits no partner. If grace does not do it all, it does nothing. If there had been any other way possible by which salvation of sinners could have been brought about but by the death of Christ, then Christ would not have died.

we make a mockery of Jesus' death. If we think that we can climb up to heaven by any other way, such as the law, then we are acting the same as the soldiers who spat on, mocked, and insulted Him.

Having come to the end of the first major section of Paul's letter to the Galatians, it will be helpful to review a few key points. Most of the first section is autobiographical as Paul defends his apostolic authority. Paul's defense is that his gospel came directly from Jesus Christ, who called him and commissioned him to be an apostle to the Gentiles. Paul makes the point that his doctrine of justification by faith is not theologically different from that of Peter or the other apostles.

The cloud over the first two chapters is that some people had brought confusion into the minds of the young converts in Galatia by their attempt to add some aspects of the law, particularly circumcision, to the gospel. These were probably the false brothers who insisted that Titus, a Gentile convert, be circumcised. Probably they were the same people who intimidated Peter at Antioch. This much we know: Paul would not give in to them one iota. To do so would be a denial of the gospel itself.

The first section launches us into the great doctrine of justification by faith, making the point that all of us must put our faith in Christ alone. As he faced objections to "his" gospel in the first two chapters, he would face further objections as he unfolds the doctrine of justification in the next two chapters. Having taken his stand without compromising, he will develop his arguments fully, historically, and beautifully.

ENDNOTES

1. John Calvin, *The Epistles of Paul to the Galatians, Ephesians, Philippians, and Colossians*, Calvin's Commentaries, vol. 11, trans. T. H. L. Parker (Grand Rapids, Mich.: William B. Eerdmans, 1965), p. 36.

2. H. Orton Wiley, *Introduction to Christian Theology* (Kansas City, Mo.: Beacon Hill Press of Kansas City, 1946), p. 276.

3. *The Book of Confessions* (New York: The General Assembly of the PC [USA], 1983).

Part Two

Doctrinal Issues: Justification by Faith and Liberty in Christ

GALATIANS 3:1–4:31

5

OBSERVE THE LAW OR LIVE BY FAITH

Galatians 3:1–12

The Pietist commentator J. Bengel described the first few verses of Galatians 3 as "the sum and marrow of Christianity."[1] Paul lays out the facts of the atonement; he explains that there is no other way for anyone, whether Jew or Gentile, to be righteous before God except through personal faith in Jesus Christ. What follows is a series of arguments based on the Scriptures to show that what Paul had preached to the Galatians was no new doctrine, but one firmly founded in the oracles and promises of God.

1. THE GALATIAN EXPERIENCE 3:1–5

The first argument Paul makes to demonstrate the fact that everyone must come to God through a personal faith in Jesus Christ is the Galatians' own experience. The cross of Christ was the great theme of Paul's preaching. He depicted it in such vivid colors and painted every detail of the story so intensely and lovingly that the Galatians were arrested, excited, charmed, and converted. While they looked to Jesus, they were secure in their faith. When they began to listen to the deceptive voices of error, their gaze turned from Christ, and the deep significance of the cross became obscured. It was then that backsliding began.

There are actually two places in the theological section of Galatians where Paul appeals directly to the experience of the people. In both passages (3:1–5; 4:12–20) Paul is exasperated when he says, **you foolish**

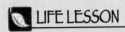

LIFE LESSON

THE CROSS

The cross is the central force and fact of Christianity. When it fades from view, Christianity declines. It is not Christ without the cross, nor the cross without Christ; it is both of them together always.

Galatians . . . I am perplexed about you (3:1; 4:20).

To strengthen his indignation, Paul characterizes them in an unflattering way as foolish, stupid, senseless, and silly. J. B. Phillips, in his paraphrase of the Scriptures, puts it like this: "Oh you dear idiots of Galatia . . . surely you cannot be so idiotic?" In 1:1, Paul called them **brothers**. In 4:19 he calls them his **children**. It is obvious he really loved them and wanted them to be theologically correct. To accomplish this he knew he needed to use strong words, the expression of a tough love. They were not unintelligent people, but they were lacking in spiritual discernment. They were like the disciples on the road to Emmaus, whom the risen Christ characterized as "foolish . . . and . . . slow of heart to believe all that the prophets have spoken" (Luke 24:25).

The churches of Galatia had lost their balance of sound doctrine and Spirit-filled living. Too often in the life of the believer there is a great divorce of the spiritual from the doctrinal, experience from theology. Paul asks, "Since you have received the Holy Spirit and witnessed His mighty works, how is it that you are now moving back from the Spirit to the flesh, from faith to works, from grace back to law?" Because they were not firmly grounded in the faith, they had been led astray by undisciplined thinking and careless theology. They were in danger of embracing doctrines that were perilous.

Paul wants to know how this had happened. **Who has bewitched you?** he asked

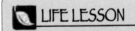

LIFE LESSON

COSMIC BATTLES

In every church, whether large or small, the devil is at work. A war is going on in every pulpit with the souls of men and women at stake. We must be certain that the content of our preaching is nothing less than Jesus Christ and Him crucified (1 Cor. 2:2).

(3:1). **Bewitched** is found nowhere else in the New Testament. It literally means to give someone the evil eye, to cast a spell over, to fascinate in the sense of being spellbound by an irresistible power. Someone had led the Galatians astray. By using the singular **who** in his question, Paul suggests that Satan himself, the father of lies, was the one behind the Galatian agitators.

Again Paul summarizes the gospel for the Galatians in 3:1. First, it is the message about Jesus Christ. Second, Jesus Christ was **clearly portrayed** before their eyes. The word *portrayed* (*prographo*) means to write beforehand or portray publicly. Paul's point was "How can you have been so deceived by these heretics when in your mind's eye you saw Jesus impaled on the cross of Calvary right before your eyes? How could you ever lose sight of that?" Finally, Paul reemphasizes the finality of the cross. The work of redemption was accomplished completely through that perfect, atoning sacrifice.

The measure of Paul's anxiety about these Galatian believers is demonstrated by the rapid fire of six questions asked in just five verses (3:1–5). He expected each question to be answered on the basis of their Christian experience. It was his way of reminding them of something they could not deny: the reality of the new life they had received in Jesus Christ.

Paul pushes the Galatians by introducing the term *Spirit* (3:2) for the first time, referring to the Holy Spirit of God. Paul put forward the crucial question in verse 2 and again in a slightly expanded form in verse 5: **Did you receive the Spirit by observing the law, or by believing what you heard?** The implied answer is that the Galatians had been saved and blessed with the Spirit as a result of Paul's preaching of "Christ crucified" long before the Judaizing disturbers of their faith appeared. If they confused the true method of moral regeneration, they would make spiritual growth and advancement impossible. Instead they would be thrown back to hopeless human effort. It is the Holy Spirit who convicts of sin; He reveals the mystery of the gospel, intercedes for the saints, baptizes, indwells, seals, fills, and empowers Christians to live a life pleasing to God. Spiritual blessings do not come from outward observances but by inward contemplation and faith.

A great deal has been written about the hearing of faith. Does it refer to the content of what was heard or the act of hearing? The content is crucial, but Paul was thinking of the process by which one comes to God's saving grace. He said to the Romans that "faith comes from hearing the message, and the message is heard through the word of Christ" (Rom. 10:17).

Hearing refers to the passive posture of the recipient. Of course physical hearing does not save, but the awakening of faith comes through the preaching of the gospel.

Paul posed a question that went to the heart of their motivation for abandoning the gospel: **are you now trying to attain your goal by human effort?** (3:3). Religious ordinances could not further the work of faith and love; Moses could not lead higher than Christ; circumcision could never accomplish what the Holy Spirit could do. Spiritual results can be brought about only by the Spirit.

The Galatian believers' experience apparently included persecution. No one could come out of a heathen society and espouse the cause of Christ in those days without being exposed to ridicule and some degree of persecution. One suspects that the Galatian Christians were subjected to the same kind of harassment and violent assaults that Paul and Barnabas experienced when they first brought the gospel to that region (Acts 13:50). If the Galatian believers so easily abandoned the gospel, for which they had suffered so much, all those early struggles against opposition amounted to nothing.

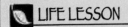

LIFE LESSON

FADING FERVOR

It is disappointing when early zeal for Christ degenerates later into apathy and worldly mindedness. If salvation is not the work of God from first to last, then the preaching of the gospel is vanity, the cross of Christ a farce, the gift of the Holy Spirit means nothing, and suffering for Christian principles and liberty foolish.

Paul concludes his argument by reminding them again that when he and Barnabas came to Galatia preaching the gospel of Jesus Christ, they heard the word and believed the message, and God poured out His Holy Spirit on them. The power of His presence was unmistakable. None of God's work was based on their acceptance of circumcision or obedience to the law. Since, therefore, they had begun in the Spirit, Paul begs them not to turn back to the flesh. What a shame it would be, after all this great experience, to turn away from the truth and follow these false teachers away from the authenticity of Christ and the gospel.

2. THE CASE OF ABRAHAM 3:6–9

Having argued from the past experience of the Galatians of hearing the gospel he and Barnabas preached to them, Paul now moved to his second argument in demonstrating the doctrine of justification by faith—the case of Abraham. The patriarch Abraham is mentioned nineteen times in Paul's letters. He is the primary figure in all Paul's arguments from Scripture in Galatians. The Judaizers were claiming the authority of Moses, the giver of the law. Paul would go back before Moses to Abraham. It was not Paul's intention to set Abraham over against Moses; He wanted to set the Abraham of "faith alone" against the Abraham of "meritorious deeds" that the rabbis used. In the Jewish literature of this period, Abraham is depicted as the "hero of faith" whose fidelity and obedience to God merited the favor of God and brought divine blessing on him and his posterity. He is called the friend of God, a man of virtue, conviction, and hospitality.

Paul uses Abraham to illustrate that the promise to Abraham contained the germ of the gospel. Though dimly apprehending its significance, Abraham trusted in God's Messianic promise (2:6). Verse 6 is a quote from Genesis 15:6. Abraham, while uncircumcised, believed in God, and his faith was reckoned to him for justification. Abraham is called the father of the faithful or of the believers. If he was justified by faith long before the law was given, then the law was not necessary for salvation.

How did Paul understand Abraham's faith? In Romans 4:3 he again quoted this same text from Genesis and described more fully how faith became the instrument of Abraham's justification. The best commentary on Galatians 3 is Romans 4. There Paul gave the example of Abraham's trust that God would fulfill His promise to give him descendents as numerous as the stars in the heavens or the sands along the seashore, even when he and Sarah were well past the normal age of childbearing. When reason would have counseled doubt and despair, Abraham was "fully persuaded that God had power to do what he had promised" (Rom. 4:21). The sacrifice of Isaac must be interpreted along these lines. Abraham was willing to slay his son of promise at God's command, believing that God could raise him back to life in order to fulfill His word. This is the kind of faith Jesus spoke of when

He announced that God was able to raise up sons of Abraham by the power of His word from inanimate objects such as lifeless stones.

In 3:7, Paul extends his argument from Abraham to his posterity. He addresses the people who insisted that one must receive the seal of circumcision to be a true child of Abraham, for circumcision was the indispensable sign of God's covenant with His people. Paul responds that Abraham was justified by faith, not because he accepted circumcision and observed the law. The true children of God are those whose faith rests on the same principle as his.

The Scripture foresaw that God would justify the Gentiles by faith, and announced the gospel in advance to Abraham (3:8). The good news of salvation was to be extended to all people, including Gentiles, who would be declared righteous on the basis of faith alone like Abraham was. The promise to Abraham contained the sum of the gospel. The gospel is, therefore, no new doctrine; it is the same in substance as was taught to Abraham and to God's followers under the Old Testament. Abraham believed in the Christ who was to come just as we trust in the Christ who has already come.

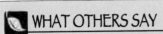

WHAT OTHERS SAY

OUR INHERITANCE

The patriarchs of old participated in the same inheritance and hoped for a common salvation with us by the grace of the same Mediator.

—John Calvin

3. CHRIST AND THE CURSE 3:10–12

The third argument Paul makes for justification by faith is a negative one. Here he argues against the possibility of justification by works.[2] The Bible says those who do not perfectly obey the law are cursed. Those who seek to be justified by works are under that curse because no one (except Jesus) ever has or ever will be able to fulfill the entire law. The law is a unit; to violate a part is to violate the whole and be guilty of breaking all of it. The law cannot justify people (3:11). The law reveals our sin and our utter helplessness to rid ourselves of its misery. The law may reveal the disease, but it cannot bring the healing.

For Paul, Christ was the "end" (*telos*) of the law because He brought to completion what the law could not do (Rom. 10:4). He did this by bearing the just curse of the law that had fallen on everyone who had not fulfilled **everything written in the Book of the Law** (Gal. 3:10). It is, therefore, only in the light of Christ that we can understand the true nature of humanity as God intended it to be and the radical character of human rebellion in this fallen world. It is not necessary for us to paint the world as dark as possible in order to illuminate the glory of Christ; it is only in the light of Calvary that we can grasp the holiness of God, the horror of sin, and the depth of divine grace.

The law ignores faith (3:12). It is likely that in Paul's day, as in ours, there were those who taught that justification by faith was a good idea so long as it was not taught to the exclusion of justification by works. How often do we hear the statement "God helps those who help themselves"? That maxim might work in other disciplines, but Paul would not tolerate it when it came to justification. To grant righteousness to faith is to deny it to works. Paul knew the law was not based on faith, and he quoted from Leviticus 18:5 as a support of his statement. In fact this passage is quoted two other times in the New Testament, and both of these references shed light on its use by Paul in Galatians 3. The first instance is the prologue to the parable of the Good Samaritan when Jesus encountered an expert in the law who asked him what he could do to inherit eternal life. Jesus replied, "What is written in the law?" The lawyer replied, correctly reciting the two great commandments about love of God and neighbor. Jesus replied, "'You have answered correctly'. . . . 'Do this and you will live'" (Luke 10:25–28). Immediately the man began "to justify himself," revealing that his life was not spotless. Then, in a response to his question "Who is my neighbor?" Jesus told the story of the Good Samaritan. His purpose was to point out how radically different the Samaritan's selfless act was from the best efforts we can put forth. He was not trying to show how much our good works resemble those of the Good Samaritan, which would encourage the self-justifying attitude of the lawyer.

Paul would not have us identify with the Good Samaritan or with the Levite or the priest, but rather with the poor man in the ditch, the man who could not "justify himself" but had to receive new life from a source outside himself.

The second citation of Leviticus 18:5 is found in the heart of Paul's great discourse on salvation and election in Romans 9–11. Having declared that Christ is the end of the law, he said, "Moses describes in this way the righteousness that is by the law: 'The man who does these things will live by them'" (10:5). He went on to explain that the way of justification by faith is for Jew and Gentile alike since "the same Lord is Lord of all and richly blesses all who call on him" (10:12).

Karl Barth, followed by C. E. B. Cranfield, has argued that Paul's citation of Leviticus 18:5 both in Romans and Galatians is a veiled reference to Christ himself. Thus, rather than assuming the law's inability to be fulfilled, Paul pointed by means of this text to the one person in human history who has obeyed the law completely and fulfilled it perfectly, qualifying Him to bear the curse of the law for others. While the exegesis behind this interpretation seems strained, the instinct to focus on Jesus Christ as the perfect fulfiller of the law is sound. Apart from Jesus' perfect obedience of the law and His resurrection, what happened at Calvary would have had no more redemptive significance than the brutal crucifixion of thousands of other young Jews before, during, and after the earthly life of Christ.[3]

ENDNOTES

1. Samuel Bengel, quoted in *Machen's Notes on Galatians* (Nutley, N.J.: Presbyterian and Reformed, 1977), p. 164.

2. J. B. Lightfoot, *St. Paul's Epistle to the Galatians* (London: Macmillan, 1986). "[H]aving shown by positive proof that justification is of faith, he strengthens his position by the negative argument derived from the impossibility of maintaining its opposite, justification by law" (p. 137).

3. Timothy George, *Galatians*, The New American Commentary (Nashville, Tenn.: Broadman and Holman, 1994), p. 236.

6

THE LAW AND THE PROMISE

Galatians 3:13–25

In verses 10–12 we have an extremely grim picture of the human situation. The law requires perfect obedience in order to be right with God, and no one can meet such a high standard. Therefore, everyone is condemned. Now Paul writes of the promised redemption.

1. THE PROMISED REDEMPTION 3:13–14

Christ brought us out of the curse of the law by voluntarily submitting himself to the terrible indignity of hanging on a tree. It was this scandal that made the cross an offense to the Jewish leaders. They thought that after He was crucified, the name of Jesus would never again be on the lips of people; no Jew would dare to profess faith in Him since **cursed is everyone who is hung on a tree** (3:13). His crucifixion did not have the results they expected. As all who trust in Jesus discover, His suffering, death, and resurrection was God's method of rescue for us; through the cross of Christ all the terrors and penalties of the law disappear.

Christ's redemption was offered to the Jew first, but not to the Jew alone; He offered redemption to the Gentile as well. This is the first time in Galatians Paul used the word *redeemed*. The idea of deliverance through the sacrifice of Christ was presupposed from the beginning of the epistle (1:4; 2:20). To redeem means to buy off, to set free by the payment of a price. So too, we have been bought with a price—nothing less than the blood of the Son of God himself who paid the ransom for our sins.

The question must be asked: How is it that Christ could become a curse for us? It is true He was "born under law" (4:4), but because He committed no sin but rather was as "a lamb without blemish or defect" (1 Pet. 1:19), He did not merit the curse for any wrongdoing. It was the manner of His death that brought Him under the curse of the law. This fact is made by Paul in quoting Deuteronomy 21:23: "Anyone who is hung on a tree is under God's curse." The Jewish Talmud recognized four modes of capital punishment: stoning, burning, beheading, and strangling. After the person had been executed, the corpse would then be hoisted onto a piece of timber, a stake, or a tree as an indication that this person had been justly condemned as a transgressor of the divine law. By being nailed onto a cross, Jesus exposed himself to the curse of the law.

The fact that Paul cites the text from Deuteronomy and the number of other references of Jesus' death by "hanging on a tree" (Acts 5:30; 10:39; 13:29; 1 Pet. 2:24) suggests strongly that there was nothing accidental or coincidental about the death of Christ. His death was a fulfillment of Old Testament Scripture. The death of Jesus by crucifixion was not some oddity of fate but the deliberate design of God. Peter affirms that when he declares in Acts 2:23 that Jesus was handed over to His executioners to be put to death by crucifixion in accordance with "God's set purpose and foreknowledge." There was a cross in the heart of God from all eternity, for Jesus was "the Lamb slain from the foundation of the world" (Rev. 13:8 KJV).

The purpose of redemption is indicated in verse 14, that **the blessing given to Abraham might come to the Gentiles**, and **by faith . . . the promise of the Spirit**. Paul is careful to intertwine justification by faith with the reception of the Holy Spirit. Those persons on whom God bestows the Spirit are justified; the persons whom God justifies by faith have the Spirit poured out on them. Paul called the gospel "good news" (Rom. 10:16), "blessing" (Eph. 1:3), and now he calls it **promise**. By using the word **promise** (3:14) he takes us back to the blessing of Abraham and forward to the new life of liberty to those who are in Christ.

From the beginning God had purposed that salvation should come through faith. He never intended that we should be justified by the works of the law. He gave the law so that the exceeding sinfulness of sin might appear. Then both Jews and Gentiles would be prepared to welcome the gospel that proclaimed salvation through the atoning passion and death of Christ.

2. THE LAW AND THE PROMISE 3:15–18

Paul calls these Galatians **brothers**, a term of endearment he has not used since 1:11. There is not a great deal of tenderness in this epistle, but the care Paul had for the Galatian believers is seen in the use of **brothers** here and again in chapters 4, 5, and 6. The Galatians might be foolish and bewitched, and Paul felt betrayed and perplexed about them, but they were still brothers.

Paul's continuing argument with regard to our justification though faith alone takes us back to the covenant relationship established with Abraham. The law needs to be understood in the context of the relationship between God and Abraham. In Genesis, God made a promise to him that was not based on

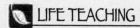

LIFE TEACHING

THE FAMILY OF GOD

As members of the body of Christ we are part of a family and truly brothers and sisters. Disagreements, theological differences, worship style preferences, denominational affiliation—none of these should be allowed either to disrupt or to destroy the true family relationship we have because of our true oneness in Christ.

any meritorious deeds, but rather on his faith in God that produced obedience to Him. This promise was unconditional. Abraham simply believed God would do what He had promised. The Genesis promise to Abraham is followed by the covenant with Moses, who delivered a new and different one that was weighted down with specific requirements, a code of behavior that made demands and issued threats.

We need to understand that this Moses covenant cannot countermand the covenant relationship with Abraham established by God prior to the covenant of Mount Sinai. It cannot for two fundamental reasons: (1) Once a will or covenant has been ratified, it cannot be altered; and (2) the law, as a temporary expedient, was not essential to the unconditional covenant granted to Abraham. Once someone's will and testament has been established, no one can change or revoke it. The point being, if this is true in human agreements, how much more is it true to God's covenant with Abraham? Jewish inheritance laws allowed for an irrevocable testament just as today our law allows us to make irrevocable trusts or wills, even giving us some tax benefits for making them. Jesus made reference to this kind of legal transaction in the parable of the prodigal son, where the father prematurely divided his property between his heirs.

Since there is civil law that lends all its force to maintain the integrity of the clauses of a human will, we can be certain that the divine covenant will be faithfully upheld. If it is likely that a human covenant will be protected, it is even more likely that a divine covenant will not be changed. Even if a human covenant may fail, the divine covenant will never fail because it is based on the word of God that cannot fail. The validity of the divine word is based on the incorruptibility of the divine character (Mal. 3:6).

In verse 16, Paul's main point was that all of these promises applied not only to one man, Abraham, but also to **his seed**. He observed that the word *seed* is singular, not plural, referring to that one person whom Paul contended was Abraham's true seed, Christ himself. The promise to Abraham was that through him "all peoples on earth will be blessed" (Gen. 12:3); this promise unites Jews and Gentiles as fellow heirs in Christ. The basis of everyone's being accepted by God is by grace through faith in Christ. The law views the Jews and Gentiles as distinct seeds. God makes His covenant of promise with the one Seed—Christ— and embraces all who are identified with and represented by Him.

In Romans, Paul contrasted Adam and Christ as two heads of humanity. Adam represents the head of sinful humanity that is doomed to die, and Christ is the head of a new humanity that has the promise of eternal life (Rom. 5:12–21). However, here in Galatians 3, the contrast is not between Adam and Christ, but Moses and Abraham, between those who base their identity on works and those who relate to God through faith in Him. When we were in the world and "under a curse" (Gal. 3:10) we were part of one family—the whole human race, lost, without hope, and incapable of pleasing God. Now we are in Christ, the true Seed of

Abraham, and we are in a new family, children and heirs of the promise through grace.

The seniority of the covenant is emphasized in verse 17, where Paul indicates that the giving of the Mosaic Law occurred nearly a half a millennium later than the original promise given to Abraham. The covenant of grace was announced to Abraham in the promise made to him and his seed long before the giving of the covenant of Sinai. Its conditions were fulfilled by Christ during the incarnation, long after the giving of that covenant. Therefore, the grace covenant given to Abraham was independent of and superior to the Mosaic covenant. Abraham's covenant was designed for the benefit of the whole human race, whereas the covenant of Sinai was confined to a single nation. The Sinai covenant was limited in its application, imperfect in its provisions, and a failure in its results.

The idea that the Abrahamic covenant was superior to the Mosaic covenant was a new idea for those who were pressing Christian converts to become Jews first. For those Judaizers, the giving of the law on Mount Sinai marked the real beginning of Israel's history in the sense it gave them a true national identity and established their unique role in the plan of salvation. They saw the period of the patriarchs (Abraham, Isaac, Jacob) as a kind of prelude to the giving of the covenant at Sinai through Moses. Paul responds to their argument by making the following points: (1) God made a covenant of grace with Abraham long before the law was given on Sinai; (2) Abraham was not present on Sinai, and, therefore, there could have been no alteration in the covenant made there by his consent; (3) Abraham never consented to any alteration in the covenant, and without his consent, the covenant could not have been altered in any way; and (4) the covenant stands firm because it was made to Abraham's seed (singular) as well as to Abraham himself. You cannot make God a dishonest broker who goes back on His word once it is given. How could He have made a promise to Abraham and then hundreds of years later changed that promise by adding to it the burdensome requirements of the law? To think God would or could do that would make Him as guilty of a deception we do not tolerate even among sinful human beings.

The conclusion of Paul's argument in 3:18 makes three succinct points: the faithfulness of God, the lateness of the law, and the graciousness of the promise. Paul uses, for the first time, the term **inheritance**, which he will develop more fully in 3:29; 4:1, 7; and 5:21. The inheritance is the blessing promised by God and ratified to Abraham and his "seed" by means of an unconditional covenant.

◖ LIFE LESSON

FREE IN CHRIST

We must not allow legalistic people to put us in bondage. The law came too late; it was preceded by 430 years of grace. We live as Abraham, a believer. We live after the revelation of Christ who has abrogated and abolished the law.

The people who opposed Paul's teaching on justification by faith sometimes gave faith a place, but they insisted that there be some place for works, a combination of law and promise. Paul insisted that the original covenant of promise given to Abraham be distinguished from the Law of Moses. The law always demands, "Do this." The promise always offers, "Accept this." In verse 18, Paul lays it out clearly: if law then not promise, if works then not grace. Knowing Christ summarizes all the arguments in support of faith and, at the same time, defends against the righteousness of the flesh, the law, works, and merit.

3. THE PURPOSE OF THE LAW 3:19–25

If the original covenant made with Abraham was a covenant of grace, and if the covenant of law made with Moses was not part of the original scheme but came in as a marginal addition or parenthesis in the dealings of God with the Jews, of what use is the law? Furthermore, is the law opposed to the promises of God? (3:21–22).

A review of Paul's logical argument will be helpful in answering these questions. Paul began his argument in 2:15 and pursued it step by step. Step 1: Everyone comes into a relationship with God through faith in Christ and not by observing the law. Step 2: While you Galatians have been bewitched by false teachers, even you must admit that you received the Holy Spirit and witnessed His miraculous works through faith, not by works of the law. Step 3: The law imposes a curse on everyone who does not obey it perfectly, and no one can or has except Christ Jesus himself.

Step 4: Christ died on the cross to redeem us from the curse of the law. Step 5: The law, given centuries after the original promise to Abraham, cannot alter the terms of the original covenant of grace. Step 6: You have to make a choice between law or promise, works or faith, grace or merit.

The question demanding an answer is "Why then the law?" If we are not justified by the law, if our receiving the Holy Spirit had nothing to do with the law, if Christ was cursed because of the law, if our inheritance depends on grace and promise not on works and law, then, what is the purpose of the law? **It was added because of transgressions until the Seed to whom the promise referred had come** (3:19). Paul stated the answer in a slightly different way in Romans 5:20: "The law was added so that the trespass might increase."

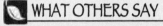

WHAT OTHERS SAY

PURPOSE OF THE LAW

The chief and proper use of the law is its provocative function, actually to increase transgressions, to make a terrible situation even more desperate, and thus to reveal to human beings their sin, blindness, misery, wickedness, ignorance, hate and contempt of God, death, hell, judgment, and the well-deserved wrath of God.

—Martin Luther

The law cannot cure the sin problem; it simply reveals and emphasizes the fact that people cannot live up to its demands. The atmosphere had changed from the time of the covenant with Abraham to that of the giving of the law. God spoke to Abraham as a man with his friend. At the time of the giving of the law, there was discord between God and the people. The law was needed as a subsidiary to the promise and as an aid toward its fulfillment. It accomplished its task by revealing sinful deeds in their true light as sinfulness in the sight of God. At the same time, it revealed the inability of people to do anything toward correcting their evil ways. Such revelation was necessary to move them toward faith that would lead them to embrace the promise.

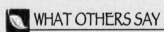

WHAT OTHERS SAY

ROLE OF THE LAW

It (the law) was given that we might know our sinfulness and the need we stood in the mercy of God. The law is the right line, the straight edge that determines the obliquity of our conduct.

—Adam Clarke

The temporary parameters and limited duration of the law is indicated in the statement **until the Seed . . . had come** (3:19). The law had a point of origin on Mount Sinai, and it has a point of termination on Mount Calvary. The work of the law was educative and preparatory. Centuries passed, and the promised Seed was long in coming. It seemed that the world would forever be under the teaching and curse of the law, but the law was doing its work. At last, "in the fullness of time" Christ the promised Seed appeared, and the law was superseded; its work was done.

Not only was the law inferior in that it was temporary but also because, unlike the covenant of God with Abraham, it was mediated by inferior beings, angels (see Acts 7:38, 53; Heb. 2:2). In the Jewish way of thinking, the administration of the law by angels enhanced its splendor. In the Christian view, this fact was evidence of its inferiority. The revelations of God by law were veiled and intermediate; the revelation by grace was direct and immediate. Under the law God was obscured and the people were unfit to enter His sacred presence; by the Gospel God is brought near to us and we are permitted to bask in the radiance of His revealed glory. He came to us "full of grace and truth."

Paul uses the word *mediator* in 3:20. There is only one other time where he used that word, in 1 Timothy 2:5, where it appears as a title for Jesus. In the Galatian use of the word, "mediator" does not apply to Christ but to Moses, who is referred to at times by Paul as a contrastive figure to Christ (2 Cor. 3:7–18). Here is another reason why the law could not annul the covenant of promise made with Abraham. In Jesus Christ, God sent a substitute or surrogate rather than angelic mediation or Moses as He did in the giving of the law. In the covenant of promise, God gave himself.

You will recall that the first question is in 3:2: "Did you receive the Spirit by observing the law, or by believing what you heard?" The Galatians would, or at least could, answer that question based on their experience with Christ. The second question is in 3:19: "What, then, was the purpose of the law?" The answer to this question required a detailed explanation by Paul. Now, Paul asks the third question with regard to the law: **Is the law, therefore, opposed to the promises of**

God? (3:21). The answer is emphatic, immediate, and almost indignant: **Absolutely not!** Paul had to ask and then answer this question because it must have been obvious to him, as it is to us in reading the epistle, that this question was in the mind of the Galatians. After all, Paul had been making the argument about the inferiority of the law, and the people must have been saying to themselves, "Why don't you tell us what you really think? Are you really saying that God's laws and His promises are totally against each other? Having said what you have about Moses and the Torah, are you really saying that the law has no place and that Moses is totally discredited?" In response to what the Galatians must have been thinking, Paul outlines three functions of the law (3:21–25).

First, the law was given to show that it fails (3:21). It was important that God show us that eternal life and blessing cannot come by way of the law but by grace alone. If the law given through Moses was able to bestow life, then a person could be justified by simply keeping that law. The point has already been made that while the law says "do this and you shall live," no human being can "do this." However, knowing from the beginning that humankind would not be able to keep the law, God intended that the law should function in this way. God always intended to save us by faith, apart from the law. He gave the law in order that it would condemn all and thus prepare us, in that negative way, for redemption on the basis of faith alone. So the law entered that it might fail, but its failure has turned into blessing. The law then was not against the promises; it was the divine method of dealing with fallen humanity. It did not profess to bestow spiritual life but, in its sacrifices and obligations, pointed to the coming of Christ who is "the end of the law so that there may be righteousness for everyone one who believes" (Rom. 10:4).

Second, the law was given to prisoners that they might be set free (3:22–23). The law declares us guilty before God, placing us under its curse and imprisoning us in sin. The Scripture makes the world one vast prison with the law the jailor and every person a prisoner held fast in chains. So the law exposes human wickedness; it eliminates any exit from prison by way of self-justification. The purpose of the law is served when we see that only grace can save us.

Third, the law disciplines that it might introduce us to Christ (3:24–25). The word used is schoolmaster, teacher, or guide. It was common in ancient Rome and Greece for wealthy parents to place their children in the care of an older woman, a nanny, who would care for their basic needs until they reached the age of six or seven. At that age they came under the supervision of another household servant, a pedagogue. The functions of the pedagogue included round-the-clock supervision, protection, and instruction in manners. Undoubtedly most of these people were kind and held in affection by their wards, but the dominant image of a pedagogue was that of a disciplinarian who used force and corporal punishment to keep the children in line. So the law was a "strict governess," as J. B. Phillips translates the word. Paul's use of the word is not that of a schoolmaster as much as it is a servant who had responsibility for the children outside school hours. So the law did not teach us the living, saving knowledge, but by its rites and ceremonies, and especially by its sacrifices, it directed us to Christ so that we might be justified by faith.

We have come now to the end of the first major doctrinal section of Galatians that began in 3:1. The chapter division is rather unfortunate, since the second doctrinal emphasis, unlike the first, is not so much historical as personal, not so much institutional as individual. From 3:1–25 Paul presented an overview of redemptive history from Abraham to Christ. He began by taking the Galatians back to their initial experience as Christian believers. He reminded them that they received the Holy Spirit through the preaching of the gospel and the hearing of faith, not by performing the works of the law. He admonished them not to fall back into thinking they could do anything to earn a right standing before God. They were a people of faith and children of Abraham, who believed God and was justified by faith. Paul taught them that this came about through the redeeming work of Christ toward which Abraham looked. Christ willingly took on himself the curse of the law and, by His death, opened the way for both Jews and Gentiles to become children of God. God's promise to Abraham is fulfilled in His Seed, Christ. To people who were hung up on the law, Paul endeavored to make it clear that the Mosaic Law, which itself cannot save us since we cannot keep it, was established through angels and a human mediator, Moses, to reveal sin. The law serves as a taskmaster, a prison warden, a public executioner, and a stern pedagogue to reveal faith and lead us to Christ. Those of us who are true children of Abraham through faith are no longer under the law or the curse of the law. We are no longer slaves—but children, no longer bound—but free, no longer condemned—but redeemed.

BEING THE CHILDREN OF GOD

Galatians 3:26–4:20

Before we examine the more personal aspects of justification by faith, the second of Paul's major theological teaching to the Galatians, the following diagram will serve to illustrate the flow of Paul's argument in chapters 3 and 4.

You will note that *faith* is the key word that links the two halves of Paul's treatment of justification together. In 3:6–25 he traces the scheme of salvation forward from Abraham through Moses to Christ. In 3:26–4:31 he argues backward from our being children of God through Christ to the use of the allegory of Abraham's two sons, Isaac and Ishmael. We know the churches of Galatia were made up primarily of Gentile converts, although

KEY IDEAS

THE PROMISE, LAW, AND FAITH

3:6–14	Promise (Covenant with Abraham)
3:15–22	Law (Through mediator, Moses)
3:23–25	Faith (Justified, Christ)
3:26	"You are all sons of God through faith in Christ Jesus."
3:27–4:7	Faith (The Spirit of His Son)
4:8–11	Law (Observance of special days)
4:21–31	Promise (Freewoman, Sarah, and son)

there was also a mingling of Jewish believers among them. In the earlier argument Paul was thinking, perhaps, primarily about the Jewish Christians in Galatia. Now in the latter, he mainly addresses the Gentile Christian community. The point is that not only are the Jews justified by faith alone, but the Gentiles, who were aliens from the commonwealth of Israel, have also become children of God and members of the new community through faith.

1. SONS AND SERVANTS 3:26–4:11

The dignity of kinship is enjoyed by all who believe in Christ because **faith in Christ Jesus** (3:26) releases us from the inferior status of being under law and lifts us to the more perfect relationship with God through Christ. The believer is no longer simply a pupil, subject to the restrictions and surveillance of the pedagogue, but a child enjoying immediate and constant relationship with the Father and all the privileges of an heir. Paul referred to the Son of God before in this letter (1:15–16; 2:20). In both instances he was referring to Christ Jesus as *the* Son of God equal with the Father from all eternity. Now he makes clear that all believers are sons and daughters of God and, as such, we no longer need a babysitter.

Not only are we children of God but we are invested with the character of Christ (**clothed . . . with Christ**, 3:27). Indeed, if Christ is the Son of God and the believer is one who has put on Christ, having the Son in us means we are being made like Him. To be baptized into Christ is not simply a mechanical rite or public observance; it is a testimony to believing and, as such, invests the soul with Christ. Baptism implies a radical and personal commitment that involves denying one's former way of life and emphatically embracing Jesus Christ. To be clothed with Christ is to assume the person and character of Christ. As Adam Clarke put it, "The profession of Christianity is an assumption of the character of Christ."[1]

Our union with Christ abolishes all secondary divisions (3:28). All distinctions of nationality (**neither Jew nor Greek**), social status (**slave nor free**), and gender (**male nor female**) disappear in the blending of all believers in the loftier relationship of children of God. The gospel is universal in its provisions and range; it elevates all who believe in Christ.

Race, money, and sex are the primal powers in human life—the stuff of which life is made. Outside of Christ these primal forces are controlled and manipulated by nations, politics, institutions, and society itself to liberate or enslave, put down or lift up, and approve or discriminate. In Christ Jesus we are freed from the tyranny of these powers and empowered to "bear . . . one another's burdens, and so fulfill the law of Christ" (Gal. 6:2 KJV). In the new Christian community Jews and Gentiles share the same table; slaves and free citizens are treated equally as brothers and sisters; women are accorded a respect equal to men. All are human beings not beasts, not Greeks and not barbarians, not citizens and not slaves, not men and not women, but all children of God, members of the aristocracy of the Most High.[2]

This section of Galatians is particularly meaningful to those of the Wesleyan persuasion who have maintained a long-standing commitment to full opportunity for women to be ordained to the ministry and, in fact, to serve in any and all ministerial and leadership capacities.

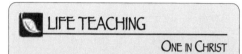

LIFE TEACHING

ONE IN CHRIST

Christianity, unlike other world religions, gives equal rights, equal blessings, equal privileges, and the opportunity for equal ministries to all. We are one family through Christ, one body of which He is the Head.

Obviously, we live in a world where these distinctions continue to play a major role in the affairs of peoples and nations. However, as Christians we are called to a new pattern of life. We must continually affirm the goodness of God's created and intended order even while we recognize it has been, and is, terribly marred by sin. Furthermore, we must attempt to bring about those changes in society at every level that approach the ideal of Christ's agenda.

In 3:29, Paul brings his argument to a conclusion and at the same time introduces the truths to be developed in the verses that follow. Through our union with Christ we have inherited this privileged status. Our kinship obviously has not come by the process of procreation but through regeneration, not by our goodness but by God's grace, not by the law but faith. We are **heirs according to the promise**.

The chapter division does not change the flow of Paul's argument. The first seven verses of this chapter outline the radical change that has taken place in the believer from slave to heir. Verses 8–11 will close the theme of children and servants by warning us of the dangers of reverting to what we once were.

Prior to becoming in Christ we were like servants and children, since minors have no legal rights until coming of age. Under the Old Testament, the bond servants, like the heirs, were recognized members of the family. In the same way, the heirs, like the servants, were in servitude because as minors they had no legal rights. There was one difference: The status of the slave was permanent. The minors were in the hands of guardians who cared for them personally and stewards who managed their estate. The guardians and trustees of the children during their minority are comparable to the pedagogue of 3:24.

Not only were we like servants. Even worse, we were **in slavery under the basic principles of the world** (4:3). The idea of worldly principles is found four times in Paul's writing, twice in this chapter (4:3, 9) and twice in Colossians (2:8, 20). It may refer to the mental thinking of the world, the moral principles of the world, the elemental things of the world, or possibly all three. It is true Jesus Christ dethroned the powers of darkness through His triumphant death and resurrection, and believers are, therefore, no longer under their domination. However, we are engaged in a lifelong struggle against the evil designs of Satan. We live on a fallen earth in bodies and minds not yet fully redeemed. We must expect continual spiritual warfare in the form of temptations, distresses, and tribulations.[3]

THE COMING OF CHRIST

This section (4:4–5) offers the basis for the Christological (the person and work of Christ) and soteriological (salvation) foundation of the doctrine of justification by faith. Perhaps this was an early confession of faith used in the earliest churches; it certainly is a passage quoted often in the celebration of the incarnation at Christmas. The expression **when the time had fully come** (4:4) is found only here in the writings of Paul. In the analogy of the heir-in-waiting just developed, the time designated by the father for his son to enter into the inheritance corresponds to the time in human history fixed and appointed by God for the ending forth of His Son. The first foundation stone for the doctrine of justification is the temporal one: the fullness of time. Christ came when a course of preparation, conducted through previous ages, was at last complete. Christ came at the precise time the Father in His infinite wisdom knew was best. So significant was the advent of Christ that believers of a later generation divided all time into A.D. and B.C., based on this event.[4]

Second, the sending formula—**God sent his Son, born of a woman, born under the law** (4:4)—presents the great fact of Christ's mission being from the Father. He was the immediate production of God by His divine power, conceived by the Holy Spirit, and thereby completely exempted from the taint of original sin. Having asserted the eternal deity of Jesus Christ, Paul also affirms His true humanity and representative role as one **born of a woman** and **born under the law**. **Born of a woman** is used elsewhere in Scripture as a common Jewish expression denoting one's status as a human being (Job 14:1; Matt. 11:11). While Jesus was the only person ever born of a virgin, Paul's purpose in this verse is to identify Jesus' full participation in the human condition. While Jesus' conception was supernatural, His birth was perfectly normal, complete with a rather crude manger, swaddling clothes, and other conditions, not very sanitary. Not only was He a man, but He was also a Jewish man because He was **born under the law**. He was circumcised the eighth day as all Jewish males were. He grew up in a Jewish home reading the Torah, praying to the Heavenly Father, attending synagogue, and faithfully fulfilling all the precepts and demands of the law as no one before or after has ever done.

Third, the design of Christ's mission is **to redeem those under law** (4:5), that is, to pay a price for them, to buy them off from the necessity of observing circumcision, offering brute sacrifices, and performing the law-required ablutions. This is the verse in which Paul turns from his great Christological statements to soteriology, from the divine person to the redemptive work. The Son of God became a human being in a most miraculous way to redeem those who were under the law and so that we might become children of God. We are redeemed from the curse of the law, from the slave market of sin, so **that we might receive the full rights of sons**. The Greek word is literally "adoption."

THE SPIRIT OF HIS SON

Paul now moves from soteriology to pneumatology. God sent His Son into the world, and now He sends the Spirit of His Son into our hearts. Readers might enjoy debating whether adoption to kinship precedes the sending of the Spirit or vice versa. Here Paul is teaching that the receiving of the Spirit is the sequel to the bestowal of kinship. Obviously, God's sovereign adoption and the regenerating ministry of the Spirit in our hearts are both aspects of the same reality. The best commentary on this text is Paul's parallel statement in Romans 8:15–16: "For you did not receive a spirit that makes you a slave again to fear, but you received the Spirit of sonship. And by him we cry 'Abba, Father.' The Spirit himself testifies with our spirit that we are God's children." The word *Abba* is a term of familial intimacy that is still heard in the Middle East as young children greet their fathers.

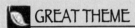

GREAT THEME

THE SPIRIT'S WITNESS

The Holy Spirit is the sign and pledge of our adoption so that by His presence in our hearts we are truly convinced that God is for us, not against us, that indeed He is our Heavenly Father.

ADOPTION

Note the points of resemblance between natural and spiritual adoption: (1) We cease to have our former name and are designated after the name of God; (2) we change our abode from being in the world to being in the church and the family of God; (3) we change our dress in that we conform to the family attire, the garments of salvation; (4) we change our status. In natural adoption only temporal advantages result, but in spiritual adoption the blessings are eternal.

In conclusion Paul declares that since all this is true—the Christology, the soteriology, the pneumatology—you are **no longer a slave but a son** (4:7). You are no longer a minor heir with no rights to the inheritance; no longer is your relationship to God determined by your race, rank, or role; no longer are you under the harsh tutelage of a schoolmaster; no longer are you under the curse of the law. Rather the promise given to Abraham and fulfilled in his prophetic Seed, Jesus Christ, has now been extended to all who through faith in Him have become His children, crying "*Abba*," and heirs of the living God.

THE DANGER OF A RELAPSE BACK TO LEGALISM

The theme begun in 3:26 and continuing to this section has been children and servants. Paul once again reminds the Galatian converts what their former way of life was like: They **did not know God,** [they] **were slaves** (4:8). They were pagans and, as such, sacrificed to imaginary deities—gods that were no gods. The Galatian pagans created a strange pantheon of gods. While Paul does not provide details concerning the nature of their gods, it is likely that some were devoted to the mystery religions of the Hellenistic cities of South Galatia, while others may have been devoted to the Roman imperial cult or to the pagan deities of ancient Greece. There was a temple to Zeus just outside the city of Lystra. After Paul and Barnabas healed a crippled man in that city, the priest of Zeus brought bulls and wreaths to the city gates and attempted to offer sacrifices to them, saying, "The gods have come down to us in human form!"[5]

Paul responded by admonishing them "to turn from these worthless things to the living God, who made heaven and earth" (Acts 14:11–15).

Having characterized the former life of the Galatians in such bleak terms, verse 9 states the glorious change that had taken place because of their conversion through faith

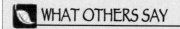

WHAT OTHERS SAY

IDOLATRY

All idolatry in the world rises from this, that people by nature have had the common knowledge that there is a God, without which idolatry would remain unpracticed. With this knowledge engrafted in mankind, they have fancied all manner of ungodly opinions about God.

—Martin Luther

in Christ: **But now that you know God—or rather are known by God.** The change from paganism to Christ is described in terms of knowledge, to be in the know. However, the kind of knowledge Paul was speaking of was not intellectual acumen, not simply intellectual assent, but rather personal intimacy. Our knowing God is conditioned on His knowing us. We do not find God so much as God finds us. Paul kept insisting on the divine initiative in salvation.

It was incredible to Paul that, having been delivered from so much and having received so much, the Galatians were now in danger of renouncing their faith. The temptation they faced was to yield to the Judaizing teachers and doubt that Jesus Christ alone was sufficient for salvation. They acted as if they needed to add circumcision and other ceremonies of the Mosaic Law to their faith in Christ. Although they once religiously observed Levitical ceremonies as a part of divine worship leading to Christ, Paul called those ceremonies **weak and miserable principles** (4:9).

KEY IDEAS

NOTHING BUT CHRIST

Whatever leads a person away from a salvation based on sole reliance on Christ, even if based on good intentions, is sub-Christian and is, therefore, to be condemned.

Paul was not, as some have supposed, suggesting that it is not proper to observe special days in the Christian calendar (4:10) such as Christmas and Easter. Paul's teaching is that while circumcision itself is neither good nor evil, so, too, the observance of special days is neither mandatory nor inherently wrong. Paul's concern was that the Galatians might be drawn into a religious system where adherence to certain calendar celebrations was necessary in maintaining a favorable standing with God. In medieval times, Roman Catholics were taught that the rituals of annual confession and Easter Communion were the minimum requirement for being members of the church in good standing. How many people attached to evangelical churches today flock to the church in semiannual pilgrimages at Christmas and Easter, assuming that this is all the Lord requires of them?

How sad is verse 11: **I have wasted my efforts on you**. Paul knew it was possible for true converts to be so thoroughly perverted from the gospel of Christ that all his labors in their conversion would be thrown away. We dare not ignore the terrible possibility of the kind of loss Paul feared. We must remember, however, that the greater scope of this letter is Paul's overall confidence and hope that the Galatians would be won back from the confusion and danger that caused Paul to write to them in the first place.

2. PAUL'S PERSONAL APPEAL 4:12–20

This section of Galatians could be considered a parenthesis in Paul's argument for justification by faith, which he resumes and concludes in verses 21–31. At the same time these verses serve as a call to Christian liberty based on Paul's personal example.

THE SPIRIT OF THE APPEAL

Paul is contrasting himself with the Judaizers in points of piety, labor, and divine blessing on his work. There are no more gripping words in the entire letter than these. Paul puts on the pastoral hat and evidences true pastoral concern. Perhaps he felt that he had written too strongly in earlier admonitions. He wants them to know that his severe rebuke came from a fatherly and apostolic spirit. He calls them "brothers" and compliments them on not treating him **with contempt or scorn** even though his **illness was a trial** to them. He indicates that they **welcomed** [him] **as if** [he] **were an angel of God** (4:14).

It is important for ministers, particularly pastors, to maintain a proper balance between theological teaching and pastoral concern.[6] Pastors must never allow themselves to become insensitive and detached from the hurts and struggles of the people of the congregation. At the same time pastors must not be absorbed so totally with meeting the congregation's needs that they neglect the weighty matters of doctrine and theology. What concerned Paul was not only that false teachers had distorted the doctrine of justification by faith, but that people whom he loved, individuals he could name, were in spiritual danger because of this doctrinal error. That is the concern that called Paul to leave, temporarily, the lofty heights of theological argumentation, and address the needs of the Galatians in this personal and emotional manner.

In 1 Corinthians 11:1, Philippians 3:17, and 1 Thessalonians 1:6, Paul admonished his readers to imitate him as he in turn imitated Christ. Here he tells the Galatians to **become like me** (4:12). "What I want is for you to become like me, living in the liberty of those who are truly the children of Abraham and of God through faith in Christ Jesus."[7]

You have done me no wrong (4:12). This is a difficult statement to understand. Certainly they had wronged Paul. He had been deeply hurt by the defection of some of his followers. Paul might have meant that the real injury is done to God when one turns from the faith. In any event, the personal, pastoral expression of Paul is unmistakable. That expression serves as an example to all those who would seek to lead people to acceptance of the gospel and in perseverance of the truth.

The reference to Paul's illness when he first came to Galatia has provoked a variety of speculations. In the early church, Jerome interpreted Paul's afflictions to have been the temptation of sexual desire that he identified with the "thorn in my flesh" of 2 Corinthians 12:7. During the Reformation, Luther dismissed this view entirely, regarding the "weakness of the flesh" as a reference to the suffering and affliction Paul bore as the result of the persecutions he endured. In recent years, most commentators have discarded both of these traditional interpretations in favor of the idea that Paul was referring to some actual bodily illness that affected his missionary labors. Some have advanced the idea that the illness was malaria, others a pain in the ear or head, and still others ophthalmia, an eye disease. Whatever the nature of Paul's illness, it apparently resulted in some kind of bodily disfigurement or unpleasant symptoms so that his condition was a "trial" to the Galatians. The culture of that time suggested that an infirmity or weakness was a sign of divine displeasure. The Galatians were tempted to reject Paul on the basis of that tradition, but, to their credit, they did not yield. Instead, they welcomed him as if he were **an angel of God** (4:14).

THE APPEAL TO JOY

The past experience in the gospel brought them happiness or blessedness. This happens when a person truly comes into a relationship with God through Christ by faith. When the vision of Christ fades and one seeks to maintain favor with God in some other way, the joy of the Lord fades as well. Joy can only be maintained by the constant realization of Christ Jesus as Savior. In writing to the Corinthians, Paul spoke of their "overflowing joy" that "welled up in rich generosity" (2 Cor. 8:2). The early joy of the Galatian believers was so great that they were willing to have their eyes transplanted and presented to Paul as an offering of their love (4:15). However, something happened, for now they regarded Paul, once their dearest friend, as an **enemy** (4:16) because he persisted in telling them the truth.

Paul certainly was deeply troubled by the shifting loyalties of his disciples in Galatia, but that would not and did not cause him to alter his message. He continued to practice tough love by speaking the truth. The

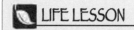

LIFE LESSON

TRUTH TELLER

The person who tells us the truth, even though it hurts deeply, is the person we can count on as a true and faithful friend—our best friend.

messenger of the gospel can never succumb to the temptation of softening the truth simply to win the favor of the people.

THE APPEAL TO ZEAL

There are various kinds of misplaced zeal: a zeal that is not according to knowledge, a mistaken zeal for the glory of God, a superstitious zeal, a persecuting zeal, and a contentious zeal. Before concluding his treatment on sons and servants, Paul has another word about those who were causing the difficulties in Galatia that distorted the gospel and damaged the relationship between Paul and the believers. Once again Paul does not identify the troubling ones but simply refers to them as **those people** (4:17). Our English word *jealous* comes from this same word translated here as "zealous." The

CHRISTIAN THEME

SINGLE FOCUS

Zeal implies unwavering steadfastness of purpose, hearty obedience to God's commands in all things, supreme devotion of heart and life to Christ, and must be uniform not periodical.

meaning of the word is to be resentfully envious or suspicious of a rival or a rival's influence. These agitators of the Galatian believers had evil intentions and selfish motives. Their purpose was to **alienate** the people, to shut them out, to exclude them. Paul does not tell us from what they wanted to exclude the believers. We must assume that they really wanted to exclude them from Christ himself.

AN APPEAL TO BE WITH THEM AND CHANGE THEIR TONE

Having zeroed in on the false teachers with their sinister motives to lead the Galatians astray, Paul now changes his mood and addresses his misled flock with great tenderness. **My dear children** (4:19) is a term of endearment, but here may connote a lack of growth and maturity. Earlier he had admonished the Galatians to move beyond infantile behavior and claim the full inheritance that was theirs as children of God through faith in Jesus Christ. Now he reminds them how deeply he has invested his life in them by comparing himself to a mother who must go through the pangs of childbirth again for the sake of her children. This image witnesses to the deep personal anguish Paul was experiencing over the defection of his spiritual offspring in Galatia.

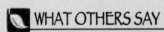 **WHAT OTHERS SAY**

TRUE CHRISTIANITY

They who know anything of religion know it is a vital union with the Son of God—Christ formed in the heart.

—George Whitefield

There is no doubt with regard to Paul's meaning as he agonizes deeply for the people. He did not want to suffer a spiritual miscarriage, but instead was anxious that Christ be formed in their hearts.

Paul brings this section to a conclusion by expressing his desire to be with the Galatians in their time of crisis (4:20). If, as we suggested in the introduction, Galatians was written on the eve of the Jerusalem Council mentioned in Acts 15, then Paul would not have been able to drop everything and return immediately to Galatia.[8] He desired to speak to them in person with his own voice, but for the moment he had to do the second best—write a letter to them.

He confesses his bewilderment over the Galatians: **I am perplexed about you!** (4:20). Earlier he said he could not bear the thought that he had "wasted [his] efforts" on them (4:11). There is no doubt he was exasperated and brokenhearted. He probably felt as he did when writing to the Corinthians: "We are hard pressed . . . perplexed . . . persecuted . . . struck "down." But "we are . . . not crushed . . . in despair . . . abandoned . . . destroyed. Therefore we do not lose heart" (2 Cor. 4:8–9, 16).

The Judaizing teachers had criticized Paul to tear him down and build themselves up. Their method of ministry was as perverted as their doctrine was corrupt. Paul was the true and faithful missionary who desired to preach the gospel to those who had not heard. He had no desire to build "on someone else's foundation" (Rom. 15:20). Unlike the Judaizers, Paul was not interested in a personality cult with a loyalty to him and not the gospel. His primary mission was that Christ would be formed in their hearts.

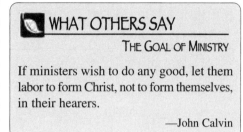

WHAT OTHERS SAY

THE GOAL OF MINISTRY

If ministers wish to do any good, let them labor to form Christ, not to form themselves, in their hearers.

—John Calvin

May God give us ministers of the gospel who refuse to turn and run when opposition threatens, but who will lovingly stand firm, weeping, praying, pleading, correcting until Christ is completely formed in the precious hearts of those who have been placed in their charge.

ENDNOTES

1. Adam Clarke, *Romans to the Revelation*, Clarke's Commentary, vol. 6 (Nashville, Tenn.: Abingdon-Cokesbury Press, 1940), p. 401.

2. See also Timothy George, *Galatians,* The New American Commentary (Nashville, Tenn.: Broadman and Holman, 1994), p. 271.

3. For a helpful interpretation of the demonic in contemporary life, see A. C. McGill, *Suffering: A Test of Theological Method* (Philadelphia: Geneva Press, 1968). On Luther's development of this theme, see H. A. Oberman, *Luther: Man Between God and the Devil* (New Haven, Conn.: Yale University Press, 1989).

4. John Calvin, *Calvin's New Testament Commentary,* vol. 11 (Grand Rapids, Mich.: William B. Eerdmans, 1965), p. 73. Calvin adds, "This ought to restrain a curiosity, if any man, not content with the secret purpose of God, should dare dispute why Christ did not appear sooner."

5. At Iconium, another south Galatian city, an inscription has been found to the goddess Dindimene, also called Mother Zizimee, a goddess with four heads and ten breasts, a goddess similar to the Ephesian Artemis, the nursing mother of all life (William M. Ramsay, *Historical Commentary on Galatians* [Grand Rapids, Mich.: Kregel Classics, 1997], pp. 219–220).

6. See T. C. Oden, *Pastoral Theology* (San Francisco: HarperSanFrancisco, 1983), for a more complete treatment of Paul's pastoral concern as related to his doctrinal content.

7. There are four other imperative verbs in chapter 4, all quotations from the Old Testament: "Be glad," "break forth," and "cry aloud" from Isaiah 54:1 and the summary verse of the Hagar-Sarah analogy at 4:30, quoting Genesis 21:10, "Get rid of the slave woman and her son."

8. See Timothy George, *Galatians*, p. 342.

CHILD OF THE SLAVE WOMAN OR THE FREE WOMAN

Galatians 4:21-31

Paul returns to his central theological treatise by picking up the theme of Abraham and his descendents. Some commentators see the Hagar and Sarah example as both a concluding proof of Scripture regarding Paul's theme of justification by faith and also a connecting link with the practical and ethical section that follows in Galatians 5–6.

Once again Paul takes them back to the historical reference by reminding them of what they would bring on themselves if they reverted back to the law. The law to which Paul referred, particularly here, was the Pentateuch, since he draws the principle argument concerning Abraham's two sons.

1. TWO SONS OF ABRAHAM 4:21-27

Actually Abraham had eight sons, six of them by Keturah (Gen. 25:1–2), whom he married after Sarah's death. It is, however, Ishmael and Isaac that Paul is describing even though their names are not mentioned. Ishmael begot twelve sons who became the ancestors of the Arab tribes. Over the course of time the descendants of Ishmael would be identified with the Gentiles in general, while the sons of Isaac were regarded as the unique possession of God and cherished above all the nations on the face of the earth.

The entire analogy involves five sets of twos: two mothers, two sons, two covenants, two mountains (Mount Sinai and Mount Zion), and two cities (the present Jerusalem and the heavenly one).

Though not mentioned by name in verse 22, Hagar was an Egyptian slave attached to the household of Abraham, while Sarah was a free woman, the lawful wife of Abraham. Paul's introduction of the contrast between slavery and freedom plays an important role in his application of the example in the closing verses of this chapter.

The two sons had different mothers—one slave, one free—and the sons were born in different ways. The son of the slave woman **was born in the ordinary way** (4:23), that is, according to the flesh and by the normal means of procreation. The son of the free woman **was born as the result of a promise**, directly fulfilling God's word to Abraham. Luther observed that the principal difference was the absence of the word of God in the birth of Ishmael:

> When Hagar conceived and gave birth to Ishmael, there was not voice or word of God that predicted this; but with Sarah's permission Abraham went into Hagar the slave, whom Sarah, because she was barren, gave as his wife as Genesis testifies . . . therefore Ishmael was born without the word, solely at the request of Sarah herself. Here there was no word of God that commanded or promised Abraham a son; but everything happened by chance, as Sarah's words indicate: "It may be," she says, "that I shall obtain children by her."[1]

The two women represented two different covenants. Hagar represented Sinai, the law with its slavish exactions and terrible threatenings—a true symbol of the working of the Law of Moses. Sarah represented Jerusalem, typical of the gospel with its freedom and fruitfulness. The two mothers, Hagar and Sarah, stand for the two covenants, one derived from Mount Sinai and capable of bearing children destined to be slaves; the other is the covenant of grace sealed in the blood of Christ, the basis for real freedom and release from sin and death.

By using the word *covenant*, Paul takes us back to 3:15–16 where he used it in a legal sense of a last will and testament. Here it has a much broader meaning, defining God's purpose for human life and all that we can be through the Redeemer, Christ the Lord.

Mount Sinai represents the earthly Jerusalem in contrast to the Jerusalem that is above (4:25–26). Hagar and Ishmael were expelled to the desert of Beersheba (Gen. 21:14), that is, to the area later known as Arabia. By emphasizing that Mount Sinai is in Arabia, the land of the Ishmaelites, Paul was preparing his readers for the dramatic contrast he was about to make in the application of the Sarah and Hagar analogy. The law came from Sinai, a mountain outside the land of promise; the gospel began at Zion, or Jerusalem, which was the heart of the Holy Land. The heavenly Jerusalem is the counterpart of Sarah, the free wife of Abraham. When Paul wrote these words to the churches of Galatia, Paul looked to the eschatological renewal God promised His people.

KEY IDEAS

SARAH AND HAGAR

HAGAR	SARAH
Ishmael, the son of slavery	Isaac, the son of freedom
Birth "according to the flesh"	Birth "through the promise"
Old Covenant	New Covenant
Mount Sinai	Mount Zion
Present Jerusalem	Heavenly Jerusalem

Paul quotes from Isaiah 54:1, applying Isaiah's joyful promise to exiled Jerusalem to the ingathering of believers. Isaiah prophesied a great reversal from barrenness to fruitfulness, from despair to joy, and from desolation to blessing. Such a change can only be accomplished by God's intervention.[2]

2. PERSONAL APPLICATION 4:28-31

Paul applies the analogy by first calling the Galatians **brothers** (4:28), indicating that there was a common bond that linked them together in the family of faith. This is the only time Isaac is mentioned by name. Paul teaches the brothers that they were like Isaac, not Ishmael. Their connection to Abraham was not physical but spiritual.

Paul observed a parallel between the mistreatment of Isaac by Ishmael and the persecution being inflicted on the believers of his day. **Get rid of the slave woman and her son** (4:30). Paul is calling on the Galatian believers to once and for all free themselves from the grip of the Judaizers and expel them from their midst. These false teachers were advocating a denial of the gospel itself. When it comes to heresy, there can be no compromise or concession.

Somehow the Galatians had become "bewitched" (3:1) about their own spiritual identity despite the fact that the Spirit had been poured out on them when they were first converted to Christ (3:1–5). The false teachers who had led them astray used Scripture itself to confuse the believers, so Paul bases his arguments against them by using a series of Scriptural passages.

First Paul reminded the Galatians of Abraham who was declared righteous by God through faith alone (3:6–9). Second, he demonstrated the primary purpose and function of the law (3:10–25). Then based on his love for them, Paul pleaded with the Galatians to "become like him" in their reliance on God's grace as the only basis for their salvation (4:12–20). He used Hagar and Sarah as an example of the difference between law and grace, slave and free, and stated that the true descendants of Isaac are those who have been justified through faith on the basis of God's unfailing promise.

The conclusion of the matter is that there is a basic incompatibility between the two systems of salvation—one of law and one of grace. They are so incompatible, in fact, that the only solution is to **get rid of the slave woman and her son** (4:30). Paul, by this time in his letter, must surely have hoped that the Galatians understood fully the concepts of slavery and freedom, grace and law, merit and faith. Believing this was the case he moves on to the third major section of his letter, the practical and the ethical. Having received the Spirit, how does one live a life controlled by the Spirit?

ENDNOTES

Key Ideas Sidebar: Timothy George, *Galatians,* The New American Commentary (Nashville, Tenn.: Broadman and Holman, 1994), p. 342.

1. Martin Luther, *Luther's Works: Lectures on Galatians Chapters 1–4*, vol. 26 (St. Louis: Concordia, 1962), p. 35.

2. See J. L. Martyn, "A Law—Observant Mission: The Background of Galatians," *Martyn Quarterly Review*, vol. 22 (1983), pp. 221–236.

Part Three

Practical and Ethical Issues

GALATIANS 5:1–6:18

9

FREEDOM IN CHRIST
Galatians 5:1–12

As indicated earlier, the epistle to the Galatians has three major divisions of approximately two chapters each. The first section (1:1–2:21) is historical and personal. The second section (3:1–4:31) is doctrinal, theological. The third section (5:1–6:10) is practical and ethical with a great deal of exhortation. Having defended his own apostolic position and personal integrity, and having laid the foundation of justification by faith alone without law or merit, Paul now gives himself to exhortation. We are justified by faith, so how do we live by faith? Paul was adamant in making the point in chapters 2 and 3 that, contrary to what the false teachers were requiring, circumcision and other requirements of the Jewish law were not necessary supplements to faith in Christ. It is true the Spirit helps Christians do good works, but we are saved by Christ through faith alone. Now Paul turns his attention to the implications of the doctrine of justification by faith alone and to describe what it actually meant for a believer who had "died to the law" to now "live for God" (2:19). We are justified by faith, a faith that must be active in love and lead to holiness of life.

Galatians is called the "Magna Carta of Christian Liberty." If it is that, and it is, then Galatians 5:1 is, without question, one of the key verses of the entire epistle. The people he was addressing were still hearing the strong notes of both slavery and freedom used by Paul in chapter 4. They were thinking of the analogy of Hagar and Sarah. Now Paul tells them to stand for freedom: **Christ has set us free . . . do not let yourselves be burdened again** (5:1).

The liberty we received in Christ was purchased at a great cost. Christ, the Son of God, became human, suffered to an unparalleled and incomprehensible degree, and died the shameful death of the crucified to win back the liberty we had forfeited by voluntary sin. Redemption was hopeless from the human point of view, and were it not for the intervention of Christ—a thoroughly competent and worthy Redeemer—we would have been in irretrievable bondage. Since Christ redeemed us, every believer has the birthright of Christian liberty.

The liberty Paul had in mind was not political liberty. The gospel of grace works in any political system, and Christianity does not guarantee "unalienable rights," as does the American Declaration of Independence. The liberty mentioned by the apostle is freedom from Jewish rites and ceremonies, called **a yoke of slavery** (5:1), and liberty from the power and guilt of sin, which only the grace of God can take away.

It is apparent that some of the believers in the churches of Galatia did not know what to do with their freedom in Christ. Some were using liberty as a license to gratify their sinful nature. Others understood liberty to mean they were free to be part of a theological anarchy, failing to proclaim the whole counsel of God and, thereby, fracturing the church.

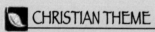

CHRISTIAN THEME

TRUE FREEDOM

Christian liberty is always grounded on both the believer's relationship with Jesus Christ and with the community of faith. We need Christ and we need each other to provide and define the parameters of liberty. Attempting to live the Christian life independently of the fellowship of other believers is dangerous. Christianity apart from Christ does not exist.

Mark my words (5:2), and strong words they are, for having told the Galatians that they ought to expel these Judaizing false teachers, Paul now speaks at length to the terrible danger posed by these people. He can hardly contain himself in emphasizing how awful these people are as evidenced by his final word in verse 12—that they ought to have themselves castrated.

The false teachers would not give in. They were insisting again and again that Paul's converts in Galatia be circumcised. Paul develops his argument against them again. First, if the believers were again to depend on external rites, doing so was an open rejection of Christ—**Christ will be of no value to you** (5:2). The defection from the gospel, as evidenced by insisting on circumcision, means the forfeiture of all Christian privileges. It is so because it means that such people would be rejecting God's all-sufficient provision for salvation through faith in Jesus Christ and His finished work on the cross. If they rejected the cross of Christ by moving again to Judaism, by accepting circumcision as a means of salvation, they would be reverting to their old paganism.

Second, Paul argues that external rites demand universal obedience: **I declare to every man that lets himself be circumcised that he is obligated to obey the whole law** (5:3). The Galatians were in grave danger of taking a step that would be their downfall; that step was circumcision. Hence, Paul warns them that circumcision, though a matter of indifference as an external rite, would in their case involve an obligation to keep the whole law. He has already shown that this was impossible. Not only would they lose Christ, they would put a burden on themselves they could never carry. Later he would point out to them that "not even those who are circumcised obey the law" (6:13).

Third, Paul insists that Christianity is superior to external rites (5:4–5). The fact is people who try to be justified by the law have **alienated** [themselves] **from Christ** (5:4). The contrast is unmistakable. On the one hand there are the Judaizers insisting on legalistic proposals, debating endlessly which of the Mosaic feasts they should celebrate and with what rites, absorbed in all the details of the Mosaic ceremony, and finally deciding to be circumcised to submit to the law. On the other hand, there is Paul with the church of the Spirit, walking in righteousness of faith and the communion of the Holy Spirit, waiting joyfully the Savior's final coming and the hope laid up for them in heaven.

Why would the believers in Galatia want to take the risk of being alienated from Christ and thus expose themselves to the peril of eternal death? We cannot have just part of Christ without losing Him entirely. The false teachers apparently did not understand that the imposition of circumcision meant their alienation from Christ. They saw circumcision as a kind of enhancement to grace. Paul makes it clear that to try to mingle the merit of works with the grace of Christ is to lose the grace of Christ.

It appears to this writer that the correct interpretation of this text suggests that Paul was teaching the actual forfeiture of salvation by a regenerated believer. A mistaken interpretation, on the other hand, suggests that Paul was writing to Christian churches that were founded on the doctrines of grace but were in danger of forsaking that sound doctrinal bedrock for a theology that could lead to ruin. But that ruin would not mean a loss of salvation. It is rather difficult to imagine how a person could become **alienated from Christ** and **fallen away from grace** (5:4) and still retain salvation.

Fourth, Paul argues that it is through Christ that we await **the righteousness for which we hope** (5:5). Righteousness does not happen because of circumcision, but **the only thing that counts is faith expressing itself in love** (5:6). Love is the working energy of faith. Faith that does not work by love is nothing, whether the person is circumcised or uncircumcised. Paul was not saying that we are justified by love, either our love for God or for our neighbor. We are justified by grace through faith, and that faith is active in leading to love and holiness. Paul here and in other places brings together the basic triad of Christian virtues: faith, hope, and love. We can generate none of these human qualities ourselves; they are gifts of God made real in the lives of His children by the presence of the Spirit in their hearts.

Who cut in on you? (5:7). The image is that of the Olympic athlete who charges out from the starting line with a great deal of energy and runs past his competitors for a while, only to have someone enter the race illegally and trip him up. Earlier Paul asked, "Who has bewitched you?" (3:1). Now he asks a similar rhetorical question: "Who cut in on you?" The Galatians had eagerly embraced the truth; their lives were changed; they were running well. The introduction and infusion of false teaching changed all this. Their spiritual progress was arrested; their faith disturbed. They wavered in their allegiance and were in danger of losing all the advantages they had gained.

The Christian life is not like a one-hundred-meter dash; it is a marathon. Beginning well is important; finishing well is critical. The gospel is not simply something to be believed; it must be obeyed. Disobedience is the major hindrance to running well and finishing strong.

It was the undermining of sound doctrine that made it possible for Satan to seduce them to careless, disobedient living.

Apparently the Judaizing teachers in Galatia were appealing and persuasive. They must have been eloquent in their speech because the believers in Galatia were persuaded by them to abandon the gospel of grace. They were accepting a new doctrine of salvation that was

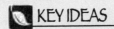

KEY IDEAS

CHRISTIAN LIFE

There is a correlation between theological correctness and spiritual vitality. People who fail in the race usually begin to trip by neglecting biblical truth and then fall into disobedience.

composed of a combination of grace on the one hand and human merit and achievement on the other hand. Paul's method was so different from theirs. He did not use "eloquence or superior wisdom;" instead the proclamation of the gospel was done "in weakness and fear, and with much trembling" (1 Cor. 2:1–5). The methodology of the false teachers and their techniques of persuasion did not come from God and were not grounded on the Word of truth. Christian doctrine is to be tested by biblical revelation, not by the persua-

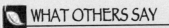

WHAT OTHERS SAY

THE DECEIVER

The devil is a juggler with a thousand tricks, by means of which he is able to impress such an obvious and shameful lie on the heart that you would swear a thousand times that it is the most certain truth.

—Martin Luther

siveness of some messenger who may have a personality that is appealing.[1]

If Paul was concerned with the methodology of the false teachers in verse 8, he was even more concerned with the end result of their interference in the gospel truth (5:9). Leaven, **yeast**, is a symbol of evil. The church of Christ and each believer must be careful to resist the beginning of sin because the least of errors and the smallest number of seduced people are like a little leaven that eventually will contaminate and destroy the whole. A slight deviation from the truth, such as the harmless rite of circumcision, can bring total ruin to the Christian community. As a little poison can destroy an entire body, so a little error can turn the gospel to something that is not the gospel.

It is the little rift within the lute,
That by and by will make the music mute,
And, ever widening, slowly silence all:
The little rift within the lover's lute,
Or little pitted speck in garnered fruit,
That rotting inward slowly moulders all.[2]

In verse 9, Paul was weighted down with concern for the Galatians as he warned them of how, with a small bit of yeast, the batch of bread could be destroyed. Immediately, however, true to the greatness of the apostle's spirit, his mood changes as he declares his confidence that after all was said and done, the Galatians would **take no other view** (5:10). What a wonderful example for all who teach: to believe the best in people. Observe that Paul's hope in the Galatians was rooted in confidence that is **in the Lord** (5:10).

Paul was not only confident that the Galatians would not turn away from the gospel of grace, he was also confident that the people responsible for **throwing [them] into confusion** (5:10) would **pay the penalty**. J. B. Phillips expressed it this way: "But whoever it is who is worrying you will have a serious charge to answer one day." Those who teach heresy must either face church discipline or divine judgment.

If I am still preaching circumcision (5:11). There was a false accusation made by Paul's opponents that Paul himself preached circumcision in certain places but not in other places, that he changed his message when preaching to the Gentiles and had a different view of circumcision when preaching to the Jews. Of course such a charge was malicious and was intended to discredit Paul.

Paul was not engaged in some anti-circumcision crusade. He taught that a person should order his life according to where he was when he came to Christ. To the Corinthians he laid down his thinking on this matter: "Was a man already circumcised when he was called? He should not become uncircumcised. Was a man uncircumcised when he was called? He should not be circumcised. Circumcision is nothing and uncircumcised is nothing" (1 Cor. 7:18–19). In other words, Jews do not need to become Gentiles and Gentiles do not need to become Jews. All can be members of the family of God.

The bottom line is that you cannot preach both the Cross and circumcision. If Paul preached the necessity of circumcision, he saw that as ceasing to preach Christ crucified. The cross is the enemy of all the rites and ceremonies to which people cling for salvation. If our security is in circumcision, then the Cross is a denial of all such security.

Paul wished that the people who were troubling the church in Galatia by insisting on circumcision would have the knife slip to the point of them castrating themselves. After all, they were emasculating the gospel by adding a Mosaic rite to it; they deserved to be emasculated themselves. The question has been raised if a minister of the gospel ever has a right to speak this way. It would be inconsistent of Paul and Christian grace if Paul actually meant that he wished his opponents to suffer physical harm. He had been severely attacked, the gospel was being threatened, and the church could

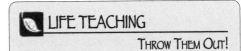

LIFE TEACHING
THROW THEM OUT!

Sometimes error is so pervasive in the church that discipline is not strong enough. For the preservation of the church there are times, limited as they may be, when excommunication is the only solution. In such instances leaders must proceed slowly, in lenity and wisdom.

have been destroyed by these false teachers. Paul knew that strong language was necessary. What he really wanted was for them to be cut off from the church and denied any influence on the believers.

ENDNOTES

1.   Compare to the comment of Ignatius of Antioch (Rom. 3:3): "Christianity is not the work of persuasiveness, but of greatness, when it is hated by the world" (*The Apostolic Fathers*, ed. K. Lake [Cambridge, Mass.: Harvard University Press, 1912], p. 1.229).

2.   Alfred Lord Tennyson, "Idylls of the King: Merlin and Vivien," http://charon.sfsu.edu/TENNYSON/poems/merlinandvivian.shtml, accessed 10/22/06.

10

FLESH AND SPIRIT

Galatians 5:13-26

Paul was concerned about another danger: antinomianism—the teaching that freedom from the law meant release from all moral restraints. Christian liberty is a great blessing, but it is also a solemn responsibility. People in today's world clamor for *liberty*, when they mean *license* to indulge in their unholy passions unchecked by the restraints of law.

Christian liberty is not the liberty of the flesh but of the Spirit. Cheap grace argues that we need not worry about moral rules or even the Ten Commandments. We may sin because God loves to forgive. The more we sin the more opportunities we give for God to display His grace. Some of the people in Rome seemed to think this way, causing Paul to ask, "What shall we say, then? Shall we go on sinning so that grace may increase? By no means!" (Rom. 6:1–2). To use Christian liberty as an occasion to indulge in any sin is to take one of the best things in the world and turn it into one of the worst.

1. CHRISTIAN LIBERTY BASED ON LOVE 5:13-15

Rather than abuse our Christian liberty, we are to **serve one another in love** (5:13). In fact, **the entire law is summed up in a single command: "Love your neighbor as yourself"** (5:14). If love does not show itself by deeds of love, then we are deceiving ourselves.[1]

The church in Galatia must have been in a state of great distress. There were, obviously, altercations among the believers as a result of their defection from the gospel. The believers were in an intense and deadly struggle. If this state continued, the churches in Galatia would cease to exist (5:15). All three verbs Paul used to describe their unholy uncivil war on one another—biting, devouring, being destroyed—were bywords commonly used in Hellenistic Greek to suggest wild animals engaged in deadly struggle.

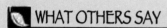

WHAT OTHERS SAY

RELIGIOUS DISPUTES

Nothing is so destructive to the peace of man, and to the peace of the soul, as religious disputes: when they prevail, religion in general has little place.

—Adam Clarke

Paul was writing to churches caught in a serious theological conflict over the doctrines of the false teachers. Some commentators think some of these churches may have divided into parties of Paul, James, and Peter, much as the Corinthians did later.

Paul spoke as a pastor to all the believers in Galatia, warning them against continuing strife and mutual destruction. The fact is these Judaizers continued to inflame a conflict that was already present among these Christians. It was the works of the flesh that Paul would deal with in the next few verses that had produced the fracture in the fellowship and broken the unity that Paul was lamenting.

2. LIFE BY THE SPIRIT 5:16–18

Now that Paul had made clear that the sins he had enumerated could and would annihilate the churches of Galatia, he moved on to something far more positive—the divinely appointed remedy for so grave a dilemma. **So I say** (5:16)—or as Phillips paraphrases it, "Here is my advice"—is a rather common way Paul introduces a new section of material.

Paul's diagnosis of the conflict that confronts every Christian begins with a command— **Walk in the Spirit** (5:16 KJV)—and a promise that **you will not gratify the desires of the sinful nature** (NIV). The Christians in Galatia might have argued that the religion of Christ had not brought to them the deliverance they had expected. Although Paul had taught them to believe in the almighty power of Christ and of Christ's grace, they found that there was within them another power antagonistic to the grace of Christ. Obviously we are to live the Christian life in the body, and the body has physical needs, desires, and impulses.

The question for us is not how to dehumanize ourselves, but rather, where do we acquire the resources for victorious Christian living? Paul's answer is the Holy Spirit, who has freed us from sin, has given us new life in regeneration, can keep us truly free from gratifying the desires of the sinful nature, and makes it possible for us to walk in the power of sanctification.

In Galatians 5 there are four distinct verbs used by Paul to describe the Spirit-controlled life of the believer. All of these verbs have a similar meaning: to **walk in the Spirit** (5:16 KJV), to be **led by the Spirit** (5:18), to **live by the Spirit** (5:25), and to **keep in step with the Spirit** (5:25). Each of these verbs suggests a dynamic relationship, direction, and purpose. They also indicate an activity now in progress. To be led by the Spirit means to go where the Spirit is going, to listen to His voice, to discern His will, and to follow His guidance. Failing to do so would mean they would succumb to their own libertine tendencies. In addition they would fall into the disputes within their churches that would destroy the churches.

There is a dualism that exists both in the world at large and in the individual believer (5:17). The word *sarx* used here and in other of Paul's writings (translated *flesh* in the KJV and **sinful nature** in the NIV) means far more than anything material or physical. It involves the mind, the will, and the emotions, as well as the physical body. To become complacent or to imagine oneself invulnerable to the flesh's attraction is a sure path to spiritual failure. None of us are so spiritually strong or mature that we need not heed this warning. At the same time, neither are any of us so weak that we cannot be free from the tyranny of flesh through the power of the Spirit.

If you are led by the Spirit, you are not under law (5:18). Before enumerating the works of the flesh, Paul states again what he had said before. Life in the Spirit stands in irreconcilable conflict with existence under the law. Paul is not saying that the moral law has been abrogated or that the Ten Commandments have become antiquated. He is teaching that believers are energized to fulfill the true intention of the law because they have been set free from the law by the indwelling of the Spirit. In Romans 8:3–4, Paul expressed this same thought: "God has done what the law, weakened by the flesh, could not do: sending his own Son in the likeness of sinful flesh and for sin, he condemned sin in the flesh, in order that the just requirement of the law might be fulfilled in us, who walk not according to the flesh but according to the Spirit."

3. THE WORKS OF THE FLESH 5:19–21

Paul's two catalogs of sinful deeds and holy traits closely parallel similar listings of virtues and vices in the writings of such moral philosophers as Seneca, Cicero, and Epictetus and Hellenistic Jewish thinkers such as Philo of Alexandria. For Paul, flesh and Spirit were two powers locked in conflict on the battlefield of every individual Christian. It is necessary to place Paul's antithesis of flesh and Spirit in its broad cosmic context if we hope to understand the tension that characterizes the church of Jesus Christ in this present evil world.

The sins enumerated may be grouped into four classes.

SINS AGAINST CHASTITY

Sexual Immorality (porneia). The word *porneia* originally meant prostitution. It is translated most frequently "fornication." In the KJV it denotes an unlawful sexual intercourse, including adultery and incest. One suspects Paul prioritizes sexual immorality because these sins display more graphically the self-centeredness and rebellion against God's norm. For believers to fall into sexual misconduct deeply grieves the Holy Spirit because it is His presence in their lives that makes their bodies temples unto the Lord (see 1 Cor. 6:18–20). Often acts of immorality are done in the name of love. In actuality they are really the antithesis of love, which is the primary fruit of the Spirit.

Impurity (akatharsia). The word *akatharsia* means uncleanness. It includes whatever is contaminating in word or look, in gesture or in dress, in thought or sentiment. The word has both a medical and ceremonial connotation. Doctors clean a wound before applying medication to it. Under the Mosaic Law, ceremonial impurity barred one from participation in worship rituals of the Temple until the impediment was removed. When Jesus cleansed a leper, He required him to complete the ritual of purification in accordance with the Old Testament provision (see Matt. 8:1–4). Uncleanness then is the defilement of sexual sin and the separation from God that it brings. In 1 John 1:9 we read, "If we confess our sins, he is faithful and just and will forgive us our sins and purify [*katharise*] us from all unrighteousness [or uncleanness]."

Debauchery (aseldeia). William Barclay defines this particular vice as "love of sin so reckless and so audacious that a man has ceased to care what God thinks about his actions."[2] Debauchery is the complete loss of restraint, decency, and self-respect. There are no limits to what a person would do if he or she had no ability to blush or be ashamed in any way. It is the final loathsome analysis of the works of the flesh.

THE SINS AGAINST RELIGION

Idolatry (eidololatria). Idolatry and sensuality have always been closely related. Some of the most popular pagan systems were purveyors of lust and placed the sanctions of religion on that lust. From the ancient fertility cult of Baal to the sacral prostitution at the temple of Aphrodite in Corinth, the homage paid to false gods was often accompanied by shameful displays of sensuality. The abuse of the gift of sex leads inevitably to the elevation of the creature to the level of the Creator. Idolatry is not limited to the sensual; it involves the worship of anything besides God—persons, gadgets, sports, cars, homes, clothes—anything!

Witchcraft (pharmakeia). We derive our word *pharmacy* from this word that literally means "drug." In the New Testament the word is associated with the occult and is usually translated as "witchcraft" or "sorcery." At times drugs were employed in the

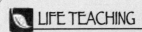

LIFE TEACHING

KILLING THE HELPLESS

In the early church both infanticide (often effected through the exposure of newborn babies to the harsh elements) and abortion (commonly brought about by the use of drugs) were regarded as murderous acts.

casting of spells and enchantments. Witchcraft conveyed the idea of black magic and demonic control often using drugs with occult properties for a number of purposes including, interestingly, abortion. As J. T. Noonan has written, "Paul's usage here cannot be restricted to abortion, but the term he chose is comprehensive enough to include the use of abortifacient drugs."[3]

SINS AGAINST LOVE (CHARITY)

Hatred (echthrai). This is the first of eight nouns Paul uses to refer to the breakdown of interpersonal relationships. Hatred is the opposite of love. Paul used the same word to describe the hostility of the sinful mind toward God in Romans 8:7. It is the antithesis to brotherly love and kindness.

Discord (eris). Paul used this word nine times to characterize the strife and discord in so many of his congregations. He spoke of those who preach Christ "out of envy and rivalry" (Phil. 1:15). When the principle of hatred breaks out into open acts, discord is evidenced by disputes, contests, altercations, even lawsuits.

Jealousy (zelos). It literally means to grieve for another's excelling us. A jealous person wants what someone else has. Jealousy often leads to bitterness and sometimes even erupts in violence as it did when Joseph's brothers seized him in anger and sold him into slavery (see Gen. 37:12–36). At the root of jealousy is ingratitude to God, a failure to accept life as a gift from Him. When we are jealous of others, we fling our own gifts before God in unthankful rebellion.

Fits of rage (thymoi). The word used here in Galatians means a "passionate outburst of hostile feeling or anger." It suggests an uncontrollable verbal violence that may be excused by some as a natural tendency, such as an "Irish temper," but it is conduct unbecoming to a Christian. The word is used in Revelation to refer to God's wrath (14:10; 19:15) and to Satan's rage (12:12).

Selfish ambition (eritheiai). This term came from the political arena in ancient Greek culture where it meant "office seeking." Obviously not all who give themselves to political life are guilty of this sin, but the vice described here is the idea of trying to get ahead by manipulation for personal gain and putting others down in the process. Not only is this bad politics in the world, but it is corrupting to the community of faith, especially when we remember that we serve the Lord, who came to serve and to give His life for us.

Dissensions (dichostasiai). Paul used this word here and in only one other place—Romans 16:17: "I urge you, brothers, watch out for those who cause divisions and put obstacles in your way that are contrary to the teaching you have learned. Keep away from them." As with the previous term, the word *dissensions* carries political overtones, suggesting the cultivation of a party spirit or exclusive elite within the church. When this happens, the unity of the church is broken, and bad-mouthing and mutual destruction often follow.

Factions (haireseis). The basic meaning of the word is "to choose," from which we also get our English word *heresy*. The idea is that one chooses a doctrine that is clearly at variance with the rule of faith. The result of such activity is further division of people and the casting of stumbling blocks before others, bringing confusion, superior attitudes, pride, and bickering.

Envy (phthonoi). Envy is the "painful or resentful awareness of an advantage enjoyed by another joined with a desire to possess the same advantage" (Webster's Dictionary). The word in the original is plural, which suggests many expressions of envious desire. In this instance, it described evil conduct and unacceptable rivalry that had sprung from the malice and ill will of the Galatians toward one another.

SINS AGAINST TEMPERANCE

Drunkenness (methai). There is no way to reconcile drunkenness with the life of a Spirit-filled believer. Alcohol abuse was a common fact of life in the Roman Empire, and Paul is making it clear that he expected a totally different, higher standard of conduct among those who belonged to Christ. He wrote to the Ephesians, "Do not get drunk on wine, which leads to debauchery. Instead, be filled with the Spirit" (Eph. 5:18). Alcoholism is such a major problem in the world and has been for so long that many Christian fellowships have taken a strict stand against the use of all alcohol, teaching that total abstinence is the wisest position for the believer. A strong case could be made for that, but this we know with certainty: Excessive drinking was portrayed by Paul as being incompatible with a real Christian commitment.

Orgies (komoi). In the KJV the word is translated "reveling," and in the RSV "carousing." It occurs three times in the New Testament: here and in Romans 13:13 and 1 Peter 4:3. In each case it is linked to the sin of drunkenness. In New Testament times, and certainly in our time, the abuse of alcohol contributed to marital infidelity, child abuse, spouse abuse, and the general breakdown of the family. It is difficult to measure how much of the moral chaos in society can also be tied directly with this sin, but it is undoubtedly considerable.

And the like (5:23) is Paul's way of saying, "I could go on and on, but I have given enough for you to understand the ugly reality of the flesh." Paul gave fifteen steps into the pit of depravity, enough to make clear that only the grace of God by the transforming power of the Holy Spirit can rescue one from the snare of such a loveless life.

4. THE END OF SIN 5:21

Exclusion from the kingdom of God is a person's own act of self-exclusion; such persons will not enter in, having loved darkness rather than light. The Galatians should not have been surprised by these repeated warnings by Paul. Apparently he was referring to his preaching of the gospel in Galatia and the earlier instruction he had given, which they were in danger of forgetting or ignoring.

Every person will be called upon to face Christ either at death or when Christ returns in a personal, visible manner. This is the blessed hope of believers, but it is also a threatening event for those outside of Christ because Christ is

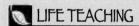

LIFE TEACHING

KILLING THE HELPLESS

The Bible uses several terms to describe sin. Sometimes sin is described as missing the mark or aim. This is the word we know as *transgression*. The word appears seven times in the New Testament and is twice applied to Adam's fall (Rom. 5:14; 1 Tim. 2:14). At times sin is described as disobedience to a voice, that is, to hear carelessly and take no heed to what is heard. This word appears three times (Rom. 5:19; 2 Cor. 10:6; Heb. 9:7). On at least one occasion sin is described as ignorance of what we ought to have done (Heb. 9:7); sometimes as disobedience to law (fourteen times in the New Testament) and is usually translated as *iniquity*.

coming again to judge the living and the dead (Acts 10:42). The people who indulge in sin and behave in sinful ways will be excluded from the celestial blessings of the kingdom of God. This is not an idle threat but a solemn warning from the pen of a divinely inspired apostle of Jesus Christ, Paul himself. Those who are slaves to the works of the flesh will not be heirs of the kingdom of God; but as Jesus said, all can be saved by repenting and turning from such wicked ways.

It is possible to be forgiven of sin and make a clear break with all the works of darkness through God's gift of transforming grace in Christ. This is the good news that we preach and teach with confidence.

5. THE FRUIT OF THE SPIRIT 5:22–26

Paul now turns to the graces of the Spirit-controlled life. What an amazing contrast! The fifteen misdeeds of the works of the flesh painted a stark picture of evil; now the catalog of grace is beautiful, harmonious, and symmetrical—a description of the life of holiness. The nine graces are grouped together into three triads: Love, joy, peace; then patience, kindness, goodness; and faithfulness, gentleness, self-control.

LOVE (AGAPE)

It has been suggested and may indeed be true that there is no word Paul used more than the word *love*. The noun *agape* occurs seventy-five times, and the verb *agapao*, to show love, thirty-four times in his writings. One is not surprised to find that love heads the list of the nine graces of the Christian life. Love is the source from which all the other graces flow. As C. S. Lewis put it,

> God, who needs nothing, loves into existence holy superfluous creatures in order that he may love and perfect them. He creates the universe, already foreseen—or should we say "seeing"? there are no tenses in God—the buzzing cloud of flies around the cross, the flayed back pressed against the uneven stake, the nails driven through the mesial nerves, the repeated incipient suffocation as the

body droops, the repeated torture of back and arms as it is time after time, for breath's sake hitched up . . . This is the diagram of love Himself, the inventor of all loves.[4]

It must never be forgotten that love, the foremost characteristic of the Christian life, is a result of God's unfathomable love toward us. Paul said earlier in this Galatian letter, "I live by faith in the Son of God, who loved me and gave himself for me" (2:20). The result of the saving, sanctifying work of the Holy Spirit in our lives is that we are enabled to love one another with the same kind of love God has toward us.

When the Holy Spirit performs His work in the believer's life, a love for God is immediate and obvious. But Paul's primary emphasis in this letter was on the Christian's love for one another. Many churches experience division because the believers fail to love one another as God has commanded. To love God and to love the Word of God means that we will surely love those who also love God. The world of the early Christian church was impressed with the love believers had for one another. The world today needs to see that same depth of love in the body of Christ, a love that transcends minor differences and any perceived wrongs.

JOY (CHARA)

This word means "to rejoice in the true acknowledgment of God, in the work of our regeneration, and in the hope of eternal life is characteristic of the life received in God through Christ." The Greek root word for *joy* is the same as that for *grace*. When we come to know God's grace in forgiveness, we celebrate the Christian life as a festival of joy. Joy is also closely related to hope, a word Paul did not list here as a fruit of the Spirit. It is hope that differentiates Christian joy from mere secular happiness. Christian joy does not mean there will be no pain; it is a joy lived out even in the midst of suffering. We have real joy, however, because of the certainty of God's ultimate victory over all the powers of sin, death, hell, and the grave. We have that certainty because of the death and resurrection of Jesus Christ, "who for the joy set before him endured the cross" (Heb. 12:2). We know that our Lord is now at the right hand of the Father and will come again in great glory.

PEACE (*EIRENE*)

The Christian's peace is not dependent on the absence of war, strife, or even violence. The concept of peace is that of a wholeness and well-bring that includes both a right relationship with God and loving harmony with one's fellow human beings. We have peace with God because we have been justified by faith. Having peace with God, we are called on to be peacemakers both within the family of faith and throughout the broader networks of humanity. To be peacemakers it is necessary that we neither take offense nor give offense; we seek to edify one another and to do good to all.

PATIENCE (*MAKROTHYMIA*)

The term *makrothymia* literally means long-mindedness, bearing with the provocation of others by considering the lengths to which God has gone in Christ in dealing with us. If God is long-suffering with us, His creatures who have been rebellious time and again, then we should display that same grace in our relationships with one another. It is particularly important for those in pastoral ministries or in church leadership to give evidence of this fruit of the Spirit. Paul instructed Timothy, "Preach the Word; be prepared in season and out of season; correct, rebuke and encourage—with great patience and careful instruction" (2 Tim. 4:2).

KINDNESS (*CHRESTOTES*)

This word for kindness is found only four times in the New Testament and used only by Paul. It carries the idea of generosity or benevolence in dealing with others, going the second mile, and blessing when we are wronged.

FAITHFULNESS (*PISTIS*)

The word for faithfulness here means "fidelity, the quality of being true, trustworthy, and reliable in all one's dealings with others." This is the term Paul used in his instructions to Timothy concerning the appointment of church leaders: "And the things you have heard me say in the presence of many witnesses entrust to reliable men who will also be qualified to teach others" (2 Tim. 2:2). Some things are more important than success,

recognition, promotion, or popular acclaim; faithfulness is first among
those things.

GENTLENESS (*PRATES*)

The word *prates* is similar to that of longsuffering but carries with it
the idea of genuine humility, a teachable spirit, and consideration of
others. In English, the word *gentleness* has become equated with weakness. As a fruit of the Spirit, however, the word has the connotation of
strength under control, power harnessed in loving service and respectful
actions. Jesus was gentle and meek, but He could act with strength, as He
demonstrated when He drove the money changers out of the Temple.

SELF-CONTROL (*ENKRATEIA*)

Self-control is temperance, the mastery of desires and appetites in the
proper use of the gifts and creatures of God. In 1 Corinthians 7:9, Paul
used this word in a context related to the control of sexual passions and
desires. The word is not confined to sexuality alone but applies to all of
life. Runners without self-control do not win the race since they run aim-
lessly. The Christian life requires strict discipline. Paul said, "I beat my
body and make it my slave so that after I have preached to others, I
myself will not be disqualified for the prize" (1 Cor. 9:27).

Against such things there is no law (5:23). If our lives are adorned
with such virtues, the fruit of the Spirit, we cannot be condemned by any
law. The whole purpose and design of the moral law of God is to produce
the virtues described here in the heart and lives of His children.

The conclusion of the two catalogs of vices and virtues is outlined by
Paul in the final three verses of chapter 5. What is the Christian life to be?
A constant tug of war between the flesh and the Spirit, or are believers to
experience real victory? Paul asserts that the Holy Spirit can provide victory and that He does so by the sanctification of the believer.
Sanctification involves two things: mortification—dying to the flesh—and
vivification—life and growth in the Spirit. In Galatians 2:20, Paul used the
passive voice in declaring, "I have been crucified with Christ." This refers
to something done for us by someone else. We have been crucified with

Christ in that He took our place on the cross; it is by His sacrifice that we are made righteous by God through faith. In 5:24, the voice is active, which describes something done by us (in contrast to the passive voice where something is done to us). The sanctified believer puts the works of the flesh to death daily by the disciplines of prayer, fasting, and self-control.

We are required as believers to take up our cross daily and follow Christ (Luke 9:23). To crucify the flesh means that we make it the business of life to overcome the evil dispositions and desires of human nature through the grace of God and to abstain from those actions to which such dispositions lead. There is cleansing from all sin, but it is a mistake to think there are shortcuts to constant spiritual victory in the Christian life. The sanctified life requires constant vigilance, obedience, and, at times, repentance.

To **keep in step with the Spirit** (5:25) is a phrase taken from the military and means "to be drawn up in line or to stand in a row." We are to show by our lives that the Spirit of Christ dwells in us. The Christian's life is growing, the walk is progressing, and the Spirit is guiding. The new birth is followed by a new life, and that life must be consistent with the fruit of the Spirit. Walking in the Spirit implies living in the Spirit. We live in the Spirit when the Spirit directs, controls, and governs.

Galatians 5:26 serves as a transitional verse connecting Paul's teaching about the Christian life with the specific situation in the churches of Galatia. The verse is linked to what has gone before since it is the negative counterpart to Paul's exhortation concerning the work of the Spirit in the

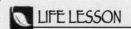 **LIFE LESSON**

BOAST ONLY IN THE CROSS

There is a great deal of egotism in the world, which makes its way in the body of believers. Many people are prone to vaunt themselves as being superior to others or to seek honor through things that do not possess moral good—such as their birth, riches, or certain gifts. The competition among believers, ministers, Christian institutions, and denominations is unbecoming and unhealthy in the family of faith. We may glory in our distinctions even when they are trivial. Such glorying is vain; it blunts our Christian witness. May God deliver us from such vanity and cause us to glory only in the cross of our Lord Jesus Christ (6:14).

life of the believer. If we walk in the Spirit, we will **not become conceited**. To be conceited is to be puffed up with pride, arrogant, boastful, and setting a value on things that are not valuable.

ENDNOTES

Life Teaching Sidebar: J. T. Noonan, Jr., *An Almost Absolute Value in History*, (Cambridge, Mass.: Harvard University Press, 1970), p. 9.

1.   G. Ebeling, *Luther: An Introduction to His Thought* (Philadelphia: Fortress, 1972), p. 212. Luther insisted that a living faith expresses itself through works of love, in service to the neighbor. That such good works are done in freedom is a consequence of justification by faith. Luther asserted: "One does not love until he has become godly and righteous. Love does not make us godly, but when one becomes godly, love is the result."

2.   William Barclay, *Flesh and Spirit: An Examination of Galatians 5:19–23* (London: SCM, 1962), p. 31.

3.   Noonan, *An Almost Absolute Value*, p. 9.

4.   C. S. Lewis, *The Four Loves* (New York: Harcourt, Brace & World, 1960), p. 176.

11

FREEDOM IN SERVICE
Galatians 6:1-10

We should disregard the chapter division since the practical and ethical section that began in 5:1 continues through 6:10. In 5:2–12, Paul warned of the danger to Christian living from the error of legalism. In 5:13–15, Paul spoke of the danger of presuming on the grace of God and, thereby, misusing the freedom in Christ as a pretext for self-indulgence, immorality, and a disregard for the moral law of God. The remainder of chapter 5 centers on Paul's description of the works of the flesh as opposed to the fruit of the Spirit. In 6:1–10, Paul applies these principles to the specific cases in the life of the Galatian churches.

Service in the church and the application of the fruit of the Spirit to ministry involves the bearing of one another's burdens and the bearing of our own burdens.

1. CARING FOR THOSE IN SIN 6:1

The sympathy toward those who stumble in the Christian way is a test of spiritual mindedness. To be **caught in a sin** (6:1) implies that a person was suddenly entrapped, overtaken, or surprised. Perhaps Paul was referring to a real-life situation he encountered in Galatia or, as seems more likely, he was giving a general admonition for dealing with moral lapses that can occur within the body of faith. It is possible to be "caught in a sin."[1] All believers must be aware of that possibility and probability. The question is what we are to do when a believer is so "caught."

The fall of any Christian should be the occasion of heart-searching and profound humility on the part of the believer. There is to be no contempt for the one who has fallen, no sense of superiority, no arrogance, since all of us are tempted. Rather, we are to thrust our shoulder beneath the weight of that person's shame and restore the fallen in a spirit of humility. The **spiritual** ones referenced here are those who walk in the Spirit, who are led by the Spirit, and keep in step with the Spirit. Those who are spiritually minded and give evidence of the fruit of the Spirit have the responsibility to take the initiative in offering restoration to and reconciliation with those who have been caught in a sin. We need to have a spirit of meekness to reprove without pride or acrimony and to stoop to the fallen without an air of condescension.

 WHAT OTHERS SAY

RESTORATION

Martin Luther's advice to a pastor charged with setting a lapsed brother back on the right path should be heeded: "Run unto him, and reaching out your hand, raise him up again, comfort him with sweet words, and embrace him with motherly arms."

The work of restoration is to be done **gently**. The word for restore means "to put in order or to restore to its former condition." In the medical profession, the same word is used to describe the setting of a fractured or dislocated bone. Gentleness does not mean that one overlooks the transgression committed. The gentle person remembers that restoration work requires wisdom, humility, and must be done in a delicate manner so as not to produce further injury. Rather than lacking firmness or being unable to confront or rebuke, the one acting gently lacks a harsh and censorious spirit. Gentleness is a Christlike grace; it does not tolerate wrong, but it does offer help.

2. CARING FOR EACH OTHER 6:2–3

The church is a family, not a civic or social club. As a family we are knit together supernaturally by the Holy Spirit in common fellowship of love. It is in this context that Paul admonished us to carry one another's burdens and so fulfill the law of Christ (6:2). The word for burden means a heavy weight or stone that someone is required to carry for a long distance. In the spiritual world it means any oppressive ordeal or hardship that is difficult to bear. The reality of the Christian life is that all believers have burdens. Our burdens are not the same. To some the burden may be a personal affliction, to others some infirmity, and to others a family crisis, but no Christian is exempt from having burdens.

God does not want us to carry our burdens alone. Isolation is not healthy for the believer either in worship or in burden bearing. The Greeks taught a Stoicism that suggested one must be aloof from both pleasure and pain and have the strength within oneself to face life without dependence on anyone else. Christian teaching does not encourage that kind of self-sufficiency, which is really a form of pride. We are to be priests to one another, bearing one another's burdens. It seems brave and strong to face life with an independent resolve to master whatever life brings to us. The Christian family, however, is one in which hurting believers seek out a Christian friend who will help carry the burden.

Bearing one another's burdens fulfills the law of Christ (6:2). The law of Christ is the law of love and is, therefore, not a fluctuating sentiment but a living principle and persistent habit. Perhaps nothing resembles Christ quite so much as living for others as He lived. As He came voluntarily and took on himself all our sin, so we should live by that same law of self-giving, sacrificing love.

3. CARRYING ONE'S OWN LOAD 6:4–5

These verses need to be taken together since they deal with two diverse aspects of the Christian's scrutiny and examination before God: (1) the serious self-examination Paul enjoined on all believers regarding their Christian walk in this present life and (2) Christ's evaluation when believers appear before His judgment seat to give account of their life.

Self-examination means not only taking our spiritual pulse on a regular basis, but also submitting our thoughts, attitudes, and actions to the will of God and Christ revealed in the Scriptures. The word **test** (6:4) is the word used for the fiery testing of gold to determine its purity. The standard against which we are to test ourselves is nothing less than the law of Christ that Paul had just referenced (6:2).

Paul's word is that **each one should test his own actions** (6:4). God will not hold anyone of us accountable for the gifts He gave to someone else or for the actions of another. There is nothing gained in comparing ourselves with someone else. It is important that we each bring our own life before the open pages of His Holy Word. We must be honest with ourselves as we test ourselves. Am I more loving, patient, and Christlike than I was last year? Individual scrutiny results in confession, not in competition.

While in 6:2 Paul instructed the Galatians to "carry each other's burdens," now in 6:5 he declares that each one **should carry his own load**. In verse 2, Paul uses a word (*bare*), which refers to a heavy load, an excessive weight, which one is expected to carry for a long distance. However, the word in verse 5 is *phortion*, which is used elsewhere to refer to a ship's cargo (see Acts 27:10), a soldier's knapsack, or a pilgrim's backpack. So, we are to bear one another's burdens that are too heavy for a person to carry alone, but there is one burden we cannot share: a burden light enough for each person to carry. It is that burden or pack that I cannot carry for you and you cannot carry for me.

4. SHARING WITH TEACHERS 6:6

Galatians 6:6 does not seem to connect either with what has gone before or what comes after. Paul is instructing the Galatians and us that those who receive instruction in Christianity by the public teaching and preaching of the Word of God must contribute to the support of the one teaching or preaching. Jesus said that "the worker is worth his keep" (Matt. 10:10). We do know that Paul himself did not receive a regular stipend from his churches, but rather used his skills to make and sell tents for a living. Perhaps Paul was uncomfortable when speaking about finances for himself, but it is interesting that he did not make his personal situation a standard for others. Rather he taught that financial stewardship was an important element of faithful service to Christ and His church. Time and again he exhorted believers to give regularly, generously, and joyfully both to the collection for the poor and for the maintenance of godly teachers.

SOWING AND REAPING 6:7–8

This is one of the strong words by Paul to the Galatians. He had warned them earlier about their being "bewitched" (3:1) by some evil deceiver. Now he makes it clear that they are not to be misled by thinking that somehow a person can mock God when it comes to sowing and reaping. The truth is plain: You can't fool God. People may cheat each other, but they cannot cheat God. To expect God to sow His bounties on them and not to let Him reap their gratitude and service is mockery. Likewise, the use of our seed-time determines exactly, and with a moral certainty greater than that which rules in the natural world, what kind of fruit will result. For each person, eternity will be the multiplied outcome of the good or evil of the present life. Heaven reveals the fruit of right-eousness. Hell is just sin ripened. There will be a payday someday because **a man reaps what he sows** (6:7). You cannot outwit God; the crop you plant in the spring will inevitably sprout forth into the harvest of the fall.

The person who indulges sensual appetites will have corruption as a crop (6:8). The sequence is inevitable. Like breeds like. The future glory of the saints is at once a divine reward and a necessary devel-opment of their present faithfulness. Like a master artist, Paul painted a vivid portrait of the dark side of reality—the certainty of judgment, the harvest of destruction and death, and the inescapable and eternal outcome of sowing to the flesh. But the destiny of those who sow to the Spirit is just as glorious as that of unrepentant sinners is horrible. If the works of the flesh issue in corruption and death, the fruit of the Spirit yields the har-vest of eternal life.

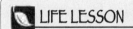

LIFE LESSON

SOWING AND REAPING

Our present life is the seed-time of an eternal harvest. The quality of the future harvest depends entirely on the present sowing. God himself is the Lord of the moral harvest. Those who reject the gospel will reap end-less disappointment and misery. Those who trust in Christ and receive the gifts and graces of the Holy Spirit will reap life ever-lasting.

NO QUITTING 6:9–10

Continuing the theme of seedtime and harvest, Paul admonished his readers to persevere in the faith, knowing that at the proper time God would fulfill His promise and bring the consummation of all things according to the good pleasure of His own divine will. In this context, it is our duty to do good, a duty enforced by both the words and example of Christ. Christianity requires its adherents not only to abstain from evil, but it demands their active service. Doing good things leads to a good harvest. A review of chapters 5 and 6 will provide an outline of the specific things Paul had instructed the Galatians to do: expel the agitators, love your neighbor as yourself, keep in step with the Spirit by manifesting the fruit of the Spirit, practice church discipline by restoring those who have fallen, bear one another's burdens, examine yourself, and provide material support for those who instruct you in the faith.

Perseverance is critical to the believer. There are many opportunities to lose heart. The Galatians faced legalism and libertinism. Having begun well in the Spirit, they were in danger of losing their first love and turning from service to petty bickering and greedy self-concern. Life has a way of causing both physical and spiritual fatigue. Servants of God become exhausted. Hence Paul's appeal: **Let us not become weary in doing good** (6:9).

The motivation in the last part of verse 9 is the reminder: **For at the proper time we will reap a harvest if we do not give up.** The word for "proper time" is *kairos*, the same word Paul used in 4:4 to describe the opportune moment, the fullness of time, in which God sent His Son into the world. It is also the same expression used in 1 Timothy 6:15 to describe the second advent of Christ.

ENDNOTE

What Others Say Sidebar: Martin Luther, *Luther's Works* vol. 27 (St. Louis: Concordia, 1963–64), 110–111.

12

CONCLUSION AND BENEDICTION

Galatians 6:11–18

We now come to the final paragraph of Paul's letter to the Galatians. The reader will remember that the introduction of this epistle differed from the usual Pauline pattern in that it contained no thanksgiving section and began with an immediate rebuke. Likewise, the concluding paragraph differs from Paul's usual practice in a number of ways. Most notably, it is longer than most, containing a summary recapitulation of the main themes Paul had addressed in the letter. Then too, there are no expressed greetings either from Paul or anyone else. Also, Paul did not give a doxology, a confession of praise, or reiterate his desire to see the Galatians. He did not even request their prayers on his behalf.

We probably should not read too much into this lack of personal touch by Paul in his concluding remarks. It would be easy to attribute this to the strained relations between Paul and the Galatians that is evident throughout the epistle. It is important that we remember Paul did use the word *adelphoi*, "brothers," just before his final **Amen**. He also gave a peace benediction in verse 16 and a grace benediction in verse 18. Taken together, they express the heart and soul of the apostle Paul as he summarizes in two majestic words the essence of the gospel he attempted to set forth in this brief but powerful letter.

1. THE APOSTOLIC SEAL 6:11-16

Paul's autograph is in 6:11: **See what large letters I use as I write to you with my own hand**.[1] Usually a secretary or amanuensis would prepare the main body of the letter, while the sender would append his signature and perhaps a few closing words of benediction. It is likely that Paul would dictate his letters and then add a personal postscript and signature in his own hand at the end of the epistle (see 1 Cor. 16:21; 2 Cor. 10:1; 2 Thess. 3:17; Col. 4:18). If that was the case, this verse (6:11) is probably the place where Paul took the stylus from the hand of his secretary and finished the writing in his own handwriting. Many have speculated that Paul's poor eyesight (see 4:15) required him to write with unusually large letters. Perhaps the large letters are a witness to the force of his convictions as in an attempt to underscore and emphasize what he was saying to them.

There are two distinctive points made in Paul's concluding remarks: his boast in the cross and his bearing the brand mark of Jesus Christ (see the next section). Throughout this epistle, Paul was relentless in his assault against the false teachers, commonly known as Judaizers, who had sown such great confusion among his recent converts. Contrary to Paul, they taught that becoming Jewish was necessary for salvation, or at the least, one must be circumcised.

In one final bold charge, Paul accused his opponents of not only dangerous doctrinal deviation but also of unworthy motivation (6:12–13). The reason they wanted to **compel** the new Christian converts to undergo circumcision was that their basic motive was self-aggrandizement: They wanted to **make a good impression outwardly** (6:12). What they really wanted was to be able to boast about all the converts they had, about how many Gentile Christians they had converted into Jewish proselytes.

Paul suggested his Jewish Christian opponents had one additional motivation for insisting that the Gentile Christians of Galatia undergo circumcision. They did this, he said, in order to **avoid being persecuted for the cause of Christ** (6:12). By insisting on the circumcision of Gentile believers, the Judaizers could cast themselves in a favorable light with the local synagogue authorities. By circumcising the converts of the missionary Paul, they could show to the fanatical Zealots that belief in Jesus as Messiah involved no breach of the Mosaic Law or the sacred ceremonies of the Jewish people.

In contrast to the false teachers, who boasted about their accomplishments, Paul had this to say: "God forbid" (6:14 KJV) that the only possible object of his boasting was the cross of the Lord Jesus Christ. The Jews stumbled at the cross, the Greeks thought it was foolishness, and the Judaizing teachers were mixing the observance of the Mosaic Law with faith in Christ as necessary for salvation. Paul, however, gloried in the cross and rejected the thought of setting up anything in competition with it.

> When false foundations all are gone,
> Each lying refuge blown to air,
> The Cross remains our boast alone;
> The righteousness of God is there.[2]

In the latter part of verse 14, Paul further developed his understanding of the cross of Christ by declaring that through it the world had been crucified to him and he to the world.

There is not only cosmological significance to Christ's death. His death also has ethical and spiritual implications for every believer. Not only is the world crucified to believers through their identification with Jesus' victory on the cross, but through the ongoing process of daily self-denial, believers are crucified to the world. The world, in this sense, means the world system, the

LIFE LESSON

CRUCIFIXION

There is a triple crucifixion in the Scriptures: The crucified Christ, the crucified world, and the crucified Christian. Obviously the crucifixion of Christ outside the city walls of Jerusalem is the most decisive and compelling event of redemptive history. Something happened to the very cosmos that day. The creation itself, cracked and groaning under the weight of sin, is yet to be redeemed on the basis of the cross of Christ. When Jesus died, the earth quaked, the sun refused to shine, and cemeteries were disturbed. God was giving notice to Satan, in these events, that his lease on the earth was about to run out. It is true that the devil is still the "God of the cosmos," but his kingdom is doomed. Jesus is Christ the All-Powerful.

basic values and orientation that are alienated from God. To be crucified to the world means to walk in the light, to bear the fruit of the Spirit, and to live in the freedom with which Christ has set us free.

In verse 15, Paul applies this truth to the situation he had been dealing with throughout this letter to the Galatians. Once again he reiterates the irrelevance of circumcision or uncircumcision. He contrasts it with the expression of the life of faith effected through the cross of Christ: **a new creation** (6:15). Paul expressed this truth in fuller terms in 2 Corinthians 5:17: "Therefore, if anyone is in Christ, he is a new creation; the old is gone, the new has come." The new creation involves the whole process of conversion: repentance and faith, the regenerating and sanctifying work of the Holy Spirit, and continual growth in holiness.

As Paul had done so often in this letter, so, too, here, in the closing verses, he reiterated the central thesis that no one is made right with God on the basis of external ceremonies or human efforts of any kind. Right standing with God comes through the unilateral action of God in the cross and resurrection of Jesus Christ. Christ alone is the object of the believer's trust and the One whose Spirit liberates and empowers all those whose sins are forgiven.

Nearing the end of his letter, Paul appends here a conditional benediction: **peace and mercy to all who follow this rule, even to the Israel of God** (6:16). Most scholars take the position that Paul was referring to the principle of justification by faith that he had just summarized in the preceding verse under the general thought of the new creation. So he was invoking peace and mercy upon those members of the congregation of Galatia who remained faithful to the truth of the gospel Paul had originally preached among them. The true Christians are called the Israel of God to distinguish them from Israel according to the flesh.

2. THE BRAND MARKS OF JESUS 6:17

The Greek word for "brand marks" is *stigmata*. Some people think Paul actually bore in his hands, feet, and side the imprinted marks of Jesus' passion and death. This phenomenon was supposed to have been true with Francis of Assisi, who had the scars of Christ's passion supernaturally imposed upon his body near the end of his life on September 17, 1224. There have been over three hundred such accounts across the centuries.

Whether this was true with Paul or Francis of Assisi or anyone at all is beside the point. The point Paul is making is that he constantly bore actual scars of persecution and marks of physical suffering received throughout his apostolic ministry because of his witness for the gospel. The Judaizing teachers gloried in the circumcision mark in the flesh of their followers. Paul, contrary to them, gloried in the marks of suffering for Christ the Lord.

3. THE BENEDICTION 6:18

The grace of our Lord Jesus Christ be with your spirit, brothers. Amen.

After a great deal of rebuke and admonition, Paul bids them farewell with the loving expression of unity as his last parting word. That word is, "I will end the letter as I began it, commending to you the awesome and marvelous grace of our Lord Jesus Christ. The only thing left for me to do is to pray from my heart that Christ will confirm my labors among you, restoring you to the truth of the gospel and granting you the gift of perseverance unto life eternal. So may it be. Amen."

ENDNOTES

1. Burton points out that "the size of the letters would have somewhat the effect of bold-face type in a modern book, or double underlining in a manuscript, and since the apostle himself called attention to it, it would impress not only the one person who might be reading the letter to a congregation but the listening congregation also" (Burton, E. deW, *A Critical and Exegetical Commentary on the Epistle to the Galatians*, International Critical Commentary [Edinburgh, Scotland: T. & T. Clark, 1921] p. 348).

2. A "Classic Hymn" quoted in J. Brown, *An Exposition of the Epistle to the Galatians* (Marshallton, Del.: Sovereign Grace, 1970), p. 360.

SELECT BIBLIOGRAPHY
For Galatians

It is not possible within the scope of the purpose of this volume to provide an in-depth treatment of the historical and critical material of the epistle of Paul to the Galatians. While on occasion the opinions of a variety of writers have been included in this discussion, a much deeper study of this epistle requires a review of both grammatical and technical material.

For a further study of the epistle of Paul to the Galatians, I have listed commentaries that I have found helpful for a deeper understanding and appreciation of the Word of God. Because of the subject matter of this particular epistle, it is important to review the opinions of scholars from a wide range of theological perspectives. The commentaries listed below offer such a view from both a Wesleyan and Reformed perspective.

Alford, Henry. *The Greek New Testament*, vol. 3. Chicago: Moody Press, 1958.

Baker, Kenneth. *Reflecting God Study Bible*. Grand Rapids, Mich.: Zondervan, 2000.

Barclay, J. M. G. *Obeying the Truth: A Study of Paul's Ethics in Galatians*. Edinburgh, Scotland: T. & T. Clark, 1988.

Bruce, F. F. *The Epistle to the Galatians*. New International Greek Testament Commentary. Grand Rapids, Mich.: William B. Eerdmans, 1982.

Burton, E. deW. *A Critical and Exegetical Commentary on the Epistle to the Galatians*. International Critical Commentary. Edinburgh, Scotland: T. & T. Clark, 1921.

Calvin, John. *The Epistles of Paul to the Galatians, Ephesians, Philippians, and Colossians*, Calvin's New Testament Commentaries, vol. 11. Translated by T. H. L. Parker. Grand Rapids, Mich.: William B. Eerdmans, 1965.

——. *Institutes of the Christian Religion*, vols. 1 and 2. Translated by Ford Lewis Battles. Philadelphia: Westminster Press, 1960.

Clarke, Adam. *The New Testament of Our Lord and Saviour Jesus Christ*. New York: G. Lane and P. P. Sandford, 1842.

Cole, R. A. *The Epistle of Paul to the Galatians*. Grand Rapids, Mich.: William B. Eerdmans, 1965.

Earle, Ralph. *Word Meanings in the New Testament*, vol. 5. Kansas City, Mo.: Beacon Hill Press of Kansas City, 1977.

Ebeling, G. *The Truth of the Gospel: An Exposition of Galatians*. Philadelphia: Fortress, 1984.

Exell, Joseph, S. *The Biblical Illustrator: Galatians*. Grand Rapids, Mich.: Baker Book House, 1952.

Fung, R. Y. *The Epistle to the Galatians*. New International Commentary on the New Testament. Grand Rapids, Mich.: William B. Eerdmans, 1988.

George, Timothy. *Galatians*. The New American Commentary, vol. 30. Nashville, Tenn.: Broadman and Holman, 1994.

Guthrie, Donald. *Galatians*. New Century Bible Commentary. Grand Rapids, Mich.: William B. Eerdmans, 1973.

Harrison, Everett, F., ed. *Baker's Dictionary of Theology*. Grand Rapids, Mich.: Baker Book House, 1960.

Henry, Matthew, and Adam Clarke, Robert Jamieson, A. R. Fausset, David Brown. *The Bethany Parallel Commentary of the New Testament: from the condensed editions of Matthew Henry, Jamieson/Fausset/Brown, Adam Clarke*. Minneapolis: Bethany, 1983.

Howard, G. Paul. *Crisis in Galatia*. Cambridge: Cambridge University Press, 1979.

Lightfoot, J. B. *Saint Paul's Epistle to the Galatians*. London: McMillan, 1986.

Longenecker, R. *Galatians*. Word Biblical Commentary. Dallas: Word, 1990.

Luther, Martin. *Luther's Works*, vols. 26 and 27. St. Louis: Concordia, 1963–64.

Machen, J. Gresham and John H. Skilton. *Notes on Galatians*. Vestavia Hills, Ala.: Solid Ground Christian Books, 2006.

McKnight, Scot. *Galatians*: The NIV Application Commentary. Grand Rapids, Mich.: Zondervan, 1995.

McLaren, Alexander. *Expositions of Holy Scripture, Second Corinthians, Galatians, and Philippians*. New York: J. J. Little and Ives, 1944.

Moulton, Harold K. *The Analytical Greek Lexicon*. Grand Rapids, Mich.: Zondervan, 1978.

Stott, John R. W. *The Cross of Christ*. Downers Grove, Ill.: InterVarsity, 1986.

Strickland, W. G., ed. *The Law, the Gospel, and the Modern Christian: Five Views*. Grand Rapids, Mich.: Zondervan, 1993.

Westerholm, Stephen. *Israel's Law and the Church's Faith: Paul and His Recent Interpreters*. Grand Rapids, Mich.: William B. Eerdmans, 1988.

Witherington, Ben III. *Grace in Galatia: A Commentary on Paul's Letter to the Galatians*. Grand Rapids, Mich.: William B. Eerdmans, 1998.

Wright, N. T. *The Climax of the Covenant: Christ and the Law in Pauline Theology*. Minneapolis: Fortress, 1991.

PHILIPPIANS

ALEX R. G. DEASLEY

PREFACE TO PHILIPPIANS

The stated purpose of the Wesleyan Bible Commentary Series is "to assist laity and ministers in the teaching ministries of the church." I have sought to keep that objective before me in the writing of this commentary. For me this has involved at least three things. First, making available to church ministers and teachers the harvest produced by the study of Philippians across the centuries. This has been done, however, not by the bare process of borrowing, so much as by allowing the work of earlier commentators to pass through my own mental filters to produce a commentary that bears the stamp of my own thought and judgment.

Second, I have sought to write in a way that would make Paul's thought accessible to those who, while not wishing to fight through the technicalities of biblical exegesis and theology, nevertheless want to be guided by those who have. I have, therefore, tried to write plainly, lapsing into technical jargon only when it seemed unavoidable, and even then attempting to include an explanation in plain speech.

Third, believing that Philippians is part of the written Word of God, I have endeavored to give some indication of its message for Christian believers today. If that message, as I understand it, exhibits coherence with the Wesleyan/Holiness tradition, it is not because I have consciously forced it to do so, but because it appears to me to be the natural import of Paul's words.

How far I have succeeded in achieving these ends is for others to judge. At all events, these are the guidelines I have sought to follow.

In writing such a commentary one inevitably acquires debts. I have already indicated my obligations to earlier commentators. Each commentator necessarily stands on the shoulders of his predecessors, and I am no exception. I am also indebted to those who unknowingly aided in the writing of this commentary by inviting me to deliver studies on

Philippians in places as far off as Fiji, or equally coincidentally asked me to write shorter studies on the epistle.

My greatest obligation however, is to my wife, Joyce, who not only lived with my obsessive preoccupation with the work, but also committed every word of it to the word processor to produce the final version. For her dedicated and skilled labor, I can only offer an inadequate word of thanks.

ALEX DEASLEY

INTRODUCTION TO PHILIPPIANS

It will help in understanding the letter to the Philippians if we can find out something about the sort of people they were and how this letter came to be written to them. It so happens that we can. Not only do we have some information from classical sources; we have a fairly lengthy account of how the gospel was brought to them (Acts 16:11–40). So it may be worth our while to sketch what we can learn about the background from both the letter itself and from Acts. We can then turn to hearing what the letter is saying.

AUTHOR

Whereas nowadays the name of the author of a letter stands at the end, in the ancient world it stood as the first word. In the case of Philippians the name is

ANCIENT GEOGRAPHY

The Roman writer Appian (writing about A.D. 160 of the civil wars of the last century B.C.) describes Philippi as "a way through . . . to Asia and to Europe like a gateway" *(Civil Wars*, IV, 105–6).

Paul, and there are no good reasons for doubting that he was the author. The language he uses and the style in which he writes coincide with these in his other writings, such as Romans and Galatians. Not only so, but it is possible to get the feel of the man in Philippians. His description of his feelings (1:18–24), his references to his friends (2:19–30), his outbursts against those who would destroy the faith of the Philippian Christians (3:2), and his revealing of the heartbeat of his own faith (3:4–11) all combine to paint a colorful picture of the living Paul.

PLACE OF WRITING

It might not seem to matter particularly where the letter was written; the important thing is the letter itself and what it says. However, it can add something to the intensity of the contents if we can find out whether the letter was written at a time of particular stress for Paul. To some extent this depends on where he was when he wrote it. The text makes clear that Paul was in prison when he wrote (1:7, 12–14). This was not an uncommon experience for Paul (2 Cor. 11:23). Clearly, however, when he wrote Philippians he recognized that he might never get out alive (1:20). It has, therefore, been thought that Philippians was written during his final imprisonment in Rome, which the early Christian historian Eusebius, tells us terminated in his execution.

An objection to this view is that Rome and Philippi are too far apart for all the comings and goings referred to in the letter to take place. Time is needed for news of Paul's imprisonment to get to Philippi from Rome, for Epaphroditus to travel from Philippi to Rome with a gift to aid Paul in prison, and for news of his illness in Rome to reach the Philippians. It would take additional time for Paul to hear of their distress over Epaphroditus and plan to send him home and to implement his emergency plan to send Timothy, who would also deliver the letter and return to him with news of the Philippians (2:25–30, 19–23). Yet all of this apparently takes place in a relatively short time span: two years, if Acts 28:30 refers to the same Roman imprisonment. The distance from Rome to Philippi has been reckoned at 730 miles plus a two-day sea voyage across the Adriatic.

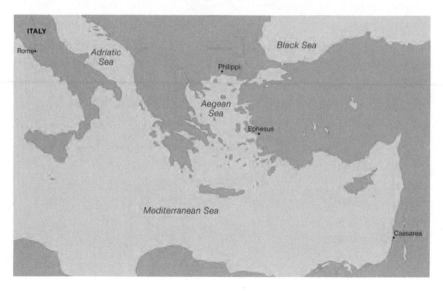

For these reasons the other place where Paul had a lengthy imprisonment has been suggested—Caesarea (Acts 24:27). The difficulty with this suggestion is that Paul could—and did—find a way out of prison by exercising his right as a Roman citizen to appeal directly to the emperor (Acts 25:9–12; 26:32). Execution was not a possibility in Caesarea. In any case, Caesarea is no nearer to Philippi than Rome was.

This has led to a third suggested place of writing: Ephesus. It is true that Ephesus is much closer to Philippi than Rome or Caesarea: about a week's journey. The main problem is that we have no evidence that Paul spent a lengthy imprisonment there. But there is another objection to Ephesus that is fatal. In Philippians 1:13 Paul says that his loyalty to Christ has become known **throughout the whole palace guard** (*praetorion*). Again, in 4:22 he refers to those **who belong to Caesar's household**. These expressions are technical terms for the praetorian guard, which protected the emperor's person and his civil servants, particularly diplomats. They were found only in provinces controlled by the emperor—imperial provinces. They were not found in provinces controlled by the Roman Senate—senatorial provinces. The province of Asia, of which Ephesus was the capital, was a senatorial province.[1]

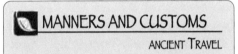

MANNERS AND CUSTOMS

ANCIENT TRAVEL

L. J. Kreitzer writes, "The most common means of travel on the network of overland roads would have been by foot, making a good day's journey about twenty miles. Travel by animals, either by riding them or in a drawn carriage, would have yielded a rate of about five to six miles an hour."

These considerations suggest that the most probable conclussion is that Philippians was written from Rome. Speed of travel could vary greatly in the Roman Empire, and uncertainties on that matter should not be allowed to override known facts.

DATE

If Philippians was written from the Roman jail in which Paul found himself in the last chapter of Acts, then clearly it comes from the later part of his missionary career. This would also be the case if Philippians was written in Caesarea. Ephesus, on the other hand, would give a date somewhere in the middle of Paul's missionary endeavors (around A.D. 54–57). But since the positive evidence points more clearly to Rome, a date in the early 60s is more probable.

AUDIENCE

In Philippians Paul was not writing (as was the case with Romans) to a church with which he had had no firsthand contact. He had founded and known the people of the Philippian church from its beginning. He had gone there from Troas in response to the vision of the man of Macedonia, calling Paul to come over and help him (Acts 16:8–10). Philippi was Paul's goal (Acts 16:11–12). There seems to have been no synagogue in Philippi, but people of various faiths and causes would seek out like-minded associates at the city gate. Paul found seven women there who had gathered for prayer. One of them, Lydia, who was in the business of selling purple cloth, became his first convert in Europe (Acts 16:13–15).

The next stage of Paul's ministry was not so easy. After Paul had cast a demon out of a slave girl who was engaged in fortune telling, her owners had Paul and Silas thrown in jail (Acts 16:16–24). Eventually, they were released, and the jailer became a believer (Acts 16:25–34). Even so, Paul and Silas had to leave Philippi (Acts 16:35–40).

Paul's converts were clearly a rather mixed bag. But then Philippi itself was rather a mixed bag. It took its name from its founder, Philip II, King of Macedon, father of Alexander the Great. With the spread of Roman power, it was incorporated into the Roman Empire and by the time of the emperor Augustus, was the chief city of the first of four districts into which the Romans had divided Macedonia. It is described in Acts 16:12 as "a Roman colony." Roman colonies were often established by successful army generals as ways of rewarding their troops, especially veterans, with free grants of land. They were modeled after the pattern of the city of Rome, and their citizens were Roman citizens.

However, not all of the inhabitants were Romans. The indigenous population would have been Greek. One scholar who has attempted to reconstruct a picture of the town based on archaeological and related evidence[2] has concluded that, of an estimated population of ten to fifteen thousand, 40 percent would be Roman citizens and 60 percent Greeks. The proportion of colonist farmers was probably about 20 percent, service groups about 37 percent, slaves about 20 percent, the poor about the same, and the elite about 3 percent.[3]

As to the makeup of the Philippian church, this would be determined in the main by the range of Paul's influence. Socially, this would mean artisans and Jews, some Romans, Asian migrants like Lydia, and religiously mostly Jews. Scholar Peter Oakes estimates the economic composition of the church to have possibly consisted of 43 percent from service groups, 16 percent slaves, 15 percent colonist farmers, 25 percent poor, and one percent elite. Ethnically, he thinks the church would have consisted of 36 percent Romans and 64 percent Greeks, a rough reflection of the population of the town.[4]

If this characterization of Paul's audience is even approximately accurate, it provides a backdrop against which the teaching of the letter comes into clearer and more exact perspective.

REASONS FOR WRITING

It is probably significant that, after the opening formalities (1:1–11), the first topic Paul takes up is his present situation in jail. The Philippians had already seen him in jail. Now he was there again. Even the hardiest believers must have wondered what effect this would have on Paul's mission (1:12–14). Consequently, they had sent one of their number, Epaphroditus, to serve as a caregiver to Paul in prison (2:25) and to convey some gifts to him (4:18). Clearly, Paul wanted to thank them for their concern. However, Epaphroditus's mission had not gone altogether according to plan. He had been taken ill, either on the journey or on arrival, and had almost died. This news had reached the Philippians and Paul thought it best to send him back to them. One reason for writing the letter was to tell them of this (2:25–30), possibly preparing his way so that the Philippians would not suspect him of failing in his mission.

There was, however, another reason Paul had for writing. It is clear that Paul was not the only one who was suffering for his faith. The Philippians were suffering too (1:29–30; 4:19). Peter Oakes has indicated how easily this could happen in a church with the makeup of the city of Philippi. Artisans might quickly find customers taking their business elsewhere. Colonist farmers might well find themselves ostracized by their fellow Romans. Any who rented their land or were in debt would be particularly vulnerable. And the poor are always vulnerable, as were the slaves. Division within families could also be a source of acute suffering. Oakes concludes that the most common form of suffering would be economic.[5]

Pressures of this sort can readily lead to tension and division within the church. This had happened at Philippi, and Paul urges the believers to come together in unity of mind and purpose (1:27; 2:1–4; 4:2–3).

However, Paul also seems to have had a further reason for writing, not necessarily unconnected (at least wholly) with those already mentioned. There is a remarkable change of tone in the letter at the beginning of chapter 3. Verses 2–4 have an explosive tone about them, differing from what goes before. We shall examine this more closely in the commentary, but Paul evidently regards the interlopers to whom he refers as a menace to the faith of the Philippian believers. In 3:18–19, he goes so far as to describe them as **enemies of the cross of Christ** whose **mind is on earthly things**.

Paul, therefore, had a number of reasons for writing Philippians. The question of how they were linked leads directly to the next section.

THE SHAPE OF THE LETTER

Letters in the Greek world were fairly standardized for a period from 300 B.C. to A.D. 300. They would begin with the names of the sender and the recipient, followed by a brief salutation: "A to B, greeting." Next would come a health wish, followed by the main themes and concerns of the letter. Finally, would come concluding elements such as good wishes and an expression of farewell. Thousands of letters conforming to this pattern have been discovered. There was no waste of words.

It is obvious that the New Testament writers were not only aware of, but made use of, this basic form. However, they did not allow themselves to be imprisoned by it. Paul frequently added a section consisting of thanksgiving and prayer (as in 1:3–11) and "Christianized" other elements such as the introductory and concluding greetings (1:1–2; 4:21–3).

There has been much discussion of the body of the letter, both in the case of Philippians and other New Testament letters. Attempts have been made to classify them according to ancient patterns of rhetoric: defense, persuasion, praise, or blame, each with clearly defined stages. But it is likely the body of the letter was flexible and adaptable in Hellenistic letters.[6] This was particularly the case in family letters. Since Philippians was something of a family letter, we should not be surprised if it moves back and forth from the more practical concerns of the Christian "family" in Philippi to matters

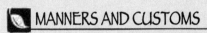

MANNERS AND CUSTOMS
ANCIENT LETTERS

A typical letter of friendship, among which the letters of the New Testament generally are categorized, reads as follows:

> Claudius Agathas Daimon to most beloved Sarapion, greetings. Since I am going to Thebes, I salute you dearest, sweetest Sarapion and I exhort you also to do the same thing. If you need anything from Thebes, I encourage you to write to me, dearest, and it shall be done. (Author's hand) I pray for your health continually together with that of your children. Farewell.

The letter dates from the early second century A.D. Private letters have been computed to be 87 words long, on average. Literary letters are much longer. Cicero's 796 letters average 295 words; Seneca's 124 average 925 words.

of Christian teaching, which, in any case, had great practical implications.

Several scholars characterize the book of Philippians as a "letter of friendship," but it was friendship conducted at a depth that incorporates guidance regarding matters of substance and significance.[7] One should not be surprised to find in Philippians the deepest expressions of friendship and affection (for example, 1:3, 7–8; 4:1) paired with the profoundest theological exhortation and instruction (2:5–11; 3:19–21).

MAJOR THEMES

Some indication of the major themes has already been given in the discussion of the reasons for the writing of the letter. It has also been noted that Paul begins Philippians—as most of his letters—with a section consisting of thanksgiving and prayer (1:3–11), frequently called the prayer-report. This section in Paul's letters usually foreshadows the main themes to follow. If that is the case here, then it appears that Paul has two main items on his agenda: first, the progress of the gospel through his ministry and theirs, despite his imprisonment (1:3–8); and second, his concern for their growth in Christian love (1:9–11). The former gives rise to the prominent place given to suffering: in Paul's case, imprisonment (1:12–26); in the case of the Philippians, persecution (1:27–30). However, their suffering has apparently given rise to dissension (perhaps some were blaming others as the cause of persecution). Accordingly, Paul strongly urges them to unity of spirit, pointing to the humility of Jesus in suffering as the example they should follow (2:1–18; 4:2–3). The second theme in the prayer-report, his concern for their growth in Christian love, is picked up in chapter 3.

However, these main themes are accompanied by, and in some cases give rise to, subordinate themes. It is clear, for example, that the visit of Epaphroditus bringing the Philippians' gift to Paul, and the illness which overtook him were more than just a footnote in Paul's mind (2:25–30; 4:10–19). Again, Paul's imprisonment, bringing with it the possibility of his execution, leads him to discuss his attitude toward death (1:18–23). His exhortation to them to have the mind of Christ (2:5–11) carries with it a profound exposition of the person of Christ, while his urging of them to grow in Christian love leads to a passionate declaration of the meaning of knowing Christ (3:10–13).

So while isolating major themes helps in gaining an overall grasp of the letter, it should not be concluded that the minor themes are of no importance. Sometimes they fill out the meaning of the larger topics.

SIGNIFICANCE IN CHRISTIAN THEOLOGY AND PLACE IN THE CANON

The classification of Philippians as a friendship or family letter—or as one commentator has put it, "like a chat"[8]—could appear to mean that it contains no theological content of any great consequence. On the contrary, the opposite is true. The writer just quoted says elsewhere in the same commentary,

> Philippians is a theological document, cast in letter form and carrying all the hallmarks of a friendship-family letter, but whose chief interest lies in what it says *about God* in the face of the many-sided problems at Philippi. Granted that Paul alludes to these problems as part of the rhetorical situation, a question still remains to be answered: How does he present his case for handling these issues of rivalry, selfishness, suffering and alien teachers? The one umbrella idea that would contain his answer to these variegated matters is that God is disclosed in the incarnation, death and vindication of Jesus Christ.[9]

Particularly since the Reformation, Romans, Galatians, and 1 and 2 Corinthians have been labeled "Paul's leading letters," with the rest being regarded as hangers-on of lesser degrees of importance. That view is being challenged, specifically with reference to Philippians. R. P. Martin concludes that "it deserves to be ranked with the 'capital epistles' of Romans, Galatians and 1 and 2 Corinthians."[10]

Traces of Philippians can be found in writers as early as Clement of Rome (A.D. 95) and Ignatius of Antioch (A.D. 107). Polycarp of Smyrna, who was martyred around A.D. 155, wrote to the Philippians and mentions that Paul had done so earlier. Philippians also appears in the earliest lists of New Testament writings, notably in the Muratorian Canon, a list of books regarded as canonical by the church of Rome about A.D. 180. Apparently there was never any question in the minds of early Christian leaders regarding either the authorship or canonical authority of the letter.

QUESTIONS OR PROBLEMS ASSOCIATED WITH THE STUDY OF PHILIPPIANS

One question that has frequently been raised is whether Philippians as it stands is a single unit or whether it is a patchwork quilt of several letters written to the Philippians by Paul at different times. Several reasons are advanced for this latter view. One is the abrupt change in tone and subject at the beginning of chapter 3. Chapter 3 verse 1 reads as though the letter is winding down, beginning as it does with "finally." But it proves to be a preacher's "finally," and Paul continues for two more chapters. Not only so, but the tone of the letter changes from friendly care to unmeasured denunciation of enemies of faith (3:1), who also prove to be **enemies of the cross of Christ** (3:18). Again, it seems odd that Paul postpones expressing his gratitude for the Philippians' gift until the final moments of the letter (4:18–19).

For these reasons it has been suggested that the first letter Paul wrote to the Philippians consisted of 4:10–20; the second of 1:1–3:1, 4:4–7 and 21–23; and the third of 3:2–21 and 4:8–9. These were later patched together into Philippians as we know it. If this in fact is what happened, the alleged editor did his work rather clumsily. The commentary will address the "awkward" features and show that they are not really as awkward as they are made out to be.

WESLEYAN/HOLINESS THEMES

There is a remarkable number of Wesleyan/Holiness distinctives that rise from themes in Philippians. Taking them roughly in their order of appearance in the letter, the first would be Paul's teaching on the relation of justification and sanctification. Righteousness by faith, already mentioned in 1:11, is expounded more fully in 3:7–19. But this extends to **knowing Christ** by sharing in His death and resurrection (3:10), leading to the resurrection on the last day (3:11). Paul says that he has not attained this resurrection perfection (3:12), but striving toward knowing Christ is a mark of Christian perfection (3:13–15). Related to the theme of sanctification and perfection is growth in love. By continuing to grow in love, believers will be kept pure and blameless until the return of Christ (1:9–11).

The life of holiness has clear ethical implications. High among these is like-mindedness and placing the interests of others before one's own (2:1–4). This is, indeed, the mind of Christ himself (2:5–11). What it comes down to is that holiness is not simply an individual affair, though it has an indispensable, individual dimension

(1:9–10). Holiness has a social dimension. Christian believers have dual citizenship in an earthly city and a heavenly city (1:27; 3:20); they are obligated to both.

Accordingly, while salvation is the work of God, this is no excuse for inertia on the part of the believer, as if "it is all up to God." The salvation worked within us by God is to be worked out by us in daily life. The technical term for this is *synergism*, working together with God. But we should never forget that it is a synergism driven by *grace*.

ENDNOTES

Manners and Customs Sidebar 1: "Travel in the Roman World" in *Dictionary of Paul and His Letters* by Gerald F. Hawthorne, Ralph P. Martin, and Daniel G. Reid (Downers Grove, Ill.: InterVarsity Press, 1993), p. 945.

Manners and Customs Sidebar 2: Stanley K. Stowers, *Letter Writing in Greco-Roman Antiquity* (Philadelphia: Westminster Press, 1986), p. 61.

1. See F. F. Bruce. "There is no known instance in imperial times of [the] use [of *praetorion*] for the headquarters of a proconsul, the governor of a senatorial province such as Asia was at this time." *Philippians*, Good News Commentary (San Francisco: Harper and Row, 1983), xxii.

2. Peter Oakes, *Philippians: From People to Letter*, Society for New Testament Studies Monograph Series 110 (New York: Cambridge University Press, 2001).

3. Oakes, *Philippians*, pp. 45–50.

4. Oakes, *Philippians*, pp. 57–61. Oakes recognizes that there are possible variables. See Table 2, p. 61.

5. Oakes, *Philippians*, pp. 89–96.

6. Loveday Alexander, "Hellenistic Letter-Forms and the Structure of Philippians," *Journal for the Study of the New Testament* 37 (1989), p. 90.

7. Stanley K. Stowers, "Friends and Enemies in the Politics of Heaven: Reading Theology in Philippians" in *Pauline Theology*, vol. 1, ed. J. M. Bassler (Minneapolis: Fortress Press, 1991), 105–21; Gordon D. Fee, *Paul's Letter to the Philippians*, New International Commentary on the New Testament (Grand Rapids, Mich.: William B. Eerdmans, 1995), pp. 2–7. The technical label for such a letter is "a hortatory letter of friendship" (Fee, pp. 12–14).

8. Ralph P. Martin and Gerald F. Hawthorne, *Philippians*, Word Biblical Commentary (Nashville, Tenn.: Nelson Reference, 2004), p. lvii.

9. Martin and Hawthorne, *Philippians*, p. lxvi. Compare the judgment of I. Howard Marshall in reference to the situation addressed in Philippians: "Paul's response to this situation in his letter is deeply theological and represents a typical use of his profound theology for pastoral purposes." (*New Testament Theology: Many Witnesses, One Gospel* [Downers Grove, Ill.: InterVarsity Press, 2004], p. 345.)

10. Martin and Hawthorne: *Philippians*, xxviii. See also Peter Oakes: "A general conclusion of my study is that Philippians ought to be moved more toward the mainstream of Paul's letters." (*Philippians*, p. 212.)

OUTLINE OF PHILIPPIANS

I. The Heart of an Apostle (1:1–11)
   A. The Opening Greeting (1:1–2)
   B. The Opening Prayer Section (1:3–11)
II. Paul's Situation and the Gospel (1:12–26)
   A. Paul's Imprisonment and Its Effects on the Proclamation of the Gospel (1:12–18a)
   B. Paul's Future Prospects and Their Effect on the Proclamation of the Gospel (1:18b–26)
III. Paul's Instructions to the Philippians (1:27–2:11)
   A. An Exhortation to Steadfastness (1:27–30)
   B. An Exhortation to Unity (2:1–4)
   C. The Secret of Stability and Unity: The Mind of Christ (2:5–11)
IV. Exhortation and Encouragement (2:12–30)
   A. A Further Exhortation to Steadfastness (2:12–18)
   B. Living Witnesses of the Christlike Mind (2:19–30)
V. The Pursuit of Perfection (3:1–4:1)
   A. True Confidence versus False Confidence (3:1–6)
   B. Knowing Christ: Righteousness by Faith and Resurrection Hope (3:7–11)
   C. The Path to Perfection (3:12–16)
   D. Some Practical Guidance (3:17–4:1)
VI. Exhortations, Thanks, and Greetings (4:2–23)
   A. Three Exhortations (4:2–9)
   B. Thanks for Their Support (4:10–20)
   C. Farewell Greetings (4:21–23)

1

THE HEART OF AN APOSTLE

Philippians 1:1–11

We saw in the introduction that there was a fairly standardized form for letters in the New Testament world. Paul, like the writers of other New Testament letters, was familiar with the form. However, although he conformed to its broad pattern, he did not allow himself to be manacled by it. The first eleven verses of Philippians are a good illustration of this. These would normally be labeled the letter-opening or some such thing, and would serve to identify the writer and the recipients and add a word of greeting. Paul does all of this in a way that opens a window on his own heart. Through the opening, he spotlights Christian character and the needs of the Philippians.

1. THE OPENING GREETING 1:1–2

Ancient letters did not begin by naming the recipients (as ours do) but by naming the senders. Paul links Timothy's name with his own. The reason for this is not that Timothy was joint author of the letter; Paul reverts to the first person almost immediately in verse 3. But Timothy had been a prominent player in Paul's mission to the Gentiles (Acts 16:1–3), and Paul had plans to send him to Philippi rather than going himself (2:19–23). Therefore, from the first line of the letter, he associates Timothy closely with himself.

The greeting continues with Paul describing himself and Timothy as **servants of Christ Jesus**. While Paul often describes himself in this way, the only other letter-greeting in which he does this is Romans 1:1, where he goes on at once to describe himself as "called to be an apostle." The absence of "apostle" from Philippians 1:1 suggests that his apostleship was not questioned there. The use of **servamt** prepares the way for the description of Jesus by that term in 2:7, where He is set forth as the example for Christians to follow. While there were different kinds of servants in Paul's day—some performing menial tasks, others discharging high responsibilities—the label (and status) carried the idea of subservience and was as demeaning then as now. But to be a servant of Christ Jesus was an honor.

The letter is addressed **to all the saints in Christ Jesus at Philippi** (1:1). In the Old Testament what makes people saints is that they belong to the holy people of God, set apart for His service (Exod. 31:13). In the New Testament this idea continues (1 Cor. 1:30). Yet this membership includes "the moral aspect of a Christlike purity and integrity which is both granted and aspired to (e.g. 2 Cor. 7:1; 1 Thess. 4:3–7; cf. Phil. 2:12, 15)."[1] Harnessed to the term **saints** is the extremely significant expression **in Christ Jesus**. It is used in Philippians no fewer than twenty-one times—more often than in the much larger letter to the Romans. Paul uses it in an intensive sense: to denote belonging to Christ, being incorporated into Him, living in and through Him. He uses the Christ-emphasis to urge Christlike living on them (2:7; 4:2). Philippians is a Christ-dominated letter because Paul wants them to be Christ-indwelt people.

The normal greeting in a secular letter of Paul's day was *chairein*, "greetings." Paul displaces it with the biblical term *charis* (**grace**) to which he adds **peace**. But it is the grace and peace of **God our Father and the Lord Jesus Christ** (1:2) that he invokes upon them. **Grace** is the undeserved favor God in His mercy shows toward sinners. **Peace** is the health, wholeness, and well-being that comes to those who are right with God through Jesus Christ. This combination of blessings appears in the greeting of every Pauline letter. These gifts may have been in shorter supply in the Philippian church than they needed to be, as we shall see from the references to them scattered throughout the letter.

2. THE OPENING PRAYER-SECTION 1:3–11

A PRAYER OF THANKSGIVING

Pagan letters often included a prayer at this point. So a young recruit in the Roman army writes to his mother from Italy, "Above all, I pray that you are in health, and I myself am in health, and I am making intercession for you before the gods here."[2] Paul typically begins his letters with prayer, and the dominant key in which they are set is that of thanksgiving (Rom. 1:8–9; 1 Cor. 1:4; Eph. 1:16; Col. 1:3). Thanksgiving, as Paul uses it, is a form of praise because the things for which he gives thanks are God's works in the lives of his converts. So the prayer both extols God and lists the features of the Philippians' lives for which he gives thanks. The intensity of the emphasis on praise is seen not only in the introductory words **I thank my God**, but in the repeated use of compounds of *all* in verses 3 and 4 which may be translated literally as follows: "at all my recollections of you, always, in all of my prayers, praying for all of you with joy."

In verses 5 and 6 he goes on to list the particular items for which he praises God. First is their **partnership in the gospel from the first day until now** (1:5). The Greek word translated **partnership** is *koinonia*, which means "having in common." Here it means that the Philippians not only accepted the gospel, but shared in Paul's mission of spreading it by their material support of him, as well as by their own steadfast witness in the midst of suffering. The second reason that moves Paul to praise is his confidence of their continuance in the faith (1:6). This is grounded in his conviction that God, who began the work of grace in them, will continue it until it is completed on the day of Christ.

If we put these two items together, we see that Paul understands there are two sides to God's saving work in human lives. On the one hand, there is human response and cooperation, and on the other, there is the initiating and continuing operation of the grace of God. Both are necessary, but they are not equal. Even though Paul (because of the way his argument develops) mentions the work of God second, the language (**he who began a good work in you**), shows that God's activity is prior.

167

AN EXPRESSION OF AFFECTION

The recollection of the Philippians' partnership with Paul causes his thanksgiving to spill over into affection (1:7). This is no passing, effervescent emotion. It is his considered attitude, his **mind**, a word that he will use often in the letter (2:2, 5; 3:15, 19; 4:2, 10). The reason: **I have you in my heart**. Paul pulls back the curtains of his heart to show that the Philippians have taken up occupancy there. It is a striking revelation of what caused the heart of the apostle to beat faster. Whether he is in prison or traveling the roads of the Roman Empire with the gospel, they are sharers with him in the grace of mission, which God has given him. The depth of emotion this stirs in Paul is indicated in the stunning words of verse 8. He longs for all of them with the affection of Christ himself. So sure is he of this that he declares that God himself can testify to it.

GREAT THEMES

FULL ASSURANCE

While we are charged to "keep [ourselves] . . . in God's love" (Jude 21), we are also "kept by Jesus Christ" (Jude 1) and serve a God "who is able to keep [us] from falling" (Jude 24). We thereby live "in full assurance of faith" (Heb. 10:22).

> The work which His goodness began
> The arm of His strength will complete;
> His promise is Yea and Amen,
> And never was forfeited yet;
> Things future, nor things that are now,
> Nor all things below nor above
> Can make Him His purpose forgo,
> Or sever my soul from His love.
>
> —Augustus Toplady

A PRAYER OF PETITION

The prayer-section in Paul's letters usually ends with a series of specific petitions (Rom. 1:11–15; Eph. 1:17–19; Col. 1:9–14). Paul's prayers indicate not only those things Paul valued, but also what he thought his correspondents needed. He addresses the specific situation in the church to which he is writing.

While verses 9–11 consist of a single sentence and so may be thought of as a single petition, there are three distinguishable parts to it. The first is the prayer that their **love may abound . . . in knowledge and . . . insight** (1:9). **Love** is probably used here in the widest sense: love for God, love for neighbor, love for each other. Particularly noticeable is the prayer that love will lead to increased understanding and insight. That this is Paul's meaning is shown by the outcome of such growth in love: the ability to test and sort out the best things from the second best. What kinds of things Paul has in mind are shown by the results of this process: that they may be pure and blameless until the day of Christ. That day will be the final inspection, and the best way of being ready for it then is being ready for it now. This prayer for an increase in their spiritual understanding is the second part of Paul's petition (1:10). The third part reinforces it. This is that their lives may be filled with righteousness, the righteousness that consists of ethical fruits such as love, joy, peace (Gal. 5:22–23). This ethical harvest comes through Christ and brings honor and glory to God (1:11).

These verses have been described as "the New Testament's most profound and precise treatment about the influence of *agape* (love) from the intellectual and moral point of view, in this world or the next. Eight words show the extent of its domain: knowledge, insight, judgment, uprightness, blamelessness, holiness, glory, and praise of God."[3] You see life, the world, and reality more clearly from the perspective of love than when you see it only from the perspective of self-interest or cold, intellectual calculation. Ultimately, the meaning of life is a question of values, and the ultimate moral value is love.

The content of Paul's prayer in verses 9–11 is strikingly similar to that of others of his prayers. A recurring theme is that his readers will

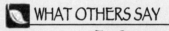

WHAT OTHERS SAY

THE GREATEST OF THESE

It were well you should be thoroughly sensible of this—the 'heaven of heavens is love' . . . There is nothing higher in religion; there is, in effect, nothing else; if you look for anything but more love, you are looking wide of the mark, you are getting out of the royal way.

—John Wesley

be strengthened in holiness so as to be found blameless on the day or at the coming of the Lord Jesus Christ (1 Cor. 1:8; 1 Thess. 3:13; 5:23), and he expresses his confidence that God will be faithful and fulfill this (1 Thess. 5:24). Yet another petition is that his hearers will come to abound in mutual love to each other and to all, a condition of heart to which he himself lays claim (1 Thess. 3:12; compare Eph. 3:17–19).

If we stand back and ask what we may expect to find in the rest of Philippians on the basis of what we have found in the opening prayer-section in 1:3–11, what answer do we get?

We may expect to find (1) Paul's concern for the Philippians' continuance in the faith and work of the gospel, and (2) Paul's concern for their spiritual maturation so that they will be found pure and blameless at the coming of Christ.

ENDNOTES

What Others Say Sidebar: John Wesley, *A Plain Account of Christian Perfection* (Kansas City, Mo.: Beacon Hill Press of Kansas City, 1966), p. 99.

1. Markus Bockmuehl, *The Epistle to the Philippians,* Black's New Testament Commentary (London: Hendrickson, 1998), p. 52.

2. J. L. White, *Light from Ancient Letters* (Philadelphia: Fortress, 1986), p. 164 (Deasley's translation). The letter dates from the second century A.D.

3. Ceslaus Spicq, *Agape in the New Testament,* vol. 2 (St. Louis: Herder, 1966), p. 277.

2

PAUL'S SITUATION AND THE GOSPEL

Philippians 1:12-26

The first thing to note about this section is its departure from Paul's normal practice of dealing with personal matters at the close of his letters (for example, Rom. 15:14–33). It is true that Paul returns to personal matters in 4:10–20, but that merely intensifies the question as to why he deals with them here also. (It is the longest personal section in all of his letters). Perhaps the reason is that in Paul's mind, it is not primarily a personal section at all. His chief concern is with how his circumstances affect his ability to preach the gospel.

1. PAUL'S IMPRISONMENT AND ITS EFFECTS ON THE PROCLAMATION OF THE GOSPEL 1:12–18A

Paul plunges directly into a description, not of the miseries of his imprisonment, but of the positive effect his imprisonment has had on the furtherance of the gospel (1:12).

It has become known, he says, that his bonds are **in Christ** (which is how the original Greek reads). This intensive expression, which Paul has used already (1:1) and will use many times again, goes deeper than **for Christ** (NIV), though it includes it. It is as one united to Christ that he is a prisoner. He is far more than merely Caesar's slave; he is Christ's slave. This has become known throughout the whole palace guard. The praetorian guard was officially responsible for carrying out the emperor's orders. Paul's status as an imperial prisoner had brought the gospel into the heart of the powerhouse of the Roman Empire, as well as beyond it (1:13). A further consequence of this imprisonment was that his brothers in Christ had been stimulated to speak more openly and fearlessly (1:14).

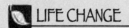

LIFE CHANGE

AT HIS SERVICE

In an age when society is turned in upon itself, and we are pressed relentlessly to think first, last, and always of how circumstances and situations affect ourselves, it is chastening to see that Paul's first thought was of how what happened to him would affect his ministry. In the piercing words of Karl Barth: "To the question how it is with *him* an apostle *must* react with information as to how it is with the *Gospel.*"

Paul expands this latter point. Not all who preached the gospel more boldly did so for altruistic reasons. Some did it for debased reasons: **out of envy and rivalry** (1:15), which he expands in verse 17 as being **out of selfish ambition, not sincerely, supposing that they can stir up trouble for me while I am in chains**. Apparently there were those who regarded Paul as a competitor. He does not deny that they preached Christ. On what grounds then, would they take advantage of his imprisonment? Probably they were Jewish Christians who opposed his preaching the gospel to Gentiles.

But besides these were others inspired by Paul's testimony who preached Christ **out of goodwill** (1:15). These had come to see that Paul's incarceration, far from being a handicap, proved to be an advantage because of the notice his case had attracted. Paul's conclusion, therefore, was that for whatever motive, Christ was preached and this was reason for rejoicing. This is the second use of some form of the word **joy**. He found joy in prayer (1:4) and now in preaching (1:18). **Joy** is one of the key words in the letter.

2. PAUL'S FUTURE PROSPECTS AND THEIR EFFECT ON THE PROCLAMATION OF THE GOSPEL 1:18B–26

Paul's imprisonment has thus far proved to be a help rather than a hindrance to the gospel. So far so good. But Paul was enough of a realist to know that the story had not ended. He would not stay in prison forever. As an imperial prisoner, he would appear before the emperor for sentencing, which could mean one of two things: He would either walk out of prison or be carried out. It is on these alternatives and their consequences for the preaching of the gospel that he reflects in these verses.

There is a degree of ebb and flow in Paul's expectations. He repeats the note of rejoicing from verse 18a and goes on to affirm his confidence that the Philippians' prayers and the help of Christ's Spirit will lead to his **deliverance** (1:19). The Greek word rendered **deliverance** is the normal Greek word for "salvation." In the Old Testament, this can mean vindication before God, or final salvation, as in Job 13:16–19. Paul too, uses it in this way, as in 2 Timothy 4:18. Indeed, that is what appears to be the meaning here, rather than deliverance from prison. This interpretation fits well with the hope he expresses in verse 20 that he will not betray the gospel by a lack of courage but **that now as always Christ will be exalted in my body, whether by life or by death**. Paul does, however, see the path to eternal salvation as taking him through present trial. His eager expectation (a strong word referring elsewhere to final salvation, for example, Rom. 8:19) and hope are that he will faithfully defend the gospel (1:16) so that, whether he is freed or executed, he will receive salvation on the last day. Significantly he sees all of this taking place not through his own innate strength and effort, but **through your prayers and the help given by the Spirit of Jesus Christ** (1:19).

LIFE CHANGE

VEINS IN THE BODY OF CHRIST

Paul's expressed dependence on the Philippians' prayers almost suggests that he sees his unity with them in even deeper terms than as fellow members of the body of Christ. His life is sustained by them as the life of the physical body is sustained by veins that carry the blood from one organ to another.

Paul's unmistakable feeling of dependence on the prayers of his fellow believers in Philippi urges evangelical Christians to temper their emphasis on the autonomy of the individual with an appreciation for the inter-connectedness of the church. . . . Paul's desire that the Philippians should ask God to supply him with the Spirit should prompt those who are not Pentecostals to re-examine their static notions of the Spirit's role in the believer's life.

—Frank Thielman

173

The mention of life or death (1:20) leads Paul to a revealing meditation on his attitude toward these. He draws up a kind of balance sheet, weighing death and life against each other. Since for him **to live is Christ** (1:21), then dying could only be gain, since he would then be in Christ's immediate presence. On the other hand, continued life on earth would mean **fruitful labor** for Him. Paul faces a dilemma, desiring **to depart and be with Christ, which is better by far** (1:23). However, it is better for the Philippians that he continue his ministry. Hence Paul is convinced that his life will be spared, and he will minister to their **progress and joy** (joy again) **in faith** (1:25). Accordingly, he expects to be with them again so that their **joy** (yet again!) **in Christ Jesus will overflow on account of me** (1:26).

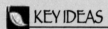

KEY IDEAS

Paul's Balance Sheet of Life and Death

Life = Christ (v. 21) = service for Christ (v. 22) = serving the Philippians (v. 24).

Death = gain (more of Christ: v. 21) = being with Christ (v. 23) = is far better (v. 23).

This is a remarkable passage in several respects. First, it reveals Paul's attitude toward death. There were many in Paul's world who regarded oblivion as preferable to existence. The dominant religion in the Roman Empire—Stoicism—regarded life with indifference, teaching people to steel their hearts against life and its experiences until eventually it was over. Paul saw it differently. To him "death is not 'gain' in the sense of escape, but in the sense of 3:8, 'gaining' more of Christ who is already our life and entering into full participation in his resurrection."[1]

In the world of today, the opposite view is held. Life on earth is prized and clung to, with people living in mortal fear of the end and banishing it to the edge of their consciousness. Paul's words speak equally to people with that mind-set, affirming that for those who share Christ's life here and now, death means entrance into a fuller dimension of life. In the words of Bishop Handley Moule, "The dying hour is to Paul the mere gateway into the 'large room' of the presence of Christ."[2]

The passage is remarkable in another respect: It demonstrates that Paul's primary concern was not with his personal future, which was secure and created no anxiety. His chief preoccupation was with the furtherance of the gospel, and his confidence is striking (1:15, 25). Whether its source was a particular revelation or an inner assurance from the Holy Spirit we cannot say. What is clear is that for Paul, the future of the gospel was more important than his personal future, and his confidence in the gospel assured him that nothing would happen to him that would hinder the progress of the faith.

The particular focus of Paul's ministry of the gospel was the Philippian believers. He was chiefly concerned with *their* progress in the faith (1:25) and *their* joy in Christ Jesus (1:26) rather than simply the progress of the gospel in general. This prepares us to expect a particular parallel between his situation and theirs. If, as we have seen, Paul's chief concern was for the proclamation of the gospel, perhaps the reason he has described his own situation as a prisoner in such detail is because this says something to the situation in which the Philippians find themselves. We shall see.

ENDNOTES

1. Markus Bockmuehl, *The Epistle to the Philippians,* Black's New Testament Commentary (London: Hendrickson Publishers, 1998), p. 88.

2. H. C. G. Moule, *The Epistle to the Philippians*, Thornapple Commentaries (Grand Rapids, Mich.: Baker Book House, 1981), p. 24.

3

PAUL'S INSTRUCTIONS TO THE PHILIPPIANS

Philippians 1:27–2:11

The letter now makes a clear shift of focus from Paul's circumstances and concerns to those of the Philippians. The two are not unrelated. They were connected as a matter of history. Paul had been roughly received in Philippi because of his message, and his followers found themselves receiving the same treatment. Further, it is because Paul was continuing to experience the rugged side of life in jail that he is well placed to speak to the situation of the Philippians, who were also enduring the rigors of persecution. This fixes the general tone of this part of the letter. It offers guidance to the Philippians in their distress from Paul in the midst of his. The guidance takes the form of instruction, particularly exhortation.

The order and extent of Paul's exhortations are worth noting. Presumably they give us some index of the needs of the Philippian Christians and Paul's view of how such needs should be resolved.

1. AN EXHORTATION TO STEADFASTNESS 1:27–30

Following the account of his own sufferings brought about by his faithfulness to the gospel, and more particularly how he has refused to be deterred by them, Paul turns to the sufferings of the Philippians. Verses 27–30 form a single sentence in Greek, suggesting that the various ideas mentioned are all part of a single idea: steadfastness in the face of persecution.

LIFE CHANGE
LIVING WORTHY OF THE GOSPEL

The most powerful stimulus to steadfastness in Christian commitment is not motivational seminars or new cultural strategies, whatever value these may have. Rather it is "the faith of the gospel" (Phil. 1:27), apprehended by heart and mind, and allowed to glow and burn in the inner being. Bunyan's Mr. Valiant-for-Truth is a classic example, characterized in the lines of the pilgrim hymn.

> Hobboblin nor foul Fiend,
> Can daunt his spirit:
> He knows he at the end
> Shall life inherit.
> Then Fancies fly away,
> He'll fear not what men say,
> He'll labor night and day
> To be a pilgrim.

In exhorting the Philippians in this way, Paul does much more than simply serve them an empty psychological platitude such as "keep your chins up!" His exhortation arises directly from his message. **Whatever happens, conduct yourselves in a manner worthy of the gospel of Christ** (1:27). He has already placed his concern for the gospel as the yardstick for measuring his own tribulations (1:4, 7, 12, 16). Now he asks them to do the same. His specific appeal is that their lives should proclaim the same message as their lips. The word translated **conduct yourselves** has a special flavor. Translated literally, it means "be a citizen." (He uses it again in 3:20). Philippi was a Roman colony (Acts 16:12), which meant its citizens had legal status and exemption from poll taxes and land taxation like all citizens of the Roman motherland. But the special privileges from the emperor brought special obligations to him. Paul is transferring this idea to Christian citizenship in the kingdom of God. This is to be their guideline, whatever happens to him: **whether I come and see you or only hear about you in my absence** (1:27). In the expression that he more commonly uses they are to "live lives worthy of God" (1 Thess. 2:12).

Now, there are two specific qualities that he enjoins as being especially needed in Philippi—both of them clues to the situation in the church there. Conduct worthy of the gospel includes both.

UNITY

The key phrase expressing unity is this: **stand firm in one spirit, contending as one man for the faith of the gospel** (1:27).[1] Steadfastness by itself is not enough. Steadfastness must be characterized by unity—and unity in a common cause: **the faith of the gospel**. This is the only instance of this phrase in the New Testament. The terms are virtually interchangeable. The foundation of their unity is not their faith *in* the gospel, but that which lies behind it: the faith *of* the gospel. Reduced to a formula, what Paul is saying is "one spirit—one mind—one faith." If they give the gospel priority, everything else becomes a priority of the second order, and unity is secure.

FEARLESSNESS IN FACE OF OPPOSITION

Fearlessly facing opposition is a second aspect of conduct worthy of the gospel. The Philippians are not to be intimidated **by those who oppose [them]** (1:28). Again, Paul gives them a substantive reason. It is not simply a matter of physical bravado. It is rather that opposition to God is a lost cause, and, therefore, their fearlessness in face of opposition points to the doom of their opponents and their own salvation. Paul adds strikingly: **And this is God's doing** (1:28 NRSV).

This sounds well enough as a morale-boosting speech for the troops in the minutes before the opening shots are fired. But Paul is not blind to what he is asking of them. He goes on to add that what they are being asked to do is simply to follow in the footsteps of Christ as well as his own. The language he uses is striking. **It has been granted to you on behalf of Christ not only to believe on him, but also to suffer for him** (1:29). The verb **granted** is derived from the word *grace*, and the use of the passive form means that God is the giver. Put together, this amounts to saying that persecution for the sake of the gospel is a gift of God's grace. Evil does not lay down its arms willingly or readily, but only after a battle that brings about its defeat. This was the battle Christ fought, and the Philippians continue it on His behalf.[2] Not only so, but they saw Paul endure the same attack, and they hear that he continues to endure it (1:30). The only way salvation will come about in a world like ours is through suffering.

We should be clear about the urgency of the need for endurance in this situation. Philippi as a Roman colony had a lot to lose if its loyalty to the emperor became suspect. This is exactly what believers were accused of in Acts 16:20–21. It also explains Paul's insistence on being publicly escorted out of the city by the magistrates (Acts 16:35–40), an open indication that he and Silas had done no wrong. The believers Paul left behind may not have been subjected to physical violence, but if they were the victims of economic pressure or social ostracism, their lives could have been made miserable indeed.

Again, in the Jewish and Greek ancient world, suffering was seen as a mark of divine disfavor. The Roman world believed in a prosperity religion, just as many today believe in a prosperity gospel. Paul's experience stood this belief on its head, as did the experience of Christ before him.

There appear to have been some in the church in Philippi who had difficulty accepting suffering. If not all suffered discrimination and persecution, those unscathed may have seen those who were persecuted as a threat to their own safety, and so the unity of the church was damaged. Paul is passing on to the Philippians what he had earlier explained to his converts in Asia Minor: "encouraging them to remain true to the faith," and that "through many hardships" they must "enter the kingdom of God" (Acts 14:22).

From this vantage point, we may raise the question as to why Paul has placed the personal information he normally reserves for the end of his letters at the beginning of this one, immediately following the opening prayer section. A summary of the import of 1:20–30 may point toward an answer. First, Paul's future was uncertain; he might be executed rather than released. Second, the Philippians might have to face (if they had not already done so) fierce opposition and persecution, and they should be fully prepared for it. Third, the best way in which to confront a hostile world was with a united church, firmly fixed to that on which they stood fast: **the faith of the gospel**.

Matter of such weight, written with such intensity, could not be reserved for the postscript of the letter. Rather, it belonged to the heart of the letter. Any interpretation that fails to see this as part of the central message of the letter is a misreading of it.

2. AN EXHORTATION TO UNITY 2:1–4

It may be asked why, since Paul has already underlined the importance of unity in 1:27, he should return to the subject at even greater length here. It is not accidental. The original text connects the two passages with the conjunction *therefore*, which is unfortunately omitted from the NIV text: "**If** [therefore] **you have any encouragement from being united with Christ** (2:1). The earlier passage is concerned with unity in face of opposition from the outside. The present passage focuses on qualities that are indispensable for the maintenance of unity *within* the church.

The heart of the exhortation is in verse 2. Paul appeals to their personal affection for him to make his joy complete **by being like-minded, having the same love, being one in spirit and purpose**. The first and last items in the list are derived from the same Greek word. We have already met it in 1:7 where the NIV translates it as **feel** and it occurs later in the letter in important verses such as 2:5, where the NIV renders it as **your attitude should be**. It is a term whose meaning is not only wide but deep. Words such as *attitude* and *outlook* capture it well. It is more than just thought, but includes conviction and disposition. The word **purpose** used by the NIV to translate the second use of it in verse 2 means literally "mind the one thing." The intervening phrases **having the same love, being one in spirit** add dashes of color to the central idea. It is not clone-mindedness, but commitment to a common purpose.

But how does this come to be? Certainly not by military (or even apostolic) order. The answer to that question is found in verse 1. Each of its four clauses begins with the conditional particle **if**, but there is nothing conditional in what Paul is saying. **If** may be translated *since*, the more probable translation here.[3] The qualities referred to in verse 1 are often taken to refer to human emotions: consolation, comfort, tenderness, and compassion. But the original makes clear that they are rooted in objective realities: **If you have any encouragement from being united with Christ, if any comfort from his love, if any fellowship with the Spirit, if any tenderness and compassion** (2:1). The most frequent meaning of the word rendered **encouragement** in the Pauline writings is consolation, which comes close to meaning salvation. The **comfort** referred to is that which comes from

Christ's love. The **fellowship** spoken of is not mushy friendliness. It refers to the fact that to be a Christian at all is to share in the Holy Spirit, and it is the fact of this sharing that creates Christian fellowship. Fellowship is a fact before it is a feeling. Any fellowship that is based on feeling will quickly evaporate. But if it is grounded in the fact that we are all possessed by the same Spirit, then its future is secure. Likewise, **tenderness and compassion** refer to the compassion and mercy shown to us by Christ.

Accordingly, it is on this basis that Paul is able to exhort them to be united. These are the bases on which unity rests, and they are not feelings which we work up, but facts of the Christian life created by the grace of God. This and only this, is what gives leverage to Paul's exhortation. If the question be asked as to why Paul refers to these particular qualities, presumably it is because he feared that **consolation, comfort, fellowship and compassion** were in short supply in Philippi.

This leads at once to a further observation. The fact that God has given His salvation, His comfort, His Spirit, and His compassion to His people does not mean that unity is automatic. We have to make space for these facts to work themselves out in life and not stifle them. Paul urges this upon the Philippians in two ways.

First, negatively, there are things to avoid (2:3). They are not to act out of **selfish ambition or vain conceit**. In a society driven by untamed entrepreneurial spirit, it is easy for the success of one person to be secured at the destruction and ruin of another. "Every man for himself and the devil take the hindmost" is a long way from "You shall love your neighbor as yourself." **In humility**

LIFE CHANGE

VEINS IN THE BODY OF CHRIST

Humility is grounded in the same facts as unity: union with Christ, the love of Christ, and participation in the Spirit (Phil. 2:1–2). It is not achieved by practicing being humble, but by acknowledging the love and lordship of Christ as the source of every good thing in us.

The biblical view of humility is precisely *not* feigned or groveling, nor a sanctimonious or pathetic lack of self-esteem, but rather a mark of moral strength and integrity. It involves an unadorned acknowledgment of one's own creaturely inadequacies, and entrusting one's fortunes to God rather than to one's own abilities or resources.

—Markus Bockmuehl

consider others better than yourself (2:3) means thinking and speaking more highly of others than of oneself, valuing their needs and achievements before one's own, giving preference without distinction. Humility was not regarded as a virtue in the ancient pagan world, and it is not regarded as a virtue in the modern pagan world either. But it is a *Christian* virtue, indeed, an apostolic command.

Second, Paul urges the Philippians to allow the grace God has shown them to work out positively by what they do (2:4). He recognizes the need for each person to care for his or her own interests. He simply insists that they should also give attention to the interests of others.

3. THE SECRET OF STABILITY AND UNITY— THE MIND OF CHRIST 2:5-11

Paul's instructions to the Philippians advance a step further. From exhorting them to be steadfast and united, he now goes on to write of the secret of stability and unity: having the mind or mind-set of Christ. This is not the first time he has referred to the mind of Christ in the letter. The NIV tends to obscure this by translating the word *mind* in 2:5 as **attitude**, but it is the same word that occurs twice in 2:2, which the NIV renders as **like-minded** the first time and **being one in . . . purpose** the second.

The passage is one of the most famous descriptions in the New Testament of Jesus' character as the Christ. It is also of central significance in the letter to the Philippians. One scholar has said that it gives "Christological and above all theological underpinning to the rest of Philippians, especially chapters 2 and 3."[4]

This passage has been the subject of much debate among scholars, and it is beyond the scope of this commentary to engage in this debate. At the same time its place in Paul's argument in this letter cannot be settled without taking a position on the debated issues. The most that can be done here is to indicate the positions adopted, with a broad statement of why one conclusion has been preferred above another. The best approach appears to be to indicate these conclusions with reasons at the start and then proceed to interpret the passage in the light of them.

The first striking feature about the passage is that it is evidently written in rhythmical prose amounting almost to poetry. Some translations (including the NIV) print it in the form of poetry, and numerous commentaries speak of it as a hymn.[5] But to describe it as such is to say something at least implicitly about its function in Paul's argument. For when it is described as a hymn, the implication is almost always that it is a faith confession of the early church that Paul is quoting. There is nothing inherently objectionable in such a suggestion, but if a confession is what it is, it constitutes a marked shift from the exhortational character of 1:27–2:4, which is picked up again in 2:12. Indeed, 2:5 is itself exhortational in form.

What the question comes down to is this: Is Paul holding up Christ to the Philippians as an example for them to follow? Or is he urging them to live up to their calling as Christians by being obedient to Christ as their Lord, who submitted for their sakes even to death on a cross? To put it otherwise, is Paul saying that having the mind-set of Christ is the natural consequence and result of being redeemed? Or is he saying that the mind of Christ is something the believer must develop through copying the example of Christ?

The distinction may appear to be slender, though scholars have covered acres of paper debating it in the last fifty years. The two are surely inseparable. Redemption is not merely *from* sin but *to* a new way of life. But, as Paul goes on to say in 2:11–12, the believer has the responsibility to work out the salvation that God has worked in. Indeed, it is precisely because of the saving power of Christ's death and resurrection that new life becomes possible. And the pattern to be followed in this "working out" is the example of Christ.

Perhaps it is a mistake to make the issue an either/or. It is hard to miss the note of exhortation that runs throughout. It is clearly an ethical result that Paul is seeking, namely, stability and unity among the Philippians. But this will be achieved only by submission to the lordship of Christ, not by sheer strength and willpower. It was through His submission to death that salvation was accomplished, and it will be through similar submission that His saving work will be fulfilled among the Philippians. So in the passage Paul reminds the Philippians of the gospel message, which they had believed, and urges upon them the corresponding attitude as those who are "in Christ."[6]

We may now turn to the text and seek to see whether it sustains such a reading. A crux is encountered immediately in verse 5, which reads literally, have this mind among you which also in Christ Jesus. As is not uncommon in Greek, connecting verbs are omitted, and the readers are left to supply them. Did Paul mean have this mind among you which *you* also *have* in Christ Jesus? That is, those who are **in Christ** and believe the gospel story summarized in these verses exhibit the mind-set found in Him. Or did he mean have this mind among you which *was* also in Christ Jesus? That is, copy the example of Christ. The former is the foundation of the soteriological understanding, the latter of the ethical understanding. It is the difference between something that is *theirs* as those who belong to Christ and something they should labor to show as those shaping their lives after the pattern of Christ's.

If the context is to be our guide, then there is clearly a note of exhortation comparable to verse 2. He picks up the same verb from there: **being like-minded**. But since the first verse assumes they are already partakers of God's grace in Christ (see above), it seems impossible to separate the two with clinical precision. *Because* they are Christ's, they may be expected to possess His mind-set, and to exhibit it more and more. Moreover, this is not an individual matter; it is a group concern. The words *in you* (left untranslated in the NIV) are plural in Greek: have this mind among yourselves. Paul proceeds to explain exactly what he means by *mind*. It is the mentality or cast of mind exhibited by Christ in the whole work by which He wrought our salvation. That work Paul traces out in two clearly defined movements.

CHRIST'S HUMBLING OF HIMSELF

The theme of Christ's humbling himself is expounded in verses 6–8. Throughout, the accent falls on the action of Christ. All that is described was the result of His initiative; nothing was forced on Him. It is also more than that He *accepted* humiliation when others thrust it upon Him. Rather He actively **humbled himself**. The passage moves progressively from His state of exaltation (2:6) to self-denial (2:7) to humiliation or debasement (2:8).

185

Paul describes Christ's exaltation in the words **being in very nature God** (2:6). The Greek text literally reads "being in the form of God" (as rendered in older translations such as the KJV). To English ears this can suggest something less than the identity or reality expressed in the NIV rendering. However, the same term is used in verse 7 to describe Christ's taking the humble position of a servant, where nothing less than the rank and reality of a servant are clearly in mind. The word *form* in Greek can denote merely outward appearance, "but it may refer to the kind of form that fully expresses the being that underlies it."[7] The following phrase specifies what is in mind in the first: **equality with God**.[8] The verse continues that Christ **did not consider equality with God something to be grasped**. The question is whether **grasped** denotes something Christ did not possess and declined to seize, or something He did possess and declined to hold on to. The drift of the passage, both what has preceded and what follows, seems clearly to support the latter. What this adds up to is that Jesus did not regard equality with God as something to be exploited or used to His own advantage. This was the dominant characteristic of Jesus' ministry (Mark 10:45) and was recognized as such by Paul: Christ did not please himself (Rom. 15:3; 2 Cor. 8:9).

On the contrary, far from using His position for His own advantage, He **made himself nothing** (2:7). Again, this is something Christ did to himself. The original reads, "he emptied himself." Much theological ingenuity has been spent in attempting to define of what He emptied himself. The verb translated "to empty" can carry the meaning "to pour out." This appears to be the meaning that fits best here, the two immediately following phrases describing the ways in which Christ poured himself out. First, He did so by **taking the very nature of a servant**. The word translated **nature** is "form" in the original and is so rendered in other versions, such as the KJV. But the meaning is not that He took merely the appearance of a servant or slave. He became a servant in the fullest sense of the word. Still more important is the point made by F. F. Bruce: "This does not mean that he *exchanged* the nature (or form) of God for the nature (or form) of a servant: it means that he displayed the nature (or form) of God *in* the nature (or form) of a servant."[9] It is doubtful that there is an implicit reference to the Servant Songs in Isaiah, such as Isaiah 53.

The institution of slavery with all its barbarities would have spoken vividly enough to the mind of the time.

The second phrase that explains the way in which Christ "poured himself out" is **being made in human likeness**. This does not mean that Christ was merely *like* human beings and not really one of them. On the contrary, it means that He **became** truly human, as the participle indicates: "being born." (For a parallel use of *likeness* see Rom. 5:14; of *being made* Gal. 4:4.) In these ways, then, Christ **made himself nothing**.

But the full depth of His humiliation has not yet been reached. The thought of the last part of verse 7 is repeated as the first part of verse 8 in the NIV: **And being found in appearance as a man**. The foundation of the remainder of verse 8 begins with the words **he humbled himself**. Christ was not humbled. He humbled himself. But this self-humbling was possible only because He assumed human form. "The implication," writes R. P. Martin, "is that at the incarnation Christ became more than God, if this is conceivable, not less than God."[10]

Verse 8 proceeds to denote the depth of Christ's self-humbling in three successive expressions, each thrusting still deeper into the completeness of Christ's humiliation. First, He **became obedient**. The note of Christ's obedience to the Father is particularly characteristic of the Gospel of John (for example, 5:19; 7:16; 8:28–29). In the Greek text, the word *became* is emphatic: "becoming obedient." Obedience was a humiliation Jesus accepted as a human being, and, therefore, it was part of His self-denial (Heb. 5:7–8).

Second, He became obedient to the point of death. Obedience can go no further than this. It is the ultimate extent of self-surrender.

Third, He became obedient not merely to death, but to **death on a cross**. Death by crucifixion was forbidden by Roman law to any Roman citizen as being too debased and degrading. Indeed, the mere discussion of it was regarded as offensive. The New Testament writers regularly refer to it as something shameful and contemptible (Heb. 12:2; 1 Cor. 1:18; Gal. 3:13).

Several things are noteworthy about the way in which Christ's death is spoken of in these verses. For one thing, His death was unique. It was necessarily so, since His person was unique. While identifying himself with humanity, He also retained His distinctiveness in such a way that He could offer obedience to God. And by definition, obedience to death is

MANNERS AND CUSTOMS

THE OFFENSIVENESS OF CRUCIFIXION

In polite Roman society the word "cross" was an obscenity, not to be uttered in conversation. Even when a man was being sentenced to death by crucifixion, an archaic formula was used that avoided the pronouncing of this four-letter word—as it was in Latin (*crux*).

—F. F. Bruce

something possible only for a divine being, since for human beings as such, death is not a matter of obedience but an inescapable necessity.[11]

With this, we reach the depth of Christ's humbling of himself. It is significant that in speaking of Christ's death, Paul describes it strictly in terms of what it meant for Christ. There is no direct mention of its redemptive effects for sinners. At the same time, it stands in the not-too-distant background. If one asks why Christ assumed human likeness and submitted to death on the cross, it is hardly satisfying to say He did so for His own benefit or that His crucifixion was a piece of empty theater. Clearly something of a large order was taking place. But the point Paul is intent on making has to do with the mind-set exhibited by Christ that Paul in turn enjoins on the Philippians. It is well summed up in the lines of Kate Barclay Wilkinson.

> May the mind of Christ my Saviour
> Live in me from day to day,
> By His love and power controlling
> All I do or say.

> May the love of Jesus fill me,
> As the waters fill the sea;
> Him exalting, self abasing,
> This is victory.

> May I run the race before me,
> Strong and brave to face the foe,
> Looking only unto Jesus
> As I onward go.[12]

GOD'S EXALTING OF CHRIST

The theme changes drastically from humiliation to exaltation. This is matched by a change in the one taking the action. **Christ** humbles himself; **God** exalts Him. It is equally noteworthy that there is a causal connection between Christ's humiliation and exaltation: **therefore God exalted him to the highest place** (2:9). It was because of His self-humbling that God lifted Him up. The declaration is significant in a number of ways.

For one thing it is significant for the doctrine of God. The plain implication is that He, who **being in very nature God** (2:6), was **made in human likeness** (2:7) **and became obedient to death** (2:8), was for that reason **exalted . . . to the highest place** (2:9). In short, the implication is Trinitarian: Jesus occupies the same place as the Father, and it is the Father who has exalted Him to that place. This is given expression in the form that God **gave him the name that is above every name** (2:9). It has been suggested that the name in mind is **Jesus**, since this is mentioned in the next verse (2:10). In this case the accent would rest on Jesus' saviorhood, since **Jesus** is the Greek form of the Hebrew *Joshua*, which is derived from the Hebrew verb "to save." However, this was Jesus' name from birth (Matt. 1:21). It is more probable that the name in mind is **Lord** (2:11)—the name of God himself. This was the earliest way in which Christians confessed their faith (Rom. 10:9; 1 Cor. 12:1).

The name **Lord** brings the homage of the universe to Jesus. The NIV correctly conveys the meaning of the original by rendering **that at the name of Jesus every knee should bow** (2:10). Martin and Hawthorne (paraphrasing Gnilka) write, "It is necessary to understand that the writer is here asserting that homage is to be paid *to* Jesus as Lord, not *through* Jesus to God."[13] Accordingly, the entire universe—**every knee . . . in heaven and on earth and under the earth** (2:10)—will bend in submission to Him. Every conscious order of life in the universe—heavenly beings, earthly beings, and the rebellious beings condemned to perdition (1 Pet. 3:18–22)—will acknowledge His lordship, admitting it as a fact, whether or not they embrace it as a reality. In the words of verses 10 and 11 there is the application to Jesus of Isaiah 45:23–24, paying divine honor to Him (compare Rom. 14:10–12). Yet this is done **to the glory of**

God the Father (2:11). Christ's lordship is a derived and related, not a solitary, lordship.

Verses 9–11 are significant not only for the doctrine of God; they are also significant for the situation of the Philippians. The point of the passage, after all, is that their **attitude should be the same as that of Christ Jesus** (2:5). It is sometimes argued that there is nothing in the life of the believer that is parallel to the exaltation of Christ described in verses 9–11. In the strict sense of course, this is true. But there is a corresponding sense in which the suffering of the believer for the sake of Christ, such as the Philippians endured (1:29), will be vindicated in the end by God. This is the plain teaching of Jesus: "Whoever wants to save his life will lose it, but whoever loses his life for me will find it" (Matt. 16:25); "Whoever exalts himself will be humbled, and whoever humbles himself will be exalted" (Matt. 23:12). To humble oneself *in order to be exalted* is a complete misreading of Paul's meaning. Yet it remains true that humble service is what God approves, and this will triumph in the end.[14] In this way the Philippians are given the key to both stability and unity: living like Christ by living in Him.

There are some far-reaching implications of 2:6–11 that deserve fuller comment than was possible when tracing the meaning of the successive clauses and phrases. While the passage is directed to the situation in Philippi, it has a significance that reaches far beyond it. Perhaps the most important arena for which this is so is the understanding of God. The implied picture is that Christ's incarnation, death, resurrection, and exaltation made a difference within the Godhead. The implied change is not,

KEY IDEAS

THE PARADOX OF CHRISTIAN SUCCESS

By the standards of worldly wisdom success is defined in terms of fame, fortune, and acclaim. Jesus reversed this standard, as Paul plainly understood. As Gerald Hawthorne puts it:

In the divine economy of things, by giving people receive, by serving they are served, by losing their lives they find them, by dying they live, by humbling themselves they are exalted. The one follows the other as night follows day, but always in this order—self-sacrifice first before the self is exalted by God.

—Gerald F. Hawthorne

indeed, on the level of God's *being*, but on the level of God's *experience*. In taking human form and sharing the conditions of human life, God in Christ experienced the realities of fallen human existence. Markus Bockmuehl, characterizing 2:6–11 as "the theological and Christological centerpiece of the letter," concludes penetratingly that there Paul "describes the work of Jesus Christ from the perspective of eternity, and in so doing offers a radically Christ-centered reaffirmation of Jewish monotheism."[15]

Yet Paul's controlling purpose is to enjoin upon the Philippians the mind-set exhibited by Christ in His incarnation, suffering, and death. This is already theirs "in Him." But it is also something to be sought, attained, and applied. Paul uses exactly the same language of the mind or mind-set in his letter to the Romans. In chapter 7 he identifies the foe as indwelling sin. In chapter 8 he identifies the deliverer as the indwelling Spirit. "For those who live according to the flesh set their minds on the things of the flesh, but those who live according to the Spirit set their minds on the things of the Spirit. To set the mind on the flesh is death, but to set the mind on the Spirit is life and peace" (Rom. 8:5–6 NRSV).

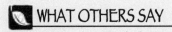

WHAT OTHERS SAY

VEHICLES OF GOD'S SELF-REVELATION

The passage sets forth "a new understanding of God," showing that "incarnation and even crucifixion are to be seen as *appropriate* vehicles for the dynamic self-revelation of God."

—N. T. Wright

Charles Wesley has given it classic expression:

God of all power, and truth, and grace,
Which shall from age to age endure,
Whose word, when heaven and earth shall pass,
Remains and stands forever sure;

That I Thy mercy may proclaim,
That all mankind Thy truth may see,
Hallow Thy great and glorious name,
And perfect holiness in me.

Give me a new, a perfect heart,
From doubt, and fear, and sorrow free;
The mind that was in Christ impart,
And let my spirit cleave to Thee.

O that I now, from sin released,
Thy word may to the utmost prove,
Enter into the promised rest,
The Canaan of Thy perfect love.[16]

ENDNOTES

Life Change Sidebar 1: John Bunyan, *Pilgrim's Progress, The World's Great Classics* (Danbury, Conn.: Grolier Enterprises Corp. n.d.), p. 342.

Life Change Sidebar 2: Markus Bockmuehl, *The Epistle to the Philippians*, Black's New Testament Commentary (London: Hendrickson Publishers, 1998), p. 110.

Manners and Customs Sidebar: F. F. Bruce, *Philippians*, Good News Commentary (San Francisco: Harper and Row, 1983), p. 47.

Key Ideas Sidebar: Gerald F. Hawthorne in Ralph P. Martin and Gerald F. Hawthorne, *Philippians*, Word Biblical Commentary (Nashville, Tenn.: Nelson Reference, 2004), p. 133.

1. Frank Thielman writes, "The phrase 'one man' is literally 'in one soul,' and most translators and commentators have understood the two phrases 'one spirit' and 'one soul' to be parallel to each other. Paul, they believe, is asking the Philippians to be united in spirit and soul. Since he uses the precise phrase 'in one spirit' elsewhere to mean 'in the one Spirit of God' (1 Cor. 12:13; Eph. 2:18), however, it is likely that in verse 27 the phrase carries at least some allusion to God's Spirit. Paul is probably saying that the Philippians should be united in spirit (because they have all experienced the work of God's Spirit) and united in soul" *(Philippians,* The New Application Commentary [Grand Rapids, Mich.: Zondervan, 1995], p. 93).

2. "The prepositional phrase . . . 'for Christ' may mean simply that the Philippians are suffering because they are on Christ's side . . . [But it] can also mean 'for the sake of Christ.' If this is the sense here, then Paul is saying that the Philippians are willing to suffer because of their love for and devotion to Christ. . . . But this prepositional phrase can also mean 'in place of' or 'instead of.' . . . If this is the idea, then the phrase has reached its most profound meaning . . . 'suffering . . . for Christ' then would indicate that the Philippians are in some way

permitted to suffer in Christ's stead. . . . By having joined 'the fellowship of his sufferings' (3:10) they have chosen to be Christ's replacements on earth in order to suffer in his absence. It is not that anyone dares put oneself on the same level with Christ in this respect. Yet there apparently is a real sense in which Christ needs people who are willing to take upon themselves the burden of his suffering in history that still remains to be borne." Martin and Hawthorne, *Philippians*, p. 75.

3. See Martin and Hawthorne, *Philippians*, p. 82.

4. N. T. Wright, *The Climax of the Covenant: Christ and the Law in Pauline Theology* (Minneapolis: Fortress Press, 1993), p. 98.

5. P. T. O'Brien describes it as "an early Christian hymn in honor of Christ" (*The Epistle to the Philippians: A Commentary on the Greek Text*, The New International Greek Testament Commentary [Grand Rapids, Mich.: William B. Eerdmans, 1991], p. 186). Martin and Hawthorne declare this as "one thing that calls forth almost universal agreement" (*Philippians*, p. 99). Frank Thielman, on the other hand, demurs from this view (*Philippians*, p. 113).

6. It is interesting to note how frequently protagonists of one view or the other feel bound to admit the presence of the opposing position in some measure. Thus P. T. O'Brien concedes that the passage "may have been originally composed for Christological or soteriological reasons," while maintaining that "Paul's object in using it here is not primarily to give instruction in doctrine but to appeal to the conduct of Christ and to reinforce instruction in Christian living" (*Philippians*, p. 262). From the other side, R. P. Martin, while championing the soteriological understanding (Martin and Hawthorne, *Philippians*, pp. 133–34), nonetheless concludes, "The thrust is not 'here is a model to be followed' so much as 'here is a Master to be obeyed.' The latter joins the soteriological with the ethical, grounding the ethical in both the salvation act and the call to obey the obedient One" (p. 135).

7. See Karl P. Donfried and I. Howard Marshall, *The Theology of the Shorter Pauline Letters* (Cambridge: Cambridge University Press, 1993), p. 131.

8. See again Donfried and Marshall, "Equality with God suggests sharing the same rank and thus possessing the same sovereign status. Thus the thought is of the supremacy possessed by God and also by this Being" (*Pauline Letters*, p. 132).

9. F. F. Bruce, *Philippians*, p. 46. Bruce goes on to cite Jesus' washing of the disciples' feet (John 13:3–5) as an excellent illustration of what is meant.

10. Martin and Hawthorne, *Philippians*, p. 127.

11. For a fuller development of this point see Martin and Hawthorne, *Philippians*, p. 120.

12. Kate Barclay Wilkinson, *Hymns of Faith and Life* (Marion, Ind.: Wesley Press), no. 423.

13. Martin and Hawthorne, *Philippians*, p. 127.

14.   The point is put in specifically theological terms by Markus Bockmuehl. Referring to Christ's exaltation he writes, "Theologically, however, his exaltation is important—not indeed in the sense of a reward, but rather as the moral counterbalance to the acceptance of suffering. Theodicy requires that innocent suffering should be vindicated: only thus can it be meaningful, and only so can God be seen to be just. From the Christian perspective, suffering is never an end in itself. It always stands in a necessary relationship to God's justice" (*Philippians*, pp. 140–141).

15.   Bockmuehl, *Philippians*, p. 148.

16.   Charles Wesley, *Hymns of Faith and Life* (Marion, Ind.: Wesley Press), no. 339.

4

EXHORTATION AND ENCOURAGEMENT

Philippians 2:12-30

It might easily have happened that the Philippians, swept off their feet by the eloquence and emotion of Paul's lofty account of the humiliation and exaltation of Christ, could have forgotten why Paul had written to them in the first place. But Paul will not allow his point to be submerged in a tidal wave of emotion—not even emotion about Christ. So he shackles what follows to what precedes by an emphatic causal conjunction: **therefore**. In effect, he is repeating verse 5: **Your attitude should be the same as that of Christ Jesus**. Verses 12–18 consist of a strong exhortation to that end.

However, exhortation by itself can lack life. So Paul shares that he intends to send two fellow believers who are examples of what he is urging the Philippians to be, adding that he hopes to come soon himself. More will be said of the linkage of verses 19–30 to what goes before when we come to interpret them.

1. A FURTHER EXHORTATION TO STEADFASTNESS 2:12-18

These verses pick up not merely the note of exhortation beginning at 1:27, but also the same themes. The calls for steadfastness and unity (1:22; 2:2), humility (2:3) and joy (2:2) are repeated in these verses (2:12, 14, 17–18) but with much greater urgency and—more importantly—with confidence. The reason for this confidence is plain: Paul believes that the mind of Christ of which he has just written in 2:5–11 can be reproduced in the Philippians.

This block of verses falls naturally by topic into three segments.

THE POWER BEHIND THE LIFE OF SALVATION

The affection Paul has for his readers is evident from the start: **my dear friends** (literally "my beloved ones"). But his affection is yoked to obedience. This is a direct link with the preceding description of the mind-set of Christ who **became obedient to death—even death on a cross!** (2:8). It is noticeable that the verb **obeyed** has no object. Paul simply says they **have always obeyed** (2:12). Commentators can be found speaking in favor of every conceivable option: They **have always obeyed** Christ or Paul or the gospel. It is doubtful whether Paul would be impressed by this kind of logic-chopping. Assuredly, obedience to Christ and still more obedience *like Christ's* was in his mind. But obedience to himself as Christ's apostle was the underpinning of his whole ministry. "A man's apostle (Heb. *shaliach*) is as himself," says rabbinic teaching,[1] and Paul certainly regarded himself as the commissioned emissary of Christ (1 Cor. 4:14–21; 2 Cor. 12:11–12; 13:10). But obedience to Paul was not obedience to Paul as the ultimate authority or embodiment of truth, but rather to Paul as the proclaimer of the gospel of Christ. It is in this sense that he combines appeal with implicit command here. Indeed, he commends them for following his directions **not only in my presence, but now much more in my absence** (2:12).

The heart of his command is that they **continue to work out** [their] **salvation with fear and trembling** (2:12). Some Christians are reluctant to use any language that seems to imply that sinners can contribute anything to their salvation other than the sin from which they are saved. The chief device they prefer to use to avoid any such suggestion is to interpret the word *salvation* in a sociological sense as referring to harmonious relations within the Philippian church rather than in a theological sense.[2] But Paul's typical use of the term will not support such a view.[3] There is clearly a sense in which the Philippians' salvation rests in their own hands, calling for their diligent and continuous effort. This is so real and serious that Paul says they must work at it **with fear and trembling**. His words from 1 Corinthians 10:12 are an apt commentary: "So, if you think you are standing firm, be careful that you don't fall!"

Immediately, however, Paul adds a further dimension to the command to **continue to work out** [their] **salvation**: namely, **for it is God who works in you** (2:13). The only reason they can work out their salvation is because God works in them. The depth at which God works within them is at the level of both will and action. The fortification of the will is achieved by the inward strengthening of the Holy Spirit (Eph. 3:16–17). Only in this way can we act in keeping with God's good purpose and pleasure.

It is important to hold together both our working and God's working in effecting our salvation. Moisés Silva writes, "It is impossible to tone down the force with which Paul here points to our conscious activity in sanctification. . . . For all that, our dependence on *divine activity* for sanctification is nowhere made as explicit as here."[4] He goes on to quote John Murray: "God's working in us is not suspended because we work, nor our working suspended because God works."[5] There is a working together, or synergism, of ourselves and God, but it is a synergism of grace, rooted in the grace of God from the start.

GREAT THEMES

A PRAYER FOR PERSISTENT RESOLVE

Grant us the will to fashion as we
 feel,
Grant us the strength to practise as
 we know,
Grant us the courage, ribb'd and
 edged with steel
To strike the blow.

Knowledge we ask not, knowledge
 Thou hast lent,
But, Lord, the will—there lies our
 deepest need.
Grant us the strength to build upon
 the deep intent
The deed, the deed.

—Alfred, Lord Tennyson

THE WITNESSING POWER OF HOLY LIVING

Paul now brings his basic teaching regarding the relation of the human and the divine in the work of salvation to focus on the particular problem in the church in Philippi. **Do everything without complaining or**

GREAT THEMES

HUMAN RESPONSIBILITY

It is God who saves—but there is a human responsibility to *take hold* of that salvation.

arguing (2:14). There have already been hints of this in the exhortations to being of one spirit (1:27) and one mind (2:2). An explicit reference to contention between two leading women in the church will appear later (4:2). The Greek words rendered "complaining" and "arguing" are the same as those used in the Greek Old Testament in the story of the murmuring of the Israelites in the wilderness wanderings, as is the language of the **crooked and depraved generation** (2:15; compare Deut. 32:5, 20).

Whether by the use of this language and its source Paul is suggesting that the church has displaced the biblical Israel is questionable. The main thrust of his argument is rather that holiness of life, as summed up in the mind of Christ, is more likely to commend Christ than congregational civil wars. As Markus Bockmuehl (with debts to Karl Barth) puts it, referring to "grumbling and bickering," "These things are not minor blemishes of morality, peripheral human weaknesses in an otherwise flawless Christian spectacle. Instead, they are part of what marks the great watershed of Christian life, the scene of the decisive Christian 'either-or' (K. Barth): either one belongs to Christ and henceforth adopts the mind of Christ, or one does not."[6]

Accordingly, Paul proceeds to spell out three characteristic marks of the holy life. The Philippians must be **blameless and pure . . . without fault** (2:15). The first denotes that which stands above reproach or accusation. The second denotes that which is unmixed and exists in an unpolluted state. The third, faultless, is frequently used in the Old Testament to describe sacrificial animals (see, for example, Num. 6:14). Only those unblemished were acceptable as offerings to God. These are the characteristic marks of the **children of God**, and Paul looks for them not in some idealistic future, but in the present. Only so will the believers stand in visible contrast with the **crooked and depraved generation** in which they live.

On the basis of the holiness of their lives, the Philippians will be able to fulfill their God-given mission. The quality of their character will make them stand out from their surroundings just as stars stand out against the blackness of the night sky. It makes little difference whether the next phrase is translated **hold fast** or **hold out the word of life** (as the NIV prefers). Either is possible. Given the image of shining as stars to give light in the darkness, the idea of "holding forth the life-giving word" is perhaps to be preferred.

But there is a further benefit that will accrue from the holiness of their lives—this, for Paul himself. It will show on the day of Christ that Paul's labors have not been fruitless. It is clear from his frequent references that Paul took the day of judgment, Christ's day—the day when Christ's lordship would be made plain—with great seriousness. Paul knew how important it was to remember that the holiness of one's life will bear scrutiny on that day (1 Thess. 3:12–13; 5:23) and equally that the worth of one's labors will be beyond dispute (1 Cor. 3:12–15; 2 Cor. 5:10). Paul's ministry to the Philippians has been like a hard-run race or strenuous toil. He is anxious that its results will give him cause for rejoicing at the final test.

THE JOY OF SACRIFICIAL SERVICE

Paul's thought now takes a step beyond the service of the Philippians to his own ministry. He likens himself to the libation or drink offering of wine (or possibly oil) frequently poured out in both Jewish and pagan sacrifice as the act that completed the sacrifice. Their sacrifice is the offering that flows from their faith. In verse 16 he has spoken of the Philippians as the occasion of his boasting on the day of Christ. Now there is a somewhat different aspect. He sees them as the central offering and his own service as simply the drink offering poured out on it to complete it.

Exactly what Paul has in mind in speaking of himself as being "poured out" is difficult to say. It may refer to his apostolic labors among them. However, the sentence begins with a strong contrasting conditional phrase: **But even if**. His thought seems to move back and forth between the possibility of his survival and the possibility of his execution (for the former see 1:25–26; 2:24; for the latter see 1:20). This reference (2:17) may belong to the latter category.[7] Paul is not dismayed or depressed by the possibility of dying. Rather he regards it as cause for rejoicing, for it will be the seal on both their service and his own. Both are offerings to God. Charles Wesley's lines express his thought perfectly:

> Ready for all Thy perfect will,
> My acts of faith and love repeat,
> Till death Thine endless mercies seal,
> And make the sacrifice complete.[8]

Hence Paul proceeds to express his joy over them and with them, and expects the same response from them (2:18). **Joy** is a recurrent note in this letter (1:25–26; 3:1; 4:1, 4, 10) and in particular, joy amid persecution. It is not that Paul was a masochist who found pleasure in pain. It was rather that, because his confidence was rooted in the suffering and exaltation of Christ (2:8–11; 3:10–11), he knew that the final victory of faith—his own and that of the Philippians—was assured.

2. LIVING WITNESSES OF THE CHRISTLIKE MIND 2:19–30

If 2:12–18 constitute an exhortation to the Philippians to live in the self-denying way that Christ has been shown to have done in 2:5–11, the remainder of chapter 2 follows the same general theme. It does so, however, from a slightly different angle. Instead of the note of exhortation, we find the note of encouragement. It comes in the particular form of two visitors whom Paul announces he will be sending to the Philippians: Timothy and Epaphroditus. If it be asked how they could be a source of encouragement to the Philippians, it may be suggested that they were living embodiments of people with a Christlike mind.

It is sometimes thought that these verses have very little of substance in them and are no more than personal chatter about Paul's future plans and movements.[9] This, however, overlooks the ways in which 2:19–30 echoes themes and ideas that occur in 2:5–11. Still more, it overlooks expressions that occur in these verses and earlier parts of the letter that are easy to underestimate. Many English translations do not help by rendering them in more than one way. Translated literally they read, "the things about you" (2:19–20), rendered in the NIV as **news about you**

(2:19) and **interest in your welfare** (2:20). Again, a kindred expression reads, literally, "the things of himself" (2:21), which the NIV renders **his own interests**. These are contrasted in the same verse with the things **of Jesus Christ**, so that the whole verse reads in the NIV: **For everyone looks out for his own interests, not those of Jesus Christ**. Paul also makes a personal reference to "the things about me," rendered in the NIV as **how things go with me** (2:23).

These expressions look bland enough until it is noticed that similar expressions are used earlier in the letter to refer to Paul's chief concerns about the Philippians. So, lurking behind the somewhat faceless words **whether I come and see you or only hear about you** (literally "the things concerning you," 1:27) is the central issue of the unity of the Philippian church. The same theme is evident in 2:4: **Each of you should look not only to your own interests but also to the interests of others** (literally "the things of others"). Once more, the personal reference to his own situation in 1:12—"Now I want you to know, brothers, that what has happened to me [literally 'the things regarding me'] has really served to advance the gospel"—points to another primary theme: Paul's personal situation and its effects on the Philippian church.

What this amounts to is that expressions we could slide over without noticing refer in fact to central concerns of the letter.[10] This means in turn that 2:19–30 does not consist primarily of social news, even though these verses convey news. Their specific intent is to indicate to the Philippians the steps Paul is taking to address the needs of their church.

It should be kept in mind, however, that there are many things lying behind Paul's language that we do not know, and about which we can only make educated guesses. Why is Timothy unique in taking a genuine interest in their welfare (2:20)? Are we to take literally the statement that **everyone looks out for his own interests, not those of Jesus Christ** (2:21)? And why does Epaphroditus have to be commended (2:29–30) to those who sent him as their messenger to Paul (2:25)?

Despite such uncertainties, our attention should be focused on what the passage tells us about the message Paul is conveying to the Philippians.

TIMOTHY

The general gist of the paragraph is clear. Paul begins by expressing his intention to send Timothy to Philippi soon (2:19, 23). In verses 20–22 he spells out his reasons for sending Timothy rather than anyone else. Finally, in verse 24, he expresses his confidence that he will visit them in person soon. We may now examine the details that fill out this outline.

Paul's hope to send Timothy is described as a hope **in the Lord** (2:19). As such it is not simply superficial optimism as in casual expressions such as "I hope it won't rain tomorrow." It is a confidence anchored in the person of Christ and the sphere of His power (1:14; 2:1; 3:9, 14; 4:1, 4, 7). Paul regarded all the details of his life as being in the overruling hand of God. Hence even his imprisonment could turn out to be an advantage for the gospel (1:12). The immediate benefit of Timothy's visit would not be for them (though that would be part of it, 1:20). The immediate benefit would be Timothy's report to Paul of "the things about them." This clearly refers to their Christian witness and unity of spirit (1:27), and equally clearly indicates that Paul expected good news by which he would be **cheered** (2:19).

He turns next to the reasons he is sending Timothy. First, Timothy shares Paul's mind-set, particularly with regard to "the things concerning you," that is, their progress and stability in the Christian life. In this respect he stands in contrast with **everyone** who looks out for their own interests, **not those of Jesus Christ**. Who **everyone** is has been widely debated, with no consensus emerging. It may be that he has primarily in mind those who **preach Christ out of envy and rivalry** (1:15), but there were others besides these as the verse indicates.

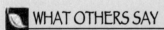
WHAT OTHERS SAY

COMMITMENT TO CHRIST AND THE GOSPEL

Paul's description of Timothy . . . lies at the heart of what Paul understands Christian life to be all about.

—Gordon D. Fee

Perhaps Paul's thought was running ahead of his words, and he was thinking of the Philippians' knowledge of Timothy's steadfast fidelity to Paul and the gospel (2:22). Paul's central concern was that Timothy would put first "the things of Christ Jesus," that is, the gospel. They know that, like his Lord who took **the very nature of a servant** (2:7), Timothy had done the same for Paul in the cause of the gospel. The overriding qualification possessed by Timothy, then, was his whole-souled commitment to the gospel.

Paul now adds a qualification or elaboration to his statement of intention to send Timothy to Philippi. He will do so **as soon as I see how things go with me** (2:23). This is a roundabout way of saying he needed Timothy's support so long as he remained in prison. While he had no doubt that he would be released (2:24), he depended on Timothy's caring for his material needs until that happened. As soon as he was freed, he would visit Philippi in person (2:24). Timothy would, thus, serve the Philippians as he had served Paul and Christ, from whose pattern of service he had learned what service meant.

If the foregoing is a sound reading of 2:19–24, it explains some otherwise puzzling features of 2:19–30. Chief among these is why the promised visits of Timothy, and indeed Paul himself, are spoken of before the announcement of the return of Epaphroditus, which would take place before either of the promised visits (2:25). First, although Epaphroditus would be returning to Philippi, he would not be returning to Paul, hence would be no source of information to Paul about the state of the Philippian church. Second, Timothy, who had served his apprenticeship under Paul (2:22) and whose heart and mind were aligned with Paul's, would not only be returning to Paul, but would be able to report with insight on the things in the Philippian church that mattered most to Paul. In the telling expression of Gordon Fee, "Paul's logic is that of concern, not chronology."[11] And the driving force of his concern is Christ and the gospel. Whatever or whoever will bring him news of the Philippians' steadfastness in the faith and will be able to reinforce that steadfastness stands first in "the things of

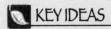

KEY IDEAS

IS THE GOSPEL ALIVE AND WELL?

Paul's chief concern, and the *ultimate* reason for this letter, is the progress of the gospel in Philippi.

Paul"—his concerns and interests. What Paul means by **news about you** (2:19) and the interests **of Jesus Christ** (2:21) is nothing other than **the work of the gospel** (2:22).

EPAPHRODITUS

Just as the paragraph about Timothy has prompted questions like those just considered, so has the paragraph about Epaphroditus. Why was he being sent back to Philippi when Paul needed someone to stay with him, and why did Paul decide to keep Timothy, though he regarded him as being better fitted to be of help to the Philippians? Why does Paul spend so much time commending him to the Philippians who knew him perfectly well, since he was one of them and was chosen by them to be their messenger to Paul? Such questions have given rise to much reading between the lines. What this reading amounts to is that Epaphroditus had let the home team down by failing in the timely performance of his mission. He had become more of a burden to Paul than a help (2:28). Paul, therefore, offloads him but tries to smooth his return to Philippi by urging his fellow Philippians to welcome rather than reproach him (2:29).

It is possible to read between the lines in this way, but it is better to read the lines themselves. Doing this, a very different picture emerges. The paragraph falls into two parts. Verses 25–27 are written from the perspective of Epaphroditus, and verses 28–30 are written from the perspective of the Philippians.

Verse 25 indicates that Paul had decided that Epaphroditus should return to Philippi. Epaphroditus had not developed cold feet. Indeed, Paul refers to Epaphroditus by three terms that express the closeness of their relationship. First he says Epaphroditus is **my brother**. The two remaining terms are compound forms Paul often used of those who worked with him closely. In Greek they are prefixed with the preposition *with*, aptly rendered by the NIV as **fellow** worker and **fellow** soldier. But the words themselves, **worker** and **soldier,** indicate that Epaphroditus had in no way become a drag on Paul's ministry. Significantly, Paul goes on to underline Epaphroditus's links with the Philippians. He is **their** messenger (apostle)[12] whom they sent to care for him (literally their liturgist, as though Epaphroditus's caring for Paul's needs was a form of priestly ministry). By linking the Philippians with Epaphroditus in this way, he is uniting them with his praise of their messenger. The appropriateness of this is shown in the immediately following words: **For he**

longs for all of you (2:26). It is unlikely that this means no more than (as some interpreters have suggested) that Epaphroditus was suffering from homesickness. Paul uses the selfsame language to describe his own feelings for the Philippians in 1:8. It more probably speaks of the depth of Christian love that characterized the Philippian believers.

Epaphroditus was distressed because his fellow Philippians had heard the news that he had been seriously ill. Paul informs them that Epaphroditus had almost died. Paul gives no indication of the nature or timing of the illness; presumably the Philippians knew both.[13] Paul does state affirmatively that Epaphroditus recovered because **God had mercy on him** (2:27). Paul saw the hand of God working through medical remedies as we rightly do today, but he and we should also recognize God's direct intervention before or when medical science has reached its limits. Whatever the means, the outcome was merciful for both Epaphroditus and Paul **to spare me sorrow upon sorrow** (2:27). We have noted already, and will do so again, how often **joy** is mentioned in Philippians. We do not know exactly what Paul had in mind when he wrote of the **sorrow** to which greater sorrow would have been added had Epaphroditus died, but he also saw mercy for himself in the sparing of Epaphroditus's life.

Paul turns to the return of Epaphroditus as seen from the Philippians' perspective. They also had been anxious about him. Paul is concerned that they should be reassured in the most convincing way possible—by seeing Epaphroditus himself. Their reassurance about Epaphroditus would

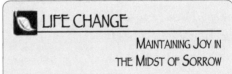

LIFE CHANGE

MAINTAINING JOY IN
THE MIDST OF SORROW

Missionary fervor did not harden Paul's heart to the human emotions of pain, loneliness and loss. Gordon Fee writes: "Joy does not mean the absence of sorrow but the capacity to rejoice in the midst of it."

diminish Paul's anxiety about them. Clearly, Epaphroditus was highly esteemed by the Philippians, which is presumably why they had chosen him to be the bearer of their gift to Paul. Paul adds his own commendation of Epaphroditus in striking terms. First comes the description of the reception they are to give to Epaphroditus, expressed in Paul's characteristic, piled-up phrases. They are to welcome him **in the Lord with great joy** (2:29). Still more powerful is the reason why they should do so. Epaphroditus **almost died for the work of Christ** (2:30), words that recall the primary mission of Paul as well as Timothy—**the work of the gospel** (2:22). But they also recall the work of Christ himself who **became obedient to death** (2:8). Epaphroditus risked[14] his own life to fulfill the priestly service (Greek *liturgy* as in verse 25) the Philippians themselves were unable to render.

LIFE CHANGE

THE LITURGY OF CHRISTIAN SERVICE

The idea of sacrificial service runs like a chain through Philippians 2. The self-giving of Christ (verse 8) gives rise to the self-giving of Paul (verse 17), which leads in turn to the self-giving of Epaphroditus (verses 25, 30) on Paul's behalf.

What are we to say of these verses that are often dismissed as conveying mere human-interest details? We have noted that language, which on the surface may appear to refer to things mundane, engages in reality with the central concerns of the epistle. The devoting of a paragraph to Epaphroditus is not intended simply to bring the Philippians up to date on the state of their messenger's health, even though it does that. It is written to show the Philippians that one of their own exhibits "the mind that was in Christ," exerting himself in the **work of Christ** (2:30) almost to the point of death. As Martin and Hawthorne put it, "Paul's high commendation of Epaphroditus does not come simply because of what he did, great as this may have been. It comes also because of why he did it. His was a self-renouncing motivation. He chose against himself for someone else: 'He came close to losing his life.'"[15]

In revealing the level at which Paul's mind was moving, these verses also display the heart of Paul. It is easy to get the impression that Paul was simply an evangelistic machine, moving relentlessly across the ancient world, bulldozing his way through all obstacles with about as much feeling as an earth mover. These verses contradict that caricature. They are infused with deep human emotion: his sense of comradeship with Epaphroditus (2:25); his agitation about the anxiety the Philippians would be feeling, wondering how he had fared (2:28); his regard for the readiness of Epaphroditus to place his life on the line (2:29–30); and above all, his fearfulness that he might lose Epaphroditus to the devouring angel of death

(2:27). This last example is perhaps the most striking, since Paul has indicated earlier that he does not fear death (1:21–23). But if Paul knew the meaning of joy in sorrow, he also knew the meaning of grief in loss.

Reading these verses, one cannot help but ask the question: Why did they do it—Paul, Timothy, and Epaphroditus? The odds against them were astronomical. The idea that they might win the world by spreading a message about a man who had been crucified and raised from the dead—a combination of the repugnant with the absurd—was so transparently ridiculous that one is bound to ask what drove them on. It is verses such as these that disclose the secret. Their entire beings had been captivated, set aflame by the things of Christ (2:21), **the work of the gospel** (2:22), and **the work of Christ** (2:30). Nothing could quench their conviction and commitment.

ENDNOTES

Great Themes Sidebar: Markus Bockmuehl, *The Epistle to the Philippians*, Black's New Testament Commentary (London: Hendrickson, 1998), p. 152.

Key Ideas Sidebar: Gordon D. Fee, *Paul's Letter to the Philippians*, The New International Commentary on the New Testament (Grand Rapids, Mich.: William B. Eerdmans, 1995), p, 270.

Life Change Sidebar: Fee, *Philippians*, p, 280.

1. Babylonian Talmud, tractate *Berakot* 34b.

2. See, for example, Frank Thielman in *Philippians* The New Application Commentary (Grand Rapids, Mich.: Zondervan, 1995), pp. 137–138, who makes a sharp distinction between justification, which once received can never be lost, and salvation, which is progressive. A similar position is espoused by Ralph P. Martin and Gerald F. Hawthorne, *Philippians*, Word Biblical Commentary (Nashville, Tenn.: Nelson Reference, 2004), p. 140.

3. Moisés Silva writes, "Out of nearly twenty occurrences of this noun in the Pauline corpus, not one instance requires the translation 'well-being;' the vast majority require—and all of them admit—the theological sense." *Philippians*, Baker Exegetical Commentary on the New Testament (Grand Rapids, Mich.: Baker Book House, 1992), p. 136.

4. Silva, *Philippians* (1992), p. 139.

5. Quoted in Silva, *Philippians* (1992), p. 140.

6. Bockmuehl, *Philippians*, p. 156.

7. It is noteworthy that in the only other example of the term "poured out" in the Pauline writings, the reference is clearly to his death (2 Tim. 4:6).

8. Charles Wesley, Hymn 327, http://wesley.nnu.edu/charles_wesley/hymns/300-399.htm.

9. It has been suggested that material like 2:19–30 usually stands at the close of Paul's letters, and that its appearance at this point indicates it is really part of a separate letter that was bundled in here by an editor who did not know what he was doing. But there is little to be said for this suggestion. For a critical account of it see Bockmuehl, *Philippians*, pp. 163–164 and P. T. O'Brien, *A Commentary on the Greek Text* The New International Greek Testament Commentary (Grand Rapids, Mich.: William B. Eerdmans, 1991), pp. 313–15.

10. So much is this the case that one commentator, Gordon D. Fee, structures his entire, lengthy commentary around these expressions, which he renders by the term "affairs." His analysis of the letter (in part) is as follows: Paul's "Affairs"—Reflections on Imprisonment (1:12–26); The Philippians' "Affairs"—Exhortation to Steadfastness and Unity (1:17–2:18); What's Next—Regarding Paul's and Their "Affairs" (2:19–30); Their "Affairs"—Again (3:1–4:3). See *Paul's Letter to the Philippians*, The New International Commentary on the New Testament (Grand Rapids, Mich.: William B. Eerdmans, 1995), pp. vii–viii.

11. Fee, *Philippians*, p. 272.

12. The use of the term *apostle* in reference to Epaphroditus shows that it had not yet acquired the exclusive sense of those appointed to witness to the resurrected Jesus (Acts 1:21–22; 1 Cor. 9:1; 15:3–11).

13. A probable reconstruction of the order of events is that of Gordon Fee, who assumes that since Epaphroditus was carrying a large sum of money, he would not have traveled alone. When he became ill on the way to Rome, one of his traveling companions returned to Philippi with that news "(which is how Epaphroditus knew they knew), while another (or others) stayed with him as he continued on his way to Rome, even though doing so put his life at great risk (v. 30). This view is favored by the way Paul phrases v. 30 . . . that he had 'risked his life in order that he might fulfill his mission to Paul on behalf of Philippi.'" (Fee, *Philippians*, p. 278.)

14. "Risked" is probably derived from a gambling term meaning "staked." Epaphroditus put his life at stake in order to minister to Paul. See Martin and Hawthorne, *Philippians*, p. 167.

15. Martin and Hawthorne, *Philippians*, p. 167.

5

THE PURSUIT OF PERFECTION

Philippians 3:1–4:1

1. TRUE CONFIDENCE VERSUS FALSE CONFIDENCE 3:1–6

At first sight, verse 1 is somewhat bewildering. Its first word, **finally**, suggests that the letter is about to end, yet it continues for two more chapters. The statement that it is no trouble for Paul **to write the same things to you again** (3:1) leaves one wondering what these **same things** are. Is he referring to things he has already written about in a previous letter that no longer survives? Or is he referring to what he is about to write in chapter 3, which he regards as a rerun of chapters 1 and 2? And how does it all connect with the explosive words with which chapter 3 verse 2 begins: **Watch out for those dogs**?

Endless suggestions have been made, some more convincing than others. But enough is reasonably clear to enable us to see the framework within which the pieces of the jigsaw puzzle should be set. First of all, **finally** need not be as final as it sounds in English. It may be no more than a transitional formula, meaning "well, then" (see 1 Thess. 4:1; 2 Thess. 3:1). Second, while Paul makes reference to teaching he has given the Philippians on other occasions (3:18), topics arise in chapter 3 that he has already dealt with in chapters 1 and 2. Among these are "gaining Christ" (3:8; compare 1:21), sharing Christ's sufferings (3:10–11; compare 1:29–30, 2:17), standing fast in the Lord (4:1; compare 1:27). So there is a measurable degree of repetition in 3:1–4:1. However, there can be no doubt that the tone is different. It is written as **a safeguard for you** (3:1). This seems to mean that the Philippians needed more than instruction in the truth; they needed defense against attack. The mood of chapter 3 is passionate—negatively toward their attackers and positively in terms of Paul's declaration of his own views.

WELL-FOUNDED CONFIDENCE

Paul begins by urging his readers to **rejoice in the Lord** (3:1). He has already used phrases of similar intensity to describe the spirit that he longs to find in them (1:26; 2:29) and that animates him (2:2, 17–18). The latter verses make clear that the source and spring of his joy is confidence in the ultimate triumph of Christ's purposes despite opposition and tribulation (1:16–17). In this Paul shows he has read (and believed) his Bible (Ps. 32:11; 33:1; 43:4).

With this confident exhortation he now turns to his opponents: **those dogs, those men who do evil, those mutilators of the flesh** (3:2). His language is strong and revealing. **Dogs** was a term of contempt used by Jews to refer to Gentiles. The bland translation of the next phrase, **men who do evil**, hardly brings out the thrust of the original, where the accent falls on *works*: "evil **workers**" or "**workers** of evil." The final expression **those mutilators of the flesh** is a clear play on the circumcision, which might be rendered in English as "cuttingcision."

If one puts these three items together—branding uncircumcised Gentiles as dogs, laying stress on the indispensability of works, and naming circumcision as the chief of these—then a picture begins to come together. Either Jews who had become Christians or Gentiles who had done the same were insisting on the observance of Jewish rites by Gentiles as being necessary for Christian salvation.

This is a crucial clue for the understanding of the whole of chapter 3. What was being claimed by the Judaizing Christians was that without the observance of Jewish rites such as circumcision—and probably also the Jewish purity laws regarding food—salvation was imperfect and incomplete. In truth, their claims seem to have gone beyond this, as our study of the chapter will show. They seem to have had a self-confidence that left little room for humility; a belief that they had already received the full benefits of the Resurrection, making them already perfect; and consequently, little—if any—place for the saving power of the Cross.[1]

Paul would have none of it. Roundly rejecting their position, he claims, **it is we who are the circumcision** (3:3)—a striking assertion since many if not most of the Philippian believers had never undergone that rite. The basis on which he rests his claim is a redefinition of the meaning of circumcision. At its heart it rests on three things: first, **worship by the Spirit of God** (3:3); that is to say, their service of God is rooted in the Spirit of God at work within them, not in effort born of human energy. The second sign that they are the true circumcision is that they **glory in Christ Jesus** (3:3): the Jesus who humbled himself and became obedient even to death on the cross. The third mark that they are the true circumcision is that they **put no confidence in the flesh** (3:3). There is a play on words here. **Flesh** evidently refers to the physical rite of circumcision. But beyond that it refers to what that rite had come to signify to the Judaizers: a ground for confidence before God, although it was a strictly human action.

Paul was saying nothing new in speaking of circumcision in this way. He was simply drawing on the teaching of the Old Testament in which circumcision is presented, not as an end in itself, but as a sign of belonging to God's covenant people (Gen. 17:9–14). Moreover, it was not the sign in itself that was important, but that which it signified: belonging to God from the heart. Hence "the circumcision of the heart" (Deut. 10:16) was always the meaning of the old covenant and was revived in the promise of the new (Deut. 30:6; compare Jer. 31:31–34; Ezek. 36:25–28). Paul himself had

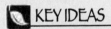

KEY IDEAS

THE HEART OF THE GOSPEL MESSAGE

The brief verses of 3:2–3 . . . bring us to the heart of Paul's religion. As he saw it, God has brought into being a new relationship through Jesus Christ, based not on our bid to please him but on what we have received, and issuing in how we are to live in grateful response.

drawn the inevitable inference from this that where the meaning of the sign was present, the absence of the sign was of no consequence (Rom. 2:25–29; 4:11).

MISPLACED CONFIDENCE

Paul now turns to the other side of the coin by referring to an example of false confidence—himself as he used to be. If anyone had reason to be sure of himself before God, it was Paul. This is demonstrated by a long list of distinctions that, in the eyes of the Judaizers, would secure Paul's place in the divine roll of honor beyond question. He had been **circumcised on the eighth day** (3:5); that is, he was a **born** Jew, not a proselyte. He was **of the people of Israel** (3:5), one who belonged to God's ancient people by descent, not by incorporation. Further, he was **of the tribe of Benjamin** (3:5). Proselytes could belong to the people of Israel, but they had no tribal roots. Paul had roots—and in the tribe that gave Israel her first king and in whose territory Jerusalem was sited. He was **a Hebrew of Hebrews**. Jews living outside Palestine preferred to be known as Hebrews rather than Jews and preferred speaking Aramaic among themselves, even if Greek was their first language (as appears to have been the case with Paul).

This characteristic of living as a Hebrew serves as a bridge-term between the first three (which were Paul's by inheritance and, therefore, inevitably) and the remaining three that were his by choice. Of his own deliberate choice, he belonged to the party known as the Pharisees, which probably means the separated ones. As Paul indicates, this was a matter that had to do with the observance of the law. As he puts it elsewhere, "according to the strictest sect of our religion, I lived as a Pharisee" (Acts 26:5). **Zeal** (3:6) was a further chosen mark of Paul's religious observance. As he said to the Jerusalem mob, which was calling for his blood, "I was thoroughly trained in the law of our fathers and was just as zealous for God as any of you are today" (Acts 22:3). The particular form of his zeal he mentions here is **persecuting the church** (3:6; compare Gal. 1:13–14). Anything that posed a threat to the law, as the sect of the followers of Jesus did, was to be harried out of existence (Acts 26:9–11). His final claim to fame in many respects encapsulates all the others: **as for legalistic righteousness, faultless** (3:6). The NIV translation is not the best rendering of the original, which reads literally "as to the righteousness which is in (or by) the law, faultless." Paul is not writing off the Old Testament in general and the law in particular as legalistic.

Elsewhere, he describes the law as holy, righteous, good, and spiritual (Rom. 7:12, 14). What he is referring to here is the visible observance of the prescriptions of the law. The law prescribed certain things to be done and others not to be done. In these regards, Paul was faultless, and he is not alone in being described in this way in the New Testament (see Luke 1:6). However, it is obvious from the tone of the argument that Paul no longer regarded this kind of righteousness as sufficient. For one thing, it was something done in human strength and, therefore, produced **confidence in the flesh** (3:4). For another, regarding the observance of the law as an end in itself blinded him to the true character of the church as the fulfillment of God's purpose, leading him to attempt to destroy it (3:6).

Here then, is one form of "complete" or "perfect" righteousness that Paul knew and rejected: the perfect or faultless observance of the law that Jewish Christians were enjoining on the Philippians. Paul had tried that way and found it to be self-defeating.

2. KNOWING CHRIST: RIGHTEOUSNESS BY FAITH AND RESURRECTION HOPE 3:7–11

In contrast to seeking confidence before God based on self-effort, Paul found another way. **But whatever was to my profit I now consider loss for the sake of Christ** (3:7). He had reversed the columns of the balance sheet. This great reversal had taken place "on account of Christ." In the light of the Christ described in 2:5–11, he had radically revised his view of the values of the religious life, beginning with his own. A more literal rendering of verse 7 would read, "What things were gains to me I have come to consider loss because of Christ." This verse provides the terms on which Paul rings the changes from verse 8 to verse 11, a single sentence in Greek. He now proceeds to show how this reversal of values had taken place.

First, he has come to consider everything a loss in comparison with the gain of knowledge of Christ (3:8). Paul writes in no measured terms. He considers **everything** a loss in this revision of values. He does so because of **the surpassing greatness of knowing Christ Jesus my Lord** (3:8). The knowledge of Christ of which he speaks is not merely factual information. It is knowledge in the sense of personal relationship. This is the only place in all his writings where Paul uses the personal pronoun to refer to Jesus: "Christ Jesus **my** Lord." It is for this intimate, interior knowledge that he has not only **lost all things**, but has lost them willingly and gladly, considering them **rubbish, that I may gain Christ** (3:8). This is a strong statement, given that he has just spoken of such a prized possession as his heritage as a Hebrew.

The reason Paul is able to speak of his Hebrew heritage in this way is given in his second step in describing the dramatic reversal of his values. This is that having a righteousness of his own is a loss in comparison with having a righteousness through faith in Christ (3:9). By **righteousness** Paul means both being in a right relationship with God and living a righteous life. His experience had showed him that there were two possible ways in which to achieve this. One was by his own efforts in keeping the law: **a righteousness of my own that comes from the law** (3:9). In this case, his righteousness rested on confidence in himself and his own powers of performance. The other was **through faith in Christ—the righteousness that comes from God and is by faith** (3:9). In this case, his righteousness rested on confidence in Christ, in whom righteousness came as a gift from God and was accepted by faith.[2]

Paul had no hesitation in deciding between these two alternatives. As noted, his language in rejecting **a righteousness of my own that comes by law** is robust. And it is important to keep in mind that Paul was not disowning his heritage or betraying his race. Rather he is rejecting his false confidence in himself as being able to use them in his own strength as the pathway to righteousness. If righteousness were to be attained at all, it would be in the power of the Spirit, not the energy of the flesh. His goal, therefore, is **to gain Christ and be found in him** when he stands before God at the last.[3]

Yet there remains a third step for Paul in describing the reversal of his evaluation of the old era of the law. He picks up his earlier passing reference to **knowing Christ Jesus** (3:8), filling out its content. In the earlier verses, he interprets **knowing Christ** in terms of having righteousness through faith in Christ rather than a righteousness of his own that comes from the law. But there is more to being right with God. Knowing Christ,

LIFE CHANGE

THE REVISION OF PAUL'S RELIGIOUS VALUES

The Old Way of Measurement	Circumcision of the flesh (verse 4)
	National and racial pedigree (verse 5)
	Observance of the letter of the law (verses 5, 9)
	Confidence in his own powers of performance (verse 4)
The New Way of Measurement	Rejection of righteousness based on personal effort (verse 9)
	Confidence in Christ alone (verse 9)
	Worship by the Spirit (verse 3)
	No confidence in human achievement (verse3)

by definition, has to be more than simply a status. It is a relationship of mutuality in which what the Christ of the incarnation was (2:5–11) is shared in and experienced by the believer. To Paul this means two things in the present, leading to a third in the future.

To begin with, it means knowing **the power of** [Christ's] **resurrection and the fellowship of sharing in his sufferings** (3:10). These two items are really one (they are governed by a single definite article in the original). Paul is apparently not thinking of the *act* of identification with Christ's death and resurrection *in* baptism (Rom. 6:1–4). He is thinking of the *life* of identification with Christ's resurrection and suffering *following* baptism. This is probably why he places resurrection first (see Eph. 1:19–20). It is only by experiencing the power of Christ's resurrection that he is able to endure the fellowship of His sufferings. In this regard, the Philippians are now following in Paul's footsteps (1:29–30).

What does **becoming like him in his death** add—if anything—to **sharing in his sufferings**? Literally, the phrase **becoming like him** can be translated "taking with him the form" (of his death). It clearly belongs to the theme of assuming the mind of Christ (2:5–11). Specifically, the term *form*, which is found in Philippians alone in Paul's writings (and indeed in the entire Greek Bible), occurs in 2:7, where Jesus is said to have taken "the **form** of a servant." The rarity of the term would have made it stand out to his readers. What Paul appears to be saying then is that he is becoming more and more conformed to the humiliation that Christ accepted in death: accepting "the form of a servant" (2:7).

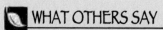

WHAT OTHERS SAY

FROM PRIDE TO HUMILITY

The apostle may be deliberately raising the issue of the "form" of Christ's death to indicate that his own former motivation of pride has given way to one of Christlike humility.

—Markus Bockmuehl

The direction of his thought now shifts from the present to the future—from experiencing the power of Christ's resurrection now to knowing it in its fullness at **the resurrection from the dead** (3:11) in the future. One striking feature about this is that he seems to speak of it with less than complete confidence: **somehow, to attain to the resurrection** (3:11). But we have already encountered this note of reserve in 2:12–13 about the need for them to "work out their salvation." The same note of reserve is found here because attaining to the resurrection from the dead presupposes sharing in Christ's sufferings (2:10). He is anxious that the Philippians and he will not flinch (1 Cor. 9:27).

Perhaps the most surprising feature, however, is the mention of the final resurrection at all. How did it get into the argument? It is possible that it may have arisen because another version of "complete salvation" was in the air at Philippi: that spiritual resurrection was the only kind of resurrection there was; bodily resurrection was not to be expected. This was present in parts of the New Testament church (2 Tim. 2:17–18), though usually where Greek thinking was influential and not where Jewish thought was prevalent, as was the case in Philippi. Paul's main point was to show that since the power of Christ's resurrection was already at work in believers, this guaranteed that it would come to complete fulfillment in the resurrection from the dead at Christ's return.

When one looks back over the message of 3:1–11 as a whole, it is difficult not to be sobered by it. Its emphases on abandoning confidence in one's own pedigree and power; of counting all one's accomplishments and achievements as valueless in comparison with knowing Christ; and of seeking to become a partner of Christ's in His sufferings, death, and resurrection are in contrast to what the world (and sometimes the church) expects or wants to hear. As Frank Thielman has put it, "Preaching Christ and him crucified . . . is a marketing strategist's nightmare."[4] But as Thielman has also said, "To become distracted from the church's primary task of Spirit-empowered obedience to God and to allow the world or a particular program to set the

LIFE CHANGE
KNOWING CHRIST

O Lord Jesus Christ, the Light of the minds that know you, the Joy of the hearts that love you, the Strength of the wills that serve you; help us so to know you that we may truly love you, and so to love you that we may truly serve you; for your name's sake, Amen.

—Adapted from a prayer of St. Augustine

church's agenda instead is to cease placing confidence in Christ and to begin placing confidence in the flesh."[5] The only effective antidote to the disease is knowing Christ in the intimacy of surrender, identification, and trust.

3. THE PATH TO PERFECTION 3:12–16

THE PERFECTION OF THE FUTURE

Having defined his goal as **to attain to the resurrection from the dead** (3:11), Paul goes on at once to repudiate any suggestion that he has already done so. He has not **already obtained all this** (3:12). **All this** refers to the full knowledge of Christ, the full power of His resurrection, the full **sharing of his sufferings**, and conformity to His death. In a word, Paul has not already been perfected, as he will be when he is raised from the dead. Such perfection belongs to the glorified body fashioned after the likeness of Christ's body at His resurrection (3:21). In that regard, Paul's attitude is to press toward it unrelentingly. It was for this that Christ laid hold of him, and he will not rest till he lays hold of it.

Paul repeats himself in the same terms so that his point is not missed. **I do not consider myself yet to have taken hold of it** (3:13). He has not yet arrived, unlike the Judaizing propagandists who claimed to have done so through the observance of the law. Paul is saying that, by implication, such a claim has the effect of making the final resurrection unnecessary. As for himself, he has but one policy—**one thing I do**. This one thing comprises several things that are aspects of the one. In depicting it, he borrows the imagery of the runner. First, he puts out of mind what lies behind, just as a runner does not spend his time contemplating the ground he has already covered. Since Paul has been speaking of what he has yet to achieve (3:12), presumably what he forgets (3:13) is what he has already accomplished in his service as an apostle. Conversely, by **what is ahead** he means the missionary ministry that lies before him, toward which he stretches. In this way he presses on **toward the goal to win the prize** (3:14). The imagery is still athletic. At Greek games, the winner was called up to receive the prize. For Paul the Christian, the upward call is from God, and the reward—as the whole passage suggests—is the full knowledge of Christ himself (3:14).

The throbbing vitality of the language with which Paul indicates his single-minded pursuit of knowing Christ conveys his own determination to remain in the race to the end. Equally, it conveys his concern that the Philippians should not be lured into a false sense of spiritual completeness on the basis of observance of ritual requirements of the Jewish law, which could only lead to spiritual stagnation. There can be no doubt that this is the overriding purpose and message of this passage.

THE PERFECTION OF THE INTERIM

Startlingly, no sooner has Paul disclaimed perfection than he immediately lays claim to it for himself and, by implication, for others. **All of us who are mature should take such a view of things** (3:15). **Mature** is derived from the verb translated **been made perfect** in verse 12, and many translations render it that way. The translation "mature" is not impossible, provided one takes into account what Paul means by maturity. It does not denote simply having been in process for a long time. It has a moral and ethical dimension, as is evident from his use of it in 1 Corinthians 2:6 and his elaboration of its opposite in 1 Corinthians 3:1–3, where he describes "infants in Christ" as those who are riven by jealousy and quarrelling. In the Old Testament the Hebrew equivalent of *perfect* is frequently used to denote those whose hearts are wholly devoted to God (Gen. 6:9; Deut. 18:13; 2 Kings 20:3). The same language is used in the Dead Sea Scrolls where members of the sect are described as *the perfect in way*.[6] In the words of M. D. Hooker, "In the present context 'perfect' (*teleios*) probably has a more specific meaning than is conveyed by the English word 'mature' . . . Paul has exchanged a life that was without fault according to the law (v. 6) for the purity and blamelessness that belong to Christ and to those who live in him."[7]

So there is a perfection of the interim to which Paul lays claim and finds in others, and he is concerned not to discredit it. It is the perfection of being "blameless and pure, children of God without fault in a crooked and depraved generation" (2:15), the perfection **of the righteousness that comes from God and is by faith** (3:9).

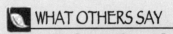

WHAT OTHERS SAY

THE BIBLICAL CALL TO PERFECTION

The call "Be perfect" (Matt. 5:48) is heard in both the Old Testament and the New Testament and is said to be a possibility in human experience.

—Ralph P. Martin and Gerald F. Hawthorne

It must be said again, however, that Paul's overriding message to the Philippians is that the goal and prize of knowing Christ in resurrection perfection lie ahead. It is this that they should fix their minds on as he does. As was noted above, Paul seems to be concerned with rebutting exaggerated claims that such perfection was already attainable. Exactly what he has in mind when he speaks of points on which the Philippians may **think differently** (3:15) was doubtless clearer to them than it is to us. It may refer to readiness to forget **what is behind** (3:13) or **sharing in** [Christ's] **sufferings** (3:10). Clearly, Paul has not changed his mind about such things, and he believes God will make them clear to the Philippians. But he expresses himself in tones of pastoral concern and restraint. Above all he is concerned that the Philippians should do nothing to cause themselves to slip backward. Hence he exhorts them—and himself also—to **live up to what we have already attained** (3:16). Spiritual progress is his prime objective.

There are few places where the teaching of Philippians 3:2–16 has been brought together more lucidly and succinctly than in two stanzas of this Charles Wesley hymn:

> Jesus, the First and Last,
> On Thee my soul is cast:
> Thou didst Thy work begin
> By blotting out my sin;
> Thou wilt the root remove,
> And perfect me in love.
>
> Yet when the work is done,
> The work is but begun:
> Partaker of Thy grace,
> I long to see Thy face;
> The first I prove below,
> The last I die to know.[8]

4. SOME PRACTICAL GUIDANCE 3:17–4:1

The whole of chapter 3 has been marked by strong emotion as Paul has described his experience and the theological issues that lie behind it. As it has progressed, however, it has moved increasingly toward what was always its intended purpose—what it all meant for the Philippians. With this, the mood has changed from passionate, almost explosive, declaration to compassionate concern. That note controls the closing verses of the section.

In concluding this part of his instruction, Paul has evidently decided that practical guidance is the best way to give direction to the Philippians. Accordingly, he begins by exhorting them to **join with others in following my example** (3:17). Paul frequently exhorts his converts to follow his example (1 Cor. 4:16–17), but he does not fail to mention that he himself follows the example of Christ (1 Cor. 11:1; 1 Thess. 1:6). Here he makes reference to those who take him as their pattern—a possible allusion to traveling Christian preachers who had visited the Philippian church. In this way he harks back to the theme of having the mind of Christ (2:5), forging a chain of imitation reaching from himself to his many followers and, he hopes, to the Philippians. Paul provided his converts not only with precepts but also with example.

Paul proceeds to define what he means by the **pattern we gave you** (3:17). The controlling idea is still that of pursuing the goal of the perfect and complete knowledge of Christ. He defines it both negatively and positively.

THE WRONG WAY TO PERFECTION: PREOCCUPATION WITH PASSING THINGS

Paul has often spoken to the Philippians of those who follow the wrong way. Again, they may well have been itinerant evangelists who visited Philippi after Paul's forced departure. Paul describes them as **enemies of the cross of Christ** (3:18). If this language sounds severe, he did not write it severely but **even with tears** (3:18). Nonetheless, it is a strong indictment. It is hard to imagine any openly rejecting the Cross of Christ (though there were various ways of soft-pedaling it). The use of the verb **live** suggests it was what they *did* rather than what they *said* that prompted Paul to describe them as enemies of the Cross.

This seems to be borne out by the list of their characteristics in verse 19 (though the exact meaning of each of these is not wholly clear). First, **their destiny is destruction**. Since the word translated **destiny** comes from the same root as the word *perfect*, there is probably a play on words here. Instead of attaining perfect salvation, they will attain perfect destruction. Second, **their god is their stomach, and their glory is in their shame** (3:19). At first glance, these words seem to point to licentiousness, but there is nothing in the language itself that would require this, nor anything earlier in the letter to suggest it. If 3:4–6 refers to the observance of Jewish ceremonial law (as 3:2 suggests), then observance of the Jewish food laws could well be Paul's target (compare Gal. 2:11–14). If **their glory is in their shame** is a reference to the nakedness involved in circumcision (which would harmonize with 3:2), then this would see a common focus on law observance in all the characteristics listed. That point would be made more forcefully if the alternative translation (which is grammatically possible and even preferable) proposed by Martin and Hawthorne is accepted: "they have made their stomach and their glory in their shame their god."[9] Third, it is on this that their proponents have fastened **their mind**.

THE RIGHT WAY TO PERFECTION: FOCUSING ON THINGS ETERNAL

Clearly such a mind-set is not that of 2:5–11, the mind Paul has been urging on them. He now proceeds to expound the mind-set that contrasts with one fixed on earthly things. The language is as lofty as the thought is profound. Fundamentally, he makes three responses, one to each of three characteristics of the earthly mind-set he has just described. He makes his responses in reverse order to that of the earlier listing. He affirms that his *focus* is different. **Our citizenship is in heaven** (3:20). This strikes the note that reverberates throughout these verses right from the start. As we have seen, Roman citizenship was highly prized in Philippi, and Paul has already used that picture to exhort the Philippians to live in a way consistent with their true citizenship in Christ's kingdom (1:27). Now, going beyond mere suggestion or implication, he tells them that their (and his) true citizenship is in heaven. Hence their lives and attitudes are to be governed not by **earthly things** but by heavenly things. There is a loftier citizenship than Roman citizenship—an affirmation that would have striking implications both for Philippian Christians who were Roman citizens and for those who were not. Not only so, but heavenly citizenship is one they already held. For the believer in Christ, heaven has already come down to earth in an important measure.

Paul passes quickly over the point that their heavenly citizenship is already a reality. His chief stress is on what is yet to be—the salvation that will come to them from heaven. **We eagerly await a Savior from there, the Lord Jesus Christ** (3:20). Thus, not only is his focus different from that of those fixated on **earthly things**, the **means of salvation** as he sees it is also different. Far from being anything he can do by way of religious observance, his hope rests squarely on Christ. The form of Christ's name that he uses is highly significant. "Savior" was a title claimed by the Roman emperors—in many formulations the climactic title summarizing all others used by them. This may be the reason why it is used so rarely by Paul. Its aptness in Philippians may be traced to the fact that Philippi's political status made it a "Rome away from Rome." But the full import of what Paul is conveying is seen in the language he uses to draw out the meaning of **Savior**. Jesus is none other than the **Lord**: the Greek equiv-

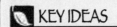

KEY IDEAS

CITIZENS OF HEAVEN

The men of faith have found
Glory begun below;
Celestial fruit on earthly ground
From faith and hope may grow.

The hill of Zion yields
A thousand sacred sweets
Before we reach the heavenly fields
Or walk the golden streets.

—Isaac Watts

alent of the term used in the Old Testament to refer to God himself. The powerful language Paul uses to describe the Lord Jesus indicates that is the meaning he intends. Such language is normally used by Paul in reference to God (as in 2:9–11, where the humiliation of Jesus is reversed by God). Here he uses it in reference to Jesus. Christ Jesus is the one who has the power that enables Him **to bring everything under his control** (3:21).

On the basis of this depiction of Jesus, Paul now proceeds to describe the completeness of the salvation Jesus will effect when He comes from heaven. He **will transform our lowly bodies so that they will be like his glorious body** (3:21). He differs from **the enemies of the cross** concerning not only their focus and their **understanding of the means of salvation**; he differs from them regarding his view of **Christian destiny**. For them, perfection is to be found in the meticulous keeping of the law. His horizon is vaster by far.

The ideas and the language in verse 21 (**transform**, **lowly**, **glory**, especially in their Greek form) are strongly reminiscent of the picture of Christ's humiliation and its reversal in 2:5–11. Particularly significant is the focus on **the body**. Paul specifically contrasts *the body of our humiliation*—our present body, with *His body of glory* or **his glorious body**, that is, the risen, glorified body of Jesus. This carries several important implications. First, it implies that since the body is subject to weakness and decay and the imperfections that necessarily go with these, perfection is not to be sought in the present life. Second, however, it also implies that human life in its wholeness carries a bodily aspect that will not be lost at death. Third, the pattern of the resurrection body of believers is none other than the risen, glorified body of Jesus himself. The risen Jesus, who was recognizably the same as the Jesus of the earthly ministry but was not bound by the limitations of time and space, is the model of the perfect life of eternity in which His followers will share.

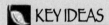

KEY IDEAS

BODILY LIFE AFTER DEATH

The blessed state is never described by Paul as a separation of the soul from the body. Salvation for him is *not* the survival of the soul alone, but the preservation and restoration of people in their wholeness—spirit, soul, and body.

But the glorified saints will not be immortal survivors in a world in which death will continue to hold sway. Rather their salvation—as the order of words in the original suggests—will encompass the entire universe. The Lord Jesus, by His sovereign power, will **make all things subject to himself** (3:21 NRSV), and His people will be renewed people in a renewed universe.

On the basis of this confidence, Paul lapses yet again (as in 1:7–8, 14; 2:12, 17–18) into the intimate language of friendship. Philippians 4:1 picks up the exhortation to **stand firm** found in 1:27, but it also continues the exhortation to **rejoice in the Lord** in 3:1 and looks forward to the same exhortation in 4:4. In one sense, therefore, it is a transitional verse. But it looks backwards more than it looks forward. His description of the Philippians as his **joy and crown** anticipates the last day when his work, like everyone else's, will be put to the test. Their fidelity to the end will be the seal on the validity of his ministry. Hence he urges them to **stand firm in the Lord**.

ENDNOTES

Key Ideas Sidebar 1: Ralph P. Martin and Gerald F. Hawthorne, *Philippians*, Word Biblical Commentary (Nashville, Tenn.: Nelson Reference, 2004), p. 178.

Life Change Sidebar: A. S. T. Fisher, An Anthology of Prayers, (London: Longraans, Green and Co., 1954), p. 35.

Key Ideas Sidebar 2: Martin and Hawthorne, *Philippians*, p. 233.

1. Expressing the matter in technical, theological terms, C. L. Mearns writes, "An analysis of the letter yields four salient features in the opponents' position. Briefly, these are the attaching of little significance to the Cross, a confident triumphalist theology, a strongly realized eschatology, and religious and moral perfectionism through obedience to Torah, especially circumcision." C. L. Mearns, "The Identity of Paul's Opponents at Philippi," *New Testament Studies* vol. 33 (1987), p. 195.

2. The phrase "faith in Christ" in Philippians 3:6 is sometimes translated "through the faithfulness of Christ" and taken to refer to Christ's obedience to death (2:8). While grammatically possible, it is improbable here since Paul is contrasting confidence or faith in himself to achieve righteousness with confidence or faith in Christ. This is confirmed by the concluding clause of the verse: **the righteousness which comes from God and is by faith**, where **by faith** can only refer to the faith of the sinner.

3. M. D. Hooker gives apt expression to both sides of the matter: "To believe in the gospel is to put one's trust in God. . . . To trust in something or someone means to rely on them, and complete trust suggests there is no need to rely on anything else. So if men and women come to put their trust in God, they must abandon all other props. It is easy to think of faith in positive terms, as acceptance—acceptance of the grace of God at work in Christ—and to forget the other, more negative aspect of faith—the need for renunciation. Before Paul could accept Christ, he had to renounce those things on which, as a Jew he had relied (3:7–11)." M. D. Hooker, *Philippians*, The New Interpreter's Bible, vol. 11 (Nashville, Tenn.: Abingdon Press, 2000), pp. 530–531.

4. Frank Thielman, *Philippians* The New Application Commentary (Grand Rapids, Mich.: Zondervan, 1995), p. 191.

5. Thielman, *Philippians*, pp. 190–191.

6. See Alex R. G. Deasley, *The Shape of Qumran Theology* (Carlisle: Paternoster Press, 2000), ch. 5, "The Way: Perfection as a Means and an End."

7. Hooker, *Philippians*, pp. 533–34.

8. Charles Wesley, Hymn 674, http://wesley.nnu.edu/charles_wesley/hymns/600-699.htm.

9. Martin and Hawthorne, *Philippians*, p. 225.

EXHORTATIONS, THANKS, AND GREETINGS

Philippians 4:2–23

The letter now moves toward its conclusion. Commentators disagree as to where the formal conclusion begins. While it is true that Paul's conclusions usually contain the same components (commands, a wish of peace, the holy kiss, greetings, and a benediction) in the same order, it is also true that Paul breaks up the pattern.[1] This seems to be the case here. It would be odd if he ended the letter without saying anything about unity, which he mentioned as early and emphatically in 1:27 as well as later (2:1–4; 3:18). Therefore, it seems as if 4:2 marks the beginning of the end.

In character these verses are marked by deep personal feeling arising from issues that lay close to the heart of Paul as well as to the hearts of the Philippians. This mutual personal concern of Paul for the needs of the Philippians and theirs for him comes aptly to expression in this letter. It exhibits the features typical of a "hortatory letter of friendship," as letters of this character have come to be called.

1. THREE EXHORTATIONS 4:2–9

AN EXHORTATION TO UNITY

There are no grammatical links between verses 1 and 2, and it seems as though verse 2 marks the beginning of a new section. It is unique in several ways. First, it is unique in that it contains personal names. We have no knowledge of Euodia and Syntyche beyond what is given here; it is remarkable that Paul mentions them by name. Reading the letter would mean reading it out loud in the Philippian church. Presumably their differences of opinion were well known in the church, so Paul is not turning a private disagreement into a public one. It is interesting, however, that whereas in the later exhortations Paul uses the language of command (4:4–9), here he uses the language of entreaty: **I plead . . . I plead**. The ground on which he urges them to find unity is that they are already united **in the Lord**, a phrase and an idea we have encountered repeatedly throughout the letter. They do not have to manufacture unity; they simply have to realize it.

Second, these verses are notable in supplying evidence that women played a large role in the propagation of the gospel. Euodia and Syntyche are described as **these women who have contended at my side in the cause of the gospel** (4:3). Historical evidence suggests that in Macedonia women played as prominent a role in public life as men. Paul did not hesitate to allow this to spill over into the church. This also suggests that the cause of the friction may have been differences of opinion regarding methods of propagating the gospel. Paul's attitude was that differences of opinion regarding methods should not be allowed to degenerate into personal quarrels. In 2:6–11 he has already enjoined upon them "the mind of Christ." He uses the same

MANNERS AND CUSTOMS
WOMEN IN PUBLIC LIFE

Here is one of those pieces of "mute" evidence for women in leadership in the New Testament . . . to deny their role in the church in Philippi is to fly full in the face of the text. Here is the evidence that the Holy Spirit is "gender-blind," that He gives gifts as He wills; our task is to recognize His gifting.

language here: **be of the same mind in the Lord**; that is, be ready to give in to those of opposite views.

Since Paul could not be present to attempt to reconcile Euodia and Syntyche, he enlists the help of one who was present, his **loyal yoke-fellow**. Paul does not give us his name, though many others have sought to supply the omission. Luke and Epaphroditus are among the leading favorites, but the best comment remains that of F. F. Bruce: "It is best to recognize that the identity of the **loyal yokefellow** was perfectly well known to the Philippian church but can only be guessed at by us."[2] A similar comment is in order regarding the identity of Clement. His Latin name may mean that he was a Philippian, but his inclusion among **the rest of my fellow workers** (4:3) may indicate that he was one of a group of evangelists who accompanied or supported Paul's missionary endeavors. The names of all of them, including Euodia and Syntyche, are **in the book of life** (see also Luke 10:20; Heb.12:23).

It is interesting to observe how Paul seeks to deal with this division within the Philippian church. First, he uses the language of appeal, not the language of denunciation. Second, he points to those things that the alienated parties have in common, especially their trust in the same Lord. Third, he seeks to use the services of a trusted colleague within the church who can act in his absence, particularly to **help** those who are at odds. They are not to be driven out or ostracized, but assisted. Differences are more likely to be dissolved by shared action than by isolation.

AN EXHORTATION TO JOY

In these verses there is a shift from the language of appeal in verses 2 and 3 to the language of command. The intensely personal character of the earlier verses explains this. There is a certain abrupt quality about the commands, though in the case of the third (4:6–7) the consequence of **not being anxious about anything** (4:6) is elaborated in the promise of **the peace of God** (4:7). Once again, Paul was not bound by matters of form.

There are indications that the precise commands given were prompted by what Paul knew of the needs of the Philippians. These were not just general commands applicable everywhere. The middle command—**Let**

your gentleness be evident to all (4:5)—suggests that this had particular appropriateness in the Philippian context. Taken together, we get the impression that the qualities enjoined are those needed for the stress of living as Christians in a hostile or unsympathetic society.

The first command given is to **rejoice in the Lord always** (4:4), a command that Paul repeats just in case they missed the point. We have noted how frequently **joy** is spoken of in this letter (1:4, 18–19, 25–26; 2:17–18). We have also noticed the frequency of the phrase **in the Lord** (1:1, 14, 26; 2:19, 24; 3:1; 4:1). Christian life is life lived in union with Christ, in the power of Christ, and in hope in Christ. Because of this, the tone of the believer's life is joy in Christ. Being related and linked to Christ is the fundamental fact of Christian existence, and no other fact can erode it.

LIFE CHANGE

THE JOY OF BELONGING TO CHRIST

The world into which Christ came was a gray world, blanketed with the dark clouds of war, privation, oppression, slavery and infanticide. Christianity brought a note of hope (John 1:12; Col. 1:27) which is the parent of joy (Rom. 15:13). In Gordon Fee's words: "Joy, unmitigated, untrammeled joy, is—or at least should be—the distinctive mark of the believer in Christ Jesus."

The second command is to **gentleness** (4:5). Paul uses the word in 2 Corinthians 10:1 in harness with meekness to refer to the meekness and gentleness of Christ. This suggests the absence of self-assertion, or claiming one's rights, which may again point to something approaching persecution in the Philippian situation. The reason Paul urges this response is that **the Lord is near**. While this could refer to the nearness of the Lord to His people (as in Ps. 119:151; 145:18), it is more likely that Paul was thinking of the nearness of the Lord's return. If that is correct, then the underlying idea may be that of leaving judgment to God (Rom. 12:19).

The third command is to avoid being overly anxious about anything (4:6). There is a clear echo of the teaching of Jesus in Matthew 6:25–34. Where Paul differs is that, while Jesus commends trust in God as the solution, Paul refines it to the specific form of prayer. **In everything, by prayer and petition, with thanksgiving, present your requests to God** (4:6). There are slight differences in meaning between the three words

used for prayer: the first is the
standard term for prayer to
God; the second denotes sup-
plication; the third, the specific
boons being sought. Together,
they cover the aspects of
prayer that bring release from
anxiety. Significantly, Paul's
command to pray includes the
directive that they are to pray

LIFE CHANGE
THE CURE FOR ANXIETY

Worry is like the worm which can destroy
the life of the loveliest rose. In contrast,
thankfulness is the fruit of confident prayer,
which is the foundation of serenity and
peace. Hence the counsel of Robert Rainy:
"The way to be anxious about nothing [is]
to be prayerful about everything.

with thanksgiving (4:6). Prayer with thanksgiving is confident prayer
because it is based on God's hearing of our prayers in the past, which gives
the assurance that He is hearing our prayers in the present.

In consequence, Paul's command against anxiety flows naturally into a
promise of God's peace. The image Paul uses is that of a sentry keeping
guard over the troubled heart and mind, thereby ensuring freedom from anxiety. Probably Paul is not thinking of peace as a thing that God gives, so
much as of God himself, who dwells above agitation, keeping guard at their
mental thresholds. Such peace does, indeed, transcend comprehension. To
those whose hearts and minds are **in Christ Jesus**, it is a lively reality.

AN EXHORTATION TO THINK AND LIVE CHRISTIANLY

There is no logical connection between 4:4–7 and 4:8–9. The latter
verses are simply a further expression of Paul's affectionate concern for
the Philippians, illustrating yet again the character of the epistle as a hortatory letter of friendship.

Not only are these verses unconnected with what precedes and follows, they also have a stylistic uniqueness. There is a staccato quality
about the individual phrases. They are not linked grammatically, but
simply piled on top of each other in a way unique in Paul's writings. Yet
their impact is increased rather than diminished because of it.

Verse 8 lists six qualities they should give their minds to. The items
listed are not typical of Paul's vocabulary. They are more characteristic
of Greek morality, though they are also found in Jewish wisdom writings.

This has led some scholars to suggest that what Paul is urging his readers to do is to recognize that there is good in human culture and to draw upon it rather than simply bury it beneath a blanket condemnation.[3]

First in Paul's list is **whatever is true** (4:8). All the qualities in the list are ethical; therefore, Paul has in mind that which conforms to truthfulness. He assumes that all are aware of the difference between truth and falsehood, but it is possible to suppress the truth (Rom. 1:18–20). Second is **whatever is noble** (4:8), that is, deserving of honor and respect. Third, **whatever is right** (4:8). Anything that offends justice and fairness is an offense against rightness and righteousness. Fourth, **whatever is lovely** (4:8); it is used only here in the New Testament and means what is loveable or calls forth love rather than hatred or contempt. Finally, **whatever is admirable** (4:8), evoking respect and admiration. The list concludes with the umbrella phrase **anything . . . excellent or praiseworthy** (4:8).

Plenty of muck-raking is possible in today's world, as in Paul's, because there is plenty of muck to rake. But thought leads to action, and what we open our minds to quickly becomes our master. Those who give their minds over to the gutter will quickly find themselves living the life of the gutter. Paul exhorts the Philippians to give their hearts and minds to what is lofty and beautiful. Even in our world it is not impossible to find.

From the sphere of thought—though it goes beyond mere thinking—Paul moves more deliberately into the realm of action. He does so decisively by calling them to **put into practice** what they saw and knew of him (4:9). They **learned** from his teaching and saw in his life an example to be imitated. If they will heed both, **the God of peace will be with** [them] (4:9). In this way, verse 8, with its list of somewhat abstract adjectives, finds concrete anchorage in Paul's personal example. The ultimate guideline for their lives is the example of redeemed living they had seen in him.

2. THANKS FOR THEIR SUPPORT 4:10–20

On the surface, these verses read rather strangely. The topic is clear enough: to thank them for the gift they had sent him by the hand of Epaphroditus. It is the tone that is bewildering. **At last** they have renewed their concern for him (4:10). He did not really need their gift anyway

(4:11), and could have done without it (4:12). It is good of them to help him (4:14), but he is not really looking for their help (4:17). Moreover, while he begins the letter with a word of thanks (1:3–5), he does not get round to spelling it out until the close. It is the last item on the agenda. These features have led one commentator to title this paragraph "Thanks, Sort Of."[4]

This, however, is to overlook several factors. First, it takes no account of Paul's settled policy of supporting himself so that he could not be charged with preaching for monetary gain (1 Cor. 9:3–18, 33–35). When he says in Philippians 4:10, **Indeed, you have been concerned, but you had no opportunity to show it**, the meaning is probably that he did not give them the chance to support him. Now that he was in prison, however, this had changed. Even so, he had **learned to be content whatever the circumstances** (4:11). Second, in the Greek-Roman world, friendship was regarded as involving **giving and receiving** (4:15), and he was ready to conform to this cultural norm. Third, the placing of this item at the end of the letter gives it a visibility it would not have had if he had dealt with it once and for all in chapter 1. It would then have slipped from sight behind the other significant matters he deals with in chapters 2 and 3. To deal with it at length at the close recalls the reason that prompted the letter in the first place, even if it was not the only matter he had to write about.

These general considerations should be kept in mind as we seek to interpret this passage.

THE SECRET OF PAUL'S STRENGTH

The paragraph begins with reference to the Philippians' gift to Paul. The gift is not mentioned directly, but rather the concern from which it sprang. This has come to life again. As if to correct any wrong impression, Paul affirms that **you have been concerned, but you had no opportunity to show it** (4:10). We have already seen that Paul's policy was to support himself by his own labor, though he notes later that when he was in need in Thessalonica, the Philippians were the only church that sent him aid (4:15–16). This would suggest that Paul's self-support policy was not absolute. He would not accept it while ministering in a given locale, but if need arose, he would accept it from outside that locale. Now that he is in a Roman jail, with only limited opportunity for work, he is ready to receive their contributions.

At the same time, the touchstone for him is not being in need, **for I have learned to be content whatever the circumstances** (4:11). His elaboration of this is remarkable. Not only does he know how to be content in want, he knows how to be content amid plenty. Frequently, plenty feeds on itself, generating an appetite for excess. Paul knows how to cope with both. This is not because he is a self-sufficient man, the ideal in the Stoicism of his day. It was because he was a Christ-sufficient man. Verse 13 should probably be translated "I can do everything *in* him who gives me strength."

The Pauline ideal is well expressed in the song of the Shepherd's Boy in *The Pilgrim's Progress*.

The boy was in very mean clothes, but of a very fresh and well-favored countenance, and as he sat by himself, he sang . . . :

> He that is down, needs fear no fall,
> He that is low, no pride;
> He that is humble, ever shall
> Have God to be his guide.
> I am content with what I have,
> Little be it, or much;
> And, Lord, contentment still I crave,
> Because thou savest such.
> Fulness to such a burden is
> That go on pilgrimage;
> Here little, and hereafter bliss,
> Is best from age to age.[5]

It is an apt word to a consumer society.

HELP FROM THE PHILIPPIANS

Paul not only picks up the note of gratitude already sounded in verse 10 for their generosity to him. He sets it in a new light by describing it as "sharing with me in tribulation." Behind everything he does lies the concern to further the gospel; therefore, to help him is to help that cause. The Philippians have done that from the start. The Greek phrase "the beginning of the gospel" may have the double sense of "when the gospel reached them" (implied by the NIV) or when Paul first became the teaching apostle to the Gentiles instead of Barnabas (compare Acts 13:2, 7 with 13:13, 16, 42, 46; 14:1). Either way, the Philippians were in it with Paul from the start.

Not only so, but they were the only church who **shared with me in the matter of giving and receiving** (4:15). As noted above, **giving and receiving** was probably a standard phrase to describe mutuality of friendship. But the phrase may also denote the Philippians' gift on the one hand and, on the other hand, the receipt Paul sent them acknowledging its arrival. Still more, their support of him was not a one-time effort. Even in Thessalonica they sent him aid again and again (4:16). The case of Thessalonica is cited perhaps because even Paul's manual labor there was insufficient to meet his needs (1 Thess. 2:9; 2 Thess. 3:8). But the Philippians came to the rescue.

However, Paul is still haunted by the fear of being regarded as a money-grubber, of whom there were many among wandering teachers then as there are now. So he repeats his disclaimer: **Not that I am looking for a gift** (4:17). Rather, he is looking **for what may be credited to your account** (4:17). The assumption on which alone he can accept their support is that involvement in his ministry is involvement in the business of God.

This explains the fine line he is treading throughout this passage dealing with their gifts. Indeed he has been helped greatly by their gifts, and he does not wish to be an ingrate. But he could have survived without them (4:12–13). In reality, their gifts to him were given to the work of God. This he now spells out at length in verse 18. The phrase **I have received full payment** was the equivalent of writing "paid in full" on an account. When he goes on to say that he is oversupplied now that Epaphroditus has delivered their gifts, he comes close to asking them to send no more. He then turns to the other side of his argument, describing their gifts to him in the language of Temple offerings made to God. **They are a fragrant offering, an acceptable sacrifice, pleasing to God** (4:18). Similar language is used of the self-giving of Christ in Ephesians 5:2 and of the self-giving that believers are called upon to make in Romans 12:1. The gifts given by the Philippians fall into that field of meaning.

But that is not all. God is in no one's debt (Rom. 11:35). The Philippians have faithfully supported Paul; God in turn will supply every need of theirs. Paul's language is carefully calculated. Verse 19 is linked to verse 18 with what may look like a faceless conjunction—**and**, but far from being without character, it expresses the conjunctive quality of the divine response to the Philippians' generosity. They have given with spontaneous generosity to Paul, and so to God; and God will respond with the same spontaneous generosity to them. Equally notable is Paul's choice of possessive pronoun: **my God**. The God in whom he trusts he knows well. He is not merely the God of the distant spaces and far-flung ranges of the universe; He is Paul's God, the one he has come to know and trust in the uncertainties of his life as an apostle. This God, Paul is confident, **will meet all your needs** (4:19). Nor is there any possibility that He might run out of resources, for the yardstick of these is **his glorious riches in Christ Jesus** (4:19). This is best understood as the wealth that belongs to God in the unbounded glory in which He dwells and that He has made available to His people in Christ Jesus. With a God like that, the Philippians need have no fear of the future. Gordon Fee comments aptly: "this sentence offers the theological basis for everything else in the letter."[6]

To such a God only one response is possible: praise or doxology. In the original text the verb "to be" is often omitted, as is the case here. Many translations supply the imperative: "To our God and Father *be* glory." But since Paul has just affirmed God's "riches in glory," it is most probably this that he is reaffirming. Accordingly, the present tense is most appropriate: **To our God and Father [is] glory for ever and ever** (4:20).

It is worthy of note that the God whom Paul has referred to in the previous verse as **my God** is now spoken of as **our God and Father**. He is the Philippians' God as much as He is Paul's.

3. FAREWELL GREETINGS 4:21–23

The closing greetings convey the burden of Paul's message as much as the heart of the letter. First, Paul greets *each* saint in Christ Jesus. This is not quite the same as **Greet all the saints in Christ Jesus** (4:21). It says that each individual is included, not one being left out—an important point in a church where there had been strain and division. Greetings were also sent by **the brothers who are with me** and **all the saints** (4:21–22). The former presumably refers to Paul's coworkers; the latter to the members of the church in Rome. Among these are **those who belong to Caesar's household** (4:22). To the Philippians who lived in a setting where Roman influence was strong, it would have been reassuring to know that there were believers at the heart of the Roman Empire, even within the official household of the emperor himself.

The letter concludes with a grace-benediction. It is interesting that while Paul begins most of his letters with a grace-greeting joining "the grace of God our Father and of the Lord Jesus Christ" (Col. 1:2; 1 Thess. 1:1 are among the few exceptions), he concludes them with a grace-benediction referring only to **the grace of the Lord Jesus Christ** (4:23). For Paul, the Lord Jesus Christ can act and speak for the Father. To know the grace of the Lord Jesus Christ is to know the grace of God.

ENDNOTES

Manners and Customs Sidebar: Gordon Fee, *Paul's Letter to the Philippians*, New International Commentary on the New Testament (Grand Rapids, Mich.: William B. Eerdmans, 1995), p. 398.

Life Change Sidebar: Fee, *Philippians*, p. 404.

1. See Fee, *Philippians*, p. 399. While Fee tends to favor finding a pattern and so sees the conclusion beginning at verse 4, M. D Hooker declares that "this final chapter of the epistle is something of a hodgepodge," *The Letter to the Philippians*, The New Interpreter's Bible, vol. 11 (Nashville, Tenn.: Abingdon

Press, 2000), p. 547.

2. F. F. Bruce, *Philippians*, Good News Commentary (San Francisco: Harper and Row, 1983), p. 115.

3. See Fee, *Philippians*, p. 416 and Ralph P. Martin and Gerald F. Hawthorne, *Philippians*, Word Biblical Commentary (Nashville, Tenn.: Nelson Reference, 2004), p. 249. The latter quote second-century Christian apologist Justin Martyr as summing up Paul's approach in the words "the truth which men in all lands have rightly spoken belongs to us" (2 Apol. 2.13).

4. Frank Thielman, *Philippians,* The New Application Commentary (Grand Rapids, Mich.: Zondervan, 1995), p. 234.

5. John Bunyan, *Pilgrim's Progress*, The World's Great Classics (Danbury, Conn.: Grolier Enterprises Corp. n.d.), p. 272.

6. Fee, *Philippians*, 455, n. 18.

SELECT BIBLIOGRAPHY
For Philippians

Bockmuehl, Markus. *The Epistle to the Philippians*. Black's New Testament Commentary. London: Hendrickson, 1998.

Bruce, F. F. *Philippians*. Good News Commentary. San Francisco: Harper and Row, 1983.

Donfried, Karl P. and I. Howard Marshall. *The Theology of the Shorter Pauline Letters*. Cambridge: Cambridge University Press, 1993.

Fee, Gordon D. *Paul's Letter to the Philippians*. New International Commentary on the New Testament. Grand Rapids, Mich.: William B. Eerdmans, 1995.

Hooker, Morna D. *The Letter to the Philippians*. The New Interpreter's Bible, vol. 9. Nashville, Tenn.: Abingdon Press, 2000.

Marshall, I. Howard. *New Testament Theology: Many Witnesses, One Gospel*. Downers Grove, Ill.: InterVarsity Press, 2004.

Martin, R. P. *Philippians*. Tyndale New Testament Commentary. London: Tyndale Press, 1959.

Martin, Ralph P. and Gerald F. Hawthorne. *Philippians* (rev. ed.). Word Biblical Commentary. Nashville, Tenn.: Nelson Reference, 2004.

Moule, H. C. G. *The Epistle to the Philippians*, Thornapple Commentaries (Grand Rapids, Mich.: Baker Book House, 1981).

Oakes, Peter. *Philippians: From People to Letter*. Society for New Testament Studies Monograph Series, 110. Cambridge University Press, 2001.

O'Brien, Peter T. *The Epistle to the Philippians*: *A Commentary on the Greek Text*. The New International Greek Testament Commentary. Grand Rapids, Mich.: William B. Eerdmans, 1991.

Silva, Moisés. *Philippians*. Baker Exegetical Commentary on the New Testament. Grand Rapids. Mich.: Baker Book House, 1992.

Spicq, Ceslaus. *Agape in the New Testament*, vol. 2. St. Louis: B. Herder, 1963.

Stowers, Stanley K. "Friends and Enemies in the Politics of Heaven: Reading Theology in Philippians." In Jouette M. Bassler, ed. *Pauline Theology*, vol. 1. Minneapolis: Fortress Press, 1991.

Thielman, Frank. *Philippians*. The NIV Application Commentary. Grand Rapids, Mich.: Zondervan, 1995.

White, J. L. *Light from Ancient Letters*. Philadelphia: Fortress Press, 1986.

Wright, N. T. *The Climax of the Covenant: Christ and the Law in Pauline Theology*. Minneapolis: Fortress Press, 1993.

COLOSSIANS

BARRY L. CALLEN

INTRODUCTION TO COLOSSIANS

The distinctive conviction of the whole New Testament is that "Jesus is Lord!" The executed peasant from Nazareth is said to be nothing short of God with us humans for our salvation. God in Jesus, through the Spirit, is set forth as the explanation of the past, the power required for the present, and the desired hope of the future for all humanity. Accordingly, the central message of the letter to the Colossians is the *all-sufficient Christ*. The Lord Jesus deserves *the* place, not *a* place, in our believing and living as Christian disciples.

No book in the New Testament more strikingly expounds the centrality and meaning of the lordship of Jesus Christ than does Colossians. This clear exposition was urgently needed in the city of Colosse because the Christian congregation there was being troubled by attractive perversions of the young faith. Alluring alternatives often arise—and they need to be faced and exposed. Such troubling of Christian believers has gained new life in the early twenty-first century. Its current outcroppings include various secular mysticisms, extreme fundamentalisms such as Islam, and "New Age" beliefs of various kinds. Therefore, it remains crucial for believers in Jesus Christ to know what is the non-negotiable essence of the Christian gospel as it interacts with a world of bewildering and sometimes enticing religious diversity.

Colossians is a theologically, ethically, and devotionally rich document. Despite being only

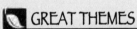

GREAT THEMES
THE CHRISTIAN YEAR

The central message of the letter to the Colossians is the *all-sufficient Christ*. The Lord Jesus deserves *the* place, not *a* place in our believing and living as Christian disciples. Christians should focus time itself around celebration of the life and ongoing ministry of Jesus. Note the following annual cycle, a year of focusing on Jesus and avoiding preoccupation with enticing religious alternatives.

The Christian Year is a way of viewing time. It is the Christian's pattern of essential memories about Jesus that inspire spiritual growth and joy.

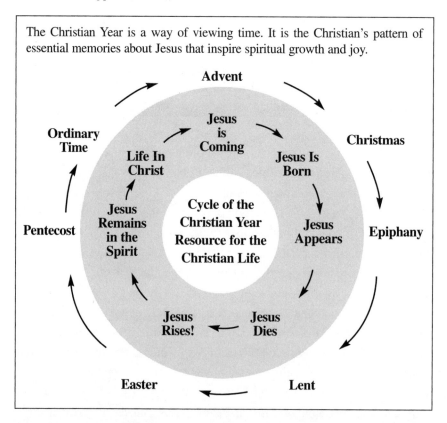

four chapters long, it contains a magnificent hymn-like passage about the cosmic scope of Christ's role in human creation and redemption (1:15–20) and a significant addressing of the theological basics and ethical implications of Christian faith. In our current age—marked by the tendency to fuse deities, rites, and interpretations of one people, region, or religious tradition with those of another—Paul still speaks a powerful word. Since the church faces unfriendly rivals, a clear word of truth about the all-sufficient Christ is as important now as ever.

AUTHORSHIP

Apparently the apostle Paul never visited the city of Colosse personally (2:1), although Epaphras, likely a convert during Paul's Ephesian ministry, is probably the one who established the Christian congregation there during the course of Paul's extended teaching ministry in Ephesus (Col. 1:7–8;

4:12–13; Acts 19:10). The Colossian congregation was founded between A.D. 52 and 55. So it was only five or six years later when Epaphras went to Paul, then a prisoner in Rome, to inform him of developments in Colosse, both good and bad. The resulting Pauline letter from Rome to the small city far to the east shows clearly that Paul was well informed about the ongoing life of the congregation and was anxious to influence its developing life.

The assumption of Paul's authorship of Colossians is affirmed consistently from the earliest Christian centuries. Some recent scholars have raised questions based on (1) the use of certain words not appearing in any other of Paul's letters, (2) the judgment that the heresy being confronted in Colosse did not exist in just this way at that time, and (3) belief that the theological thought about Jesus that appears in this letter evolved only after Paul's time. However, close examination of these matters does not require an abandonment of the traditional claim of Pauline authorship. It is possible "to understand any shift in Paul's thinking as reflecting the dynamic of a single person who is intent on communicating theological convictions in practical ways to different audiences at different moments in the course of a long career."[1]

Even if the letter is not directly from Paul's hand, the authority of its message is well established. After all, "what was canonized by the church were not the complete thoughts of Paul, but those texts in which it recognized apostolic tradition."[2] Colossians was a letter recognized as truly inspired by God and carrying the authority of the apostle Paul.

DATE AND PLACE

We assume that the Colossian letter came from Paul, as the letter itself suggests (1:1; 4:18), probably with the report of Epaphras in hand and possibly with Timothy's substantial writing assistance. The letter came from prison (4:10, 18), maybe in Ephesus, but more likely while Paul was a prisoner in Rome (A.D. 60–62).

AUDIENCE

There is significant evidence in this letter of Pauline concerns, ideas, and approaches. The Colossian letter appears to contain lines from an early Christian hymn used skillfully by Paul in writing to people familiar with such material.[3] Obviously, he was anxious that his readers recall the apostolic faith and accept it as foundational for their faith and life (2:6–8). We will focus less on literary speculation and more on theological message and life application.

Although nothing of a physical nature is now left, the site of ancient Colosse is located in present-day western Turkey and was the home region of Epaphras. It was in Phrygia, about one hundred miles east of Ephesus in the valley of the River Lycus, near where it joins the Meander River. The area immediately around Colosse featured flocks of sheep and a large woolen industry. Colosse sat at the base of the Cadmus range of mountains and commanded the roads leading to the mountain passes. Since it was located on the ancient route from Ephesus and Sardis to the Euphrates River, it is mentioned in the itineraries of the armies of King Xerxes and Cyrus the Younger.

By the time of Paul's writing, Colosse was in decline and not particularly large in population or important commercially. Paul mentions the more prominent nearby cities of Laodicea and Hierapolis, where there also were Christians (2:1; 4:13, 15–16). The local population consisted of indigenous Phrygians, Greek settlers, and a significant community of Jews, who originally came to the area in the time of Antiochus the Great (223–187 B.C.E.). Based on the volume of Temple taxes paid and sent to Jerusalem from Phrygia in 62 B.C., there would have been some 50,000 Jews living in the greater Colosse area. Such a community would have had a real influence on the young Christian movement that came there much later. All of this influence was not good in Paul's view.

The nature of Judaism in Phrygia was itself influenced by other religious communities. It is known that the Jews remaining in Palestine were strict in religious observance and lamented the large number of their fellow believers who had settled elsewhere and largely abandoned the rigors of their ancestral land for the wines and baths of Phrygia. Christianity had come to the cities of the Lycus Valley during the years of Paul's Ephesian ministry recorded in Acts 19 (A.D. 52–55). Because of his effective work of evangelization, not only the people of Ephesus but "all the Jews and Greeks who lived in the province of Asia heard the word of the Lord" (Acts 19:10). That would have included the city of Colosse and the man Epaphras.

Colosse was a cosmopolitan city in Paul's day, a blending of diverse cultural and religious elements. The Christian community apparently had become a strange potpourri of religious ideas, even though some Christian foundations were being altered subtly but significantly by non-Christian content. Paul's writing to this church was intended to address forthrightly these heretical tendencies. If left unchallenged, this false teaching might have been the ruin of the local Christian movement. Paul would not leave it unchallenged, and neither should we when similar trends invade our churches today.

Along with Paul's letter to the church in Colosse came a second writing, a personal message from Paul to Philemon, who apparently was a prosperous Christian man of the immediate area. This man owned slaves, including Onesimus who had run away, met Paul, became a Christian, and now was being returned to Philemon with Paul's written hope that he would be received as a Christian brother. Since the note to Philemon has been preserved and treasured as part of Scripture, it is reasonable to assume that Paul's request was honored. What Paul also hoped was that his addressing of the heretical teaching in the congregation in Colosse might be heard well and heeded fully.

REASON FOR WRITING: ADDRESSING A DANGEROUS RELIGIOUS ALTERNATIVE

There are many allusions in the book of Colossians to the pagan past of many of the letter's recipients, inferring that they were Gentile converts (1:27; 3:5–7). They once were spiritually dead because of the **uncircumcision of [their] sinful nature** (2:13), a statement indicating a godless and non-Jewish background. God, however, had graciously forgiven their sins, united them with Christ (2:11–12, 20), and brought about great change in their lives (1:5, 13–14; 3:1–4). Initially, then, Paul had heard about these Christians from Epaphras and rejoiced in their faith with sincere thanksgiving (1:4–6).

The occasion of Paul's letter to Colosse, however, went beyond expressing his delight in them. Apparently Epaphras had brought to Paul both encouraging news and a significant concern. He needed advice about how to deal with a false teaching that had arisen in the Colossian congregation. Likely, Epaphras was not able on his own to counter the arguments of the false teachers. Epaphras, the congregation's theological mentor, may have been under attack, as Paul was elsewhere. The more matured wisdom and reasoning ability of Paul were needed urgently.

Nowhere in the letter does Paul provide a formal description of the theological heresy. Why should he? His readers would know perfectly well what he was addressing without any explanations. Some of the chief characteristics of the heresy can be detected by piecing together Paul's comments about it, his arguments against it, and from the slogans of the heresy that he quotes. In brief, the problem teaching was a **hollow and deceptive philosophy** calling for submission to the **basic principles of this world** (2:8).

Some of the Colossian Christians appear to have been convinced by wayward new teachers that they needed something more than Jesus Christ to free them from subjection to elemental and demonic powers (1:16; 2:9–10, 15). These powers were to be placated and maybe even worshiped (2:15, 18–19). One way of placating them was to engage in a rigorous subduing of the body. Supposedly the participant would gain visionary experiences of the heavenly dimension of life, thus invoking the help of good angels in controlling hostile spirits.

It appears that the form of Judaism around Colosse was a religious mixture of the Hebrew heritage, Greek philosophy, astrology, and mysticism. The result was strange, alluring, and dangerous. Especially misleading was the tendency to share ideas foreign to original Christian teaching in language typically used by prominent Christian leaders such as the apostle Paul. It is reasonable to conclude, "When the gospel was introduced to the area, a Jewish-Hellenistic syncretism would find no great difficulty in expanding and modifying itself sufficiently to take some Christian elements into its system."[4]

We know from Paul's Colossian letter that the heresy was attacking the supremacy, total adequacy, and singular glory of Jesus Christ. The Colossian air was filled with the desire to tap into occult powers and astrological forces, sometimes emphasizing the mediating role of angels (2:18).

Many special disciplines and rituals were being encouraged among Colossian Christians, moving them beyond freedom in Jesus Christ (2:16, 21) and even causing some to think lightly of bodily sins (3:5–8). In fact, the body was presumed to be evil, leading to a denial that Jesus had been fully human. Such people were arguing that God is pure spirit, the world is evil, and thus no direct "incarnation" is thinkable because it would be an impossible mixture of divine spirit with fallen flesh.

This thinking reflects aspects of what later came to be called Gnosticism, finally judged heretical by the larger Christian community. Such false belief was subtle, alluring, and increasingly influential in Colosse. Derived from the Greek word *gnosis*, knowledge, Gnosticism taught that salvation comes through the gaining of mystical knowledge available only to those properly initiated into the mysterious spiritual world. Whether appearing in gross or subtle forms, the bottom line for Paul was the same. Even when not *denying* completely the full deity and adequacy of Jesus Christ, it was *dethroning* Him functionally. This had to be challenged; it still does.

THEMES: A PREVIEW OF PAUL'S RESPONSE

Paul had been born into Roman citizenship and nurtured in the cosmopolitan atmosphere of his hometown, Tarsus. He was used to thinking in larger categories than local and restricted provincialisms. Eventually he had been forced to face a critical question for the early apostles of Jesus. How could the apostolic faith concerning Jesus move from its Jewish home base without abandoning the crucial Hebrew heritage or failing to relate constructively to the mainly non-Jewish world? Paul was well positioned by God to work at this difficult but essential task. Bridging the multiple worlds, he wrote to the Colossians "not with the message of a reformed Judaism, but with the proclamation of the all-sufficient Christ."[5]

In the letter to the Colossians, Paul functions much like John Wesley did in the setting of the troubled English church of the eighteenth century. Wesley focused on "nurturing and shaping the worldview that frames the temperament and practice of believers."[6] His primary theological concern was not so much to build an elaborate system of truth claims as to correct the thought and practice of believers where necessary, encouraging them to embody their full inheritance as reborn children of God. In the Colossian case, Paul acts as a deeply appreciative and concerned missionary/theologian/pastor who sees a church in confusion and offers sorely needed guidance. He resisted the tendency of believers to accommodate their faith to surrounding cultures in ways that degrade witness to the all-sufficiency of Jesus Christ for human salvation.

Paul's letter to the Colossians is like two men who were gazing into the wonder of a night sky. One asked the other whether he ever pondered the great scheme of things. The response was that he never thought about the grand scale of life's drama because he was having enough trouble with life's daily subplots! Wesley and Paul cared much for life's practical subplots, but assumed that they must be controlled by getting the big picture straight. The theological and the practical cannot be separated. *Who Jesus Christ is* in the grand scheme of things has everything to do with *how disciples of Christ should think and act.*

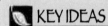 KEY IDEAS

The theological and the practical cannot be separated. Who Jesus Christ is in the grand scheme of things has everything to do with how disciples should think and act. To argue that theology is only a collection of ivory-tower abstractions, implying that clarity about the real identity of Jesus is relatively unimportant for the Christian life, is a serious and dangerous mistake.

The apostle Paul directly addresses the theological danger facing the Colossians. They are told to be on their guard lest they be kidnapped from the truth and led blindly into the slavery of error (2:8). The error at hand is labeled a **human tradition** (2:8), a fabrication standing against the apostolic tradition that centers on Christ Jesus, the true and only Lord. Paul insists that anyone, including any self-professed spiritual saint, who claims exalted heavenly experiences or visions leading to new and extra-Christ revelations is merely a deluded believer full of twisted ideas and unjustified pride (2:18). In short, the Colossian heresy, with all its taboos and spiritual arrogance, was "no syllabus of advanced wisdom; it bore all the marks of immaturity."[7] Christian freedom should be unencumbered by false inhibitions and humanly created religious regulations that distract from the centrality of Jesus Christ.

Paul's letter to Colosse may be the earliest Christian "apology" or public statement explaining and defending the faith. It presents the confrontation of Christianity with a theological trend that the church would have to defend itself against from that time to the present. Paul counters this heretical trend with direct statements of a lofty view of Jesus Christ and an insistence on His completeness and finality. Jesus Christ is the image of the invisible God. In Him all fullness dwells (1:15, 19). In Him there is resident all the treasures of knowledge and wisdom (2:2). In Him the fullness of the Godhead dwells in bodily form (2:9). In Christ all things were created (1:16) and cohere (1:17). By His Cross the cosmic powers of evil were conquered, once and for all time. These are lofty claims indeed, not to be discounted, accommodated, or compromised.

Three aspects of Christ's gospel were threatened by the Colossian heresy. They are as follows: (1) the uniqueness and full adequacy of Jesus Christ for human salvation; (2) the incomparable person and centrality of the cross of Jesus for authentic Christian faith; and (3) the spiritual liberty to be enjoyed by all who believe in and are united to Christ. Humble Christian believers need no higher wisdom than that of Jesus to mediate between themselves, God, and the spiritual world. They need not live in fear of demons or yield to any fatalism, as though all is predestined by the stars or by unseen and uncontrollable powers. They need not seek for spiritual highs or practice mandatory and rigorous rituals to be more mature in their faith.

Christians must resist the twin temptations of becoming severely ascetic, punishing their bodies to advance spiritually (2:20) and of living with license, justifying the doing of almost anything with the body since only the soul is presumed important (3:5). To the contrary, creation is good, insists Paul, and we humans are accountable for our bodily actions. There is no need for secret sources of wisdom or multiple mediators between God and the fallen world. The Christ of God is fully adequate, final, truly all in all!

The Colossian church had become a melting pot of the local thinking, resulting in (1) a reduction of Christ to only one element in a system of divine mediators between God and the fallen creation and (2) a restriction of Christian living by imposing an alien pattern of "spiritual" disciplines thought necessary for any successful salvation. Paul saw deadly danger on both counts. No reduction of the centrality of Jesus Christ is tolerable. Further, people cannot put off the "sinful nature" by religious activity of any kind. The need is for the power of divine grace as seen in God's triumph of evil by the cross of Jesus (2:13–15) and then as reflected in transformed human relationships (3:5–4:6). Paul's confrontation with the Colossian problem was no intellectual game. His own practical theology led him to fear that the "hollow and deceptive" (2:8) wisdom beginning to be followed by many in Colosse would lead to an untenable discipleship that denies the inherent goodness of God's creation and would lack the life-changing power resident in God's new creation, the church.

The apostle makes clear to the Colossians and believers of all times what he understands to be the apostolic faith of Christians. The gospel is the **word of truth** (1:5) that alone provides trustworthy insight into God's will and provision for lost humanity. This word comes in and through *the Word*, God actually present with us in Jesus. As the **word of God** (1:25), the good news has its source in God; as **the word of Christ** (3:16), it has the historical Jesus as its central content. Salvation is found in Christ alone and in active participation with Christ in the power of new creation (1 Cor. 1:18–25). The lordship of Jesus Christ extends over everything spiritual and material, external and internal (1:15–20).

This stunning series of claims is no abstract theorizing. Paul was a missionary with good news for present life. When we read Paul's letters, we should study them less as academic documents and more as living, pulsating letters poured out to meet immediate threats. Salvation's validity is to be judged finally in terms of its actual impact on human life.

According to Paul, the individual believer and the church as a whole must be raised with Christ from sin and death (2:11–15) and made alive **with Christ in God** (3:3). Believers are privileged to share in nothing less than God's Easter triumph in Christ! Since every blessing may be obtained in Christ, it is to Christ and Christ alone that believers are to hold fast. Lines from a hymn of Charles Wesley convey Paul's deepest thought in the Colossian letter:

Sent by my Lord, on you I call!

The invitation is to all!

Come all the world, Come sinner thou!

All things in Christ are ready now![8]

ENDNOTES

1. Robert W. Wall, *Colossians and Philemon*, The IVP New Testament Commentary Series (Downers Grove, Ill.: InterVarsity Press, 1993), p. 19.

2. Andrew T. Lincoln, *The Letter to the Colossians*, The New Interpreter's Bible (Nashville, Tenn.: Abingdon Press, 2000), vol. 11, p. 582.

3. See George E. Cannon, *The Use of Traditional Materials in Colossians* (Macon, Ga.: Mercer University Press, 1983).

4. F. F. Bruce and E. K. Simpson, *Commentary on the Epistles to the Ephesians and Colossians*, The New International Commentary on the New Testament (Grand Rapids, Mich.: William B. Eerdmans, 1957), pp. 166–67.

5. William Barclay, *The All-Sufficient Christ* (Philadelphia: Westminster Press, 1963), p. 19.

6. Randy L. Maddox, *Responsible Grace: John Wesley's Practical Theology* (Nashville, Tenn.: Kingswood Books, Abingdon Press, 1994), p. 17.

7. F. F. Bruce, *Paul: Apostle of the Heart Set Free* (Grand Rapids, Mich.: William B. Eerdmans, 1977), p. 418.

8. As quoted by T. Chrichton Mitchell, *Charles Wesley: Man with the Dancing Heart* (Kansas City, Mo.: Beacon Hill Press of Kansas City, 1994), p. 162.

OUTLINE OF COLOSSIANS

Part One

Beginning with Christian Basics

COLOSSIANS 1:1–14

1

THE ESSENCE OF
THE GOSPEL

Colossians 1:1–8

In significant ways, not to know one's personal heritage is to be orphaned in the present. What could be more important than knowing origin, family, and personal identity? In his letter to the Colossians, Paul addresses directly the identity question for them as Christians. He rehearses the good news of the gospel of Jesus Christ as the necessary touchstone for their remembering who and whose they were.

Paul immediately makes clear certain foundational theological assumptions. He knew there would be some critical questions among the letter's recipients. By what right did he compose a letter he hoped would be received with appreciation and followed with care? By what authority did he claim that this congregation should rethink and reverse key elements of its religious life? Definite answers had to be given.

The considerable critique of aspects of belief and practice in the Colossian congregation will come soon into the letter. First, however, Paul chooses the traditional approach of offering gracious greetings. Included is a reminder of what he judged the essence of the gospel of Jesus Christ. That essence was being threatened and needed to be set forth initially and clearly, although gently and in the context of Paul's genuine gratitude for much that apparently was truly good in this church.

The essence of the true gospel of Jesus Christ, the basic theological identity of Christian believers, is said to include several things. They are (1) a right view of God as known in Jesus; (2) an apostle sent to share accurately the good news that is centered in Christ and based on divine revelation; and (3) a commitment to holiness of life that leads to peace, hope, deep gratitude, and sacrificial service. In brief, the gospel is good news about God's initiative in Jesus Christ and the related divine grace, summons, sending, and enablement, all resulting in thanksgiving and joy.

1. SENT AND SANCTIFIED BY GOD 1:1–2

The letter begins with Paul identifying himself as an **apostle**, one who has been sent, an officially authorized spokesperson. His apostleship is **of Jesus Christ** and **by the will of God** (1:1). It had not come through people (Gal. 1:1) but from the Lord himself. Used early by the Greeks for the leader of a band of colonists, Paul also uses the concept of an apostle to establish a sense of clear authority for his Colossian communication. He had been sent to the Gentile world in general and now, by this letter, was being sent to the Colossian believers in particular. The purpose was to "colonize" foreign religious territory for the true gospel of Jesus.

Paul's Gentile mission was quite controversial in early Christianity. The first believers in Jesus were Jews who had accepted Jesus as their expected Messiah. They were, in effect, a Jesus movement *within* Judaism. Paul's teaching was freed from strict Jewish laws (as explained in Galatians) and highlighted by his acceptance of Gentile converts who did not have to comply with the usual proselyte requirements of Greek-speaking Judaism (as explained in Romans). This was difficult for traditional Jews to accept. Even some Jewish Jesus-believers would not soon forget how Paul once had persecuted Christ's disciples. Yes, he had been changed by his Damascus Road experience, but he had not been with Jesus from the beginning. These facts created ambivalence toward Paul's apostolic credentials, and sometimes overt hostility and opposition to his ministry.

If Paul were a true apostle, then who had sent him with an urgent and authoritative message for the Colossians? The sender is *God himself*. Paul is **an apostle of Christ Jesus by the will of God** (1:1). Here is an opening theological assumption of great magnitude. Jesus had told His disciples that they had not chosen Him, but He had chosen them (John

15:16). Paul docs not present himself as self-made or self-called, not ministering because of the political decision of some religious body or about to instruct the Colossians out of his own wisdom. The overriding realities are divine providence and grace. Paul presents himself as only what God had enabled him to be. He was being sent because God had a mission in mind and God's apostle had been graciously chosen as a humble instrument of that mission.

Where is a Christian to get dependable direction for living the life intended by God? John Wesley wisely pointed to "scriptural Christianity," believing that the "primitive church" of Paul's general time gained its guidance from divine revelation and the activity of the Holy Spirit within the community of believers. Paul knew himself to have been sent by God as part of the Spirit's ministry to congregations like Colosse.

Timothy is acknowledged as a valued coworker, **our brother** (1:1), who had been with Paul for much of his Ephesian ministry. Naming Timothy probably helped to answer the anticipated criticism that Paul was alone in his coming critique of the religious life of the Colossians. To the contrary, the concerns of Paul were of divine origin in line with the revelation in Jesus Christ. The reference in 1:2 to the Colossian congregation as **faithful brothers in Christ** expresses the desire that the close relationship enjoyed by Paul and Timothy be shared among Paul's readers—and hopefully between Paul and the Colossians.

Prison life likely put some constraints on Paul, who in turn may have chosen to rely on Timothy to function as the scribe of the Colossian letter (see Phil. 2:19). Note the letter's closing benediction, where Paul writes the final blessing **in my own hand** (4:18). The implication is that the rest of the letter was written by another hand, probably Timothy's. Jewish scribes often functioned as composing editors of what the revered teacher said. If this was the case here, it explains in part the differences in writing style and vocabulary between this letter and others of Paul's, supporting the judgment of the primary Pauline authorship of Colossians.

We learn from 1:1 that the essence of the Christian gospel is God's initiative, grace, summons, sending, and enablement. The reference is to **God our Father** (1:2). The **our** is significant when addressed to a congregation largely Gentile in background. A special relationship with God was traditionally claimed for Israel (Deut. 32:6; Isa. 63:16). This claim now is appropriated for Gentile believers in Jesus, the Jewish Messiah. By accepting the gospel of Christ, Paul's **our** implies that, given belief in Jesus the Christ, Gentiles were incorporated freely into Israel, the family of God, those who "belong to the family of believers" (Gal. 6:10). This was and still is really good news!

2. TWIN TRUTHS OF THE GOSPEL 1:2

Colossians 1:2 sets forth three sets of twin truths that round out the picture of the heart of the good news in Christ as it should be embraced by all believers, whether with Jewish background or not. They are: **holy** and **faithful**; in **Colosse** and **in Christ**; and **grace and peace**. These pairs of Christian truth elements are combined to yield what should be characteristic descriptions of basic Christian reality.

Paul greets the Colossians as a **holy** and **faithful** congregation (1:2). The concepts of holiness and faithfulness are rooted in the Hebrew Scriptures. Israel was God's holy people (Exod. 19:6), chosen, set apart, and commissioned by God for divine service. Such holiness was necessary and possible only because God is holy (Lev. 11:44; 19:2) and desires holiness of those chosen to be His people. The heart of holiness is the reign of love. In his sermon "On Zeal," John Wesley said, "In a Christian believer, love sits upon the throne which is erected in the inmost soul; namely, love of God and man, which fills the whole heart, and reigns without a rival."

To be holy (*hagios*) implies a quality of relationship with God that issues in conduct corresponding to that relationship. Persons committed to a God of absolute moral purity must reflect that purity. Christians are to be "saints" because of the cleansing reality of their relationship to God through Jesus Christ and in the power of Christ's Spirit. Together, such saints comprise the elect community of the end time, the age of the Spirit. They are to continue growing in their faithfulness.

The words *faith* and *faithful* in Paul's context tend to mean less the act of believing and more the resulting relationship with Christ that brings about a distinctive Christ identity in the believer. This relationship is distinguished from Judaism because it is fashioned by practices related to

Jesus the Christ and not by moral codes. In the Colossian context, there is a call for the believers to be (1) loyal to the truth when pressed by false-hood and (2) faithful to Jesus Christ, who alone should shape personal identity. The call of the Christian life is to be open to divine grace that wills and enables the flowering of a holy heart and life, that is, the mind of the Christ.

The phrase **in Christ** makes clear that God's grace positions the believing community to participate in the glorious results of the redemp-tive work of Jesus. Because Jesus lives, we, too, can live in the newness of resurrected life. Paul presents the twin facts that the Colossian believers were to be both **in Christ** and **in Colosse**. These two uses of **in** are sig-nificant for clarifying Christian identity in general and analyzing the troubling issue to be dealt with later in this letter. Believers are to be faithful in Jesus Christ and in their citizenship and witnesses in given loca-tions. To be in Colosse without being in Christ is to be without a vital message. To be in Christ but separated from "the world" of Colosse is also to fail in the Christian mission. The true believer in Jesus is to live in two spheres simultaneously. The Greek uses the same word (ἐν) for *in* Christ and *in* Colosse, even though the NIV translates the one "*at* Colosse."

To believe *in* is necessarily to speak *out*. The life of faith is to be both shaped by the resurrection reality of the Christ and related redemptively to the particular place of one's immediate witness and service. Christian belief is stable in its essential message and fluid in its forms of expres-sion and places of implementation. In the case of the Colossian believers, Paul was actively reaffirming the apostolic message. He was concerned, however, that the fluidity of local application in Colosse had gone too far, compromising the integrity of the message itself.

By stressing the **in Christ**, Paul reaffirms that believing "outsiders" (non-Jews) really do belong among God's chosen people. The decisive factor in determining the identity of God's people is no longer Temple loyalty or ethnic kinship, but oneness in Jesus. Contemporary Christians should be more accepting of each other on the basis of their common life in Christ, avoiding division because of human factors such as race, social class, and preferences of personality type, worship style, and the-ological trivia.

Christians are to be *of Christ* in character and will, *in the world* at a distinctive location, and living locally in a way that reflects and shares the Christ reality. Holiness that is not "social" lacks maturity and mission. Christ is not merely for inward experiencing, but for sharing with a world in desperate need. Paul had heard that the Colossians were being tempted to move their spirituality inward to a dangerous degree. Their religious orientation was tending toward a spiritual mysticism that disconnected them from their surrounding world in ways that derail discipleship and mission. Their philosophical speculation and religious experimentation were giving rise to a variety of attitudes and practices that were much too private and largely irrelevant to unbelievers in Colosse.

God's grace transforms the inner life of individuals. But, as Paul's letter will explain, it also intends to impact the more public arenas of life, including the social (3:5–14; 4:2–6), the family (3:18–4:1), and corporate worship (3:15–17). Too much of Christianity in North America today is focused on the myth of the self-sufficient individual who practices a private discipleship based on personal religious experiences. According to Paul, "a theology that makes the spiritual mutually exclusive of the material distorts the truth of the gospel and will contaminate its fruit (1:3–12). Foundational to both theological (2:4–15) and ethical (2:16–4:1) formation is the confession that Christ is Lord over both realms (1:15–20)."[1]

Finally, there is the beautiful doublet of **grace** and **peace** that come **from God our Father** (1:2). Grace (*charis*) denotes the unmerited favor of God, the essence of God's saving activity in Christ. Paul's message was the "gospel of God's grace" (Acts 20:24). This emphasis on grace in his opening salutation is

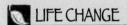

LIFE CHANGE

Too much of Christianity in North America today is focused on the myth of the self-sufficient individual who practices a private discipleship based on personal religious experiences and felt spiritual needs. In fact, believers need each other for help in better understanding of the faith, gaining resources for nurturing in the faith, and enabling maximum effectiveness in the church's mission. The church is not a convenience fellowship, but a spiritual necessity. Are you approaching your church involvement with the right attitudes? Remember that Jesus Christ is the sole Lord of individuals, churches, societies, and all things.

more than mere convention. For Paul, grace highlights the core theology of his entire Gentile mission and stands in sharp contrast to the alternatives swirling around the Colossians and throughout the Roman world of the time. Salvation is seen here as a work of divine grace. God elects a people (3:11–12), sends Jesus (1:15–20), leads people on a new exodus from sin (1:13–14), and calls apostles to spread the good word (1:24–2:5). All of this is so that, in Christ, even Gentiles can triumph over evil (1:21–22).

Presented throughout Colossians is great news about the sheer grace of God that inspires and empowers holy and faithful lives. Salvation is *a free gift*. As opposed to the mentality of ruling elites, civic and religious, God's salvation is offered to those with no moral merit, social status, or political clout. It is truly universal, really free—amazing! Teaching that presses believers to practice various disciplines to increase God's favor toward them is a serious diversion from the true gospel of grace. This is especially true if such disciplines are thought of as mandatory and possible only for a limited number of properly initiated people.

The dual greeting of **grace and peace** is traditional in Pauline prayers (1 Thess. 1:1; 1 Cor. 1:3; Gal. 1:3). The effect of receiving divine grace is wonderful peace, wholeness, and harmony as the new order of Christ yields healing and unity according to the Creator's plan. Peace (*eirene*), like the Hebrew greeting *shalom*, is not an idealizing of the absence of conflict. Among the Jews, accustomed to persecution, peaceful well being denoted wholeness and good relations, including social wholeness and harmony even in conflict (Ps. 72:1–7). The source of such peace is God alone. In the Colossian setting, the immediate focus probably was on spiritual health since it was a faith community where personal and corporate tensions were threatening harmony.

3. REASONS FOR TRUE THANKSGIVING 1:3–8

The thanksgiving prayer found in 1:3–8 is based on the condition of the Colossian church. It reads "we" rather than "I" give thanks, probably allowing for the inclusion of at least Timothy. The tone is in marked contrast to the Galatian correspondence where the crisis at hand called for abrupt language and immediate action. Even though the problem in Colosse was significant, there was no urgency about confronting it until after the writer had shared his joy and laid some groundwork for the needed correction.

Paul's prayer is one of sincere thanksgiving for the Colossians despite his deep concern. These believers had expressed true faith and faithfulness in many ways. The news that had reached Paul was heartwarming. Paul pays tribute to their faith, love, and hope. This threefold reality of God's grace sums up what Epaphras had relayed to Paul in prison and suggests Paul's view that these three form what is essential for authentic Christian experience (compare 1 Cor. 13).

Love (*agape*) often carries an article with it in Paul's writing (literally, "*the* love"). This makes his concept of love definitive and concrete, not an abstract moral idea, but a transforming reality, faith in motion (Gal. 5:6). God's love was seen in Christ's death. In grateful response, it was reported to Paul that the Colossians' love was being acted out **for all the saints** (1:4). It then follows that the believing community's shared faith and mutual love, being graciously acted out toward each other, results in a common *hope* for God's coming grace that finally will resolve all evil, answer all questions, and fulfill all divine promises. What will be should already be begun among the saints—obviously, concretely, relationally begun.

Our present experiences of God's salvation are real but limited. Our love, wonderful as it is, remains imperfect; and our faith, reassuring as it can be, is nonetheless incomplete (1 Cor. 13:10–12). But there is a future where the fullness of love and the finality of faith are assured. There always is hope because there always is God.

The thanksgiving of Paul is addressed to God, recognizing that God is finally responsible for all the virtues, spiritual fruit, and ultimate success of the gospel mission in the world. The God to whom Paul prayed and gave thanks is the God made known in Jesus Christ, the one whose character is a loving and saving **Father**. The high view of Jesus Christ (Christology) to be addressed shortly in the letter is to be kept within the strict constraints of Jewish monotheism. Jesus taught His disciples to pray, beginning with "Our Father . . ." (Matt. 6:9). The divine Father is in such intimate relationship with the Son that Jesus Christ himself was held to be Lord (*kyrios*), with all the connotations that term carried when the Jews referred to God as Yahweh (compare Rom. 10:13; Phil. 2:11).

The Colossians already had heard **the word of truth** (1:5). This phrase echoes the Hebrew prophets who proclaimed "the word of the Lord" (Ezek. 1:3; Dan. 9:2; Joel 1:1; Micah 1:1; Zeph. 1:1; Hag. 1:1; Zach. 1:1; Mal. 1:1), the source of which was God. This divine word can be trusted because God is the truth. This emphasis on divine revelation anticipates Paul's coming argument against the Colossian "philosopher" who is bringing a word of falsehood based on human speculation rather than divine revelation.

Colossians 1:4–8 detail the occasion and ground of Paul's thanksgiving. Three things are reported, the first being the good report to Paul about the Colossian Christians. Paul had **heard** (1:4) about the progress of the Colossian believers, further suggesting that he had not visited the congregation personally (1:9; 2:1). What he wanted to emphasize now was that the gospel of Christ they had received is the sole source of the Christian hope. His own hope had been reassured on hearing that the Colossians were fulfilling the two key aspects of the Christian faith, namely, faith in Jesus Christ and love for others in Christ's name.

Jesus himself had said that the burden of the law and prophets and the proper summation of the Ten Commandments come down to two basic things: love for God and neighbor (Matt. 22:37–39). The Christian must know and believe the message about the Christ and place this knowledge and belief into loving, relating, and reconciling action. The Colossians were doing these two essential things, and thus Paul rejoiced.

Paul further rejoiced in the progress of the gospel of Christ in the world. This gospel had evidenced fruit-bearing power wherever it had been preached. Surely a mark of the gospel's authenticity is the fact of its life-changing influence on believing recipients. The references to **bearing fruit** and **growing** (1:6) speak both of the inner working and outward extension of Christ's gospel. The tense of both verbs is present, suggesting action that is continuing. Paul is truly grateful for this: The gospel of Christ had taken root in the lives of his readers and was producing among them good deeds consistent with the saving message. It also was attracting an increasing number of believers in widening circles of witness.

The second thing Paul reports as a cause for his thanksgiving is that the gospel conveys the knowledge of **God's grace in all its truth** (1:6). He prefaces the rest of his letter by hinting that the competing "gospel" recently introduced to the Colossians by new teachers is a dangerous diversion. The gospel of Jesus, and only this gospel, is available to all and can make the needed difference for all. It is the way of grace, featuring less what we humans must do for our salvation and more what God already has done for us. Rather than a message of divine grace, what was being confronted by Paul in Colosse was more a developing system of human traditions leading to a legalistic bondage and eventually to a failed faith and aborted mission.

The emphasis on divine grace and its power to change lives implies the corresponding fact that there must be a faithful human channel through whom God's good news can be communicated. Thus, the third thing for which Paul is thankful is that the Colossians initially had been privileged to have a trustworthy teacher, Epaphras, who had brought to them the true gospel of the life-changing grace of God in Jesus Christ. Known only in a few brief references (1:7; 4:12–13; Philem. 23), Epaphras was a native of Colosse who had ministered faithfully there and in nearby Laodicea and Hierapolis.

Epaphras was Paul's **dear fellow servant, . . . a faithful minister of Christ on our behalf** (1:7). Likely, he was a convert of Paul's ministry in Ephesus, established the gospel work in Colosse, had been imprisoned (during which theological opponents may have taken control from him in Colosse), and now had brought the report to Paul that occasioned the present letter. Epaphras is an example of what Paul desires for all believers: a life filled with the fruit that should follow a faithful hearing and receiving of God's word. Even so, the readers of Paul's letter had begun to fail in the central goal of incarnating their faith in practical ways. They now were exchanging the **word of truth** (1:5) for **fine-sounding arguments** (2:4) that were rooted in a **hollow and deceptive philosophy** (2:8).

Congregations of Christians must have reliable leaders who themselves embody the spiritual lives they encourage in others. A failure of leadership is a disastrous failure indeed, something suffered too often in the contemporary church. Education for inspired church leadership is crucial, although not enough. Effective preaching and informed teaching may either function as God's true instruments or tickle people's ears and lead them astray.

The final phrase of Paul's thanksgiving are the words **in the Spirit** (1:8). This is the only place in the Colossian letter where the Holy Spirit is mentioned explicitly, although the immediacy and importance of this divine reality are assumed everywhere. The Colossian believers had a real love for spiritual things, a love that, when commonly experienced **in the Spirit**, brings unity among believers, insight into truth, and effectiveness in church mission. The love among believers that properly reflects the love of God as seen in Jesus can be inspired and maintained only by the Spirit of God. True love and right teaching are Spirit enabled (Rom. 2:29; 1 Cor. 14:16; 1 Thess. 1:5).

The church is to be a place where the Spirit reigns, cleansing sin and liberating from sin's power and consequences. Faith is God's way into Jesus Christ. Once in Christ, the Spirit provides believers with the resources needed for faithful, thankful, and Christlike growing and living. To be the true church requires rich life in the Spirit of God.

ENDNOTE

1. Robert W. Wall, *Colossians and Philemon*, The IVP New Testament Commentary Series (Downers Grove, Ill.: InterVarsity Press, 1993), 28.

2

THE PRIME PURPOSES OF PRAYER

Colossians 1:9–14

To the warm greetings and heartfelt thanksgivings already extended to the Colossian believers (1:1–8), Paul, the apostle sent to this people of God yet a prisoner in Rome, now adds his prayer and petitions to God on their behalf. **Since the day we heard about you** (1:9) refers to when the news about the Colossians came to Paul from Epaphras. Clearly, the intercessions in this prayer are in light of what Paul now knew of the Colossian situation.

We are wise to study the content of the prayer of a spiritually mature Christian. Paul offers an important opportunity for us to sample the prime purposes of Christian prayer. These purposes are appropriate for prayer that is offered at any time and in any circumstance.

1. TEACHING IN A CONTEXT OF WORSHIP 1:9A

Significant and sometimes stern theological and ethical instruction will be given to the Colossians later in the letter, but first Paul's intent is to establish a context of worship. Teaching about spiritual things proceeds best when enveloped in an ethos of worship—thanksgiving, praise, and prayer directed to a sovereign and loving God. The concerns of Paul are preceded by a warm pastoral affirmation of the readers and sincere intercession for their spiritual growth (1:9–11).

Paul's prayer assumes a certain spiritual immaturity remaining among the Colossian believers that was causing difficulty in their discerning what is important to believe and what practices are appropriate for Christian disciples. He prays first that the Colossians may be filled with the knowledge of God's will (1:9) that they will be enabled to live worthy of their Lord, pleasing Him in everything (1:10). Then he asks God that, in all their growing knowledge and proper doing, the Colossians may be blessed with endurance, patience, and joy.

This prayer is more than devotional musings independent of the rest of the letter. Knowing God rightly in Jesus Christ should yield an active spiritual life that grows in obedience to God and is guarded from error by its focus on the full adequacy of Jesus Christ for human salvation. Obedience to God and focus on Christ constitute the logical basis for the coming admonitions to be offered by Paul to the Colossians.

Two basic requests are to be set before a gracious God on a regular basis. The first is that discernment be given to the one praying so that God's will can be understood properly. The second is that God may grant the power necessary to perform that divine will, accomplish the proper goal, run the right race, achieve the intended prize, and serve well and with the right attitudes in the assigned tasks of Christian ministry.

Hearing God's word and receiving it in faith is a necessary beginning. However, in order to resist the inevitable pressures of false teaching and wrong acting, a believer needs to grow in Christ under the sure guidance of the Spirit and at the hands of dependable teachers like Epaphras. The progress of Christian spiritual formation follows rebirth with retraining. To be born and not grow is the leading edge of death. Rebirth and spiritual growth, nurtured by God's Spirit, launch the intended life of holiness.

Growth is rarely an accident; intentionality is required. For instance, the Wesleyan revival in eighteenth-century England was aided greatly by the organizational and discipling skills of John Wesley. For him, new life in the Spirit necessarily called for nurturing the new life with personal discipline, community support, and clear accountability. The centerpiece of his plan was the "class meeting." The genius of the Wesleyan revival was "an instructional tool [the class meeting], more so than a theological distinctive or an organizational structure."[1] Wesley had confidence in the church practices that were divinely instituted as "means of grace" to promote spiritual growth: communion, baptism, Bible reading, prayer, preaching, and confession. He added to this list some "prudential means," such as the class meeting, that he believed would promote progressive growth if believers would "partake" of them seriously and regularly. These means put people in touch with the dynamic power of God's sustaining and maturing grace.

Beyond the question of means is the critical question of right goals for growth. How can true spiritual growth be described and measured? For what should believers pray and plan? Paul identifies three aspects basic to the Christian maturing process. He tells the Colossians that Christians are (1) to be filled with knowledge of God's will, (2) to live in ways worthy of the Lord, and (3) to be blessed with endurance, patience, and joy. All of this is to be marked by a crowning Christian virtue, gratitude to God for the blessings of redemption (1:12–14).

2. BE FILLED WITH KNOWLEDGE 1:9B

Prayer is the daily spiritual breathing that sustains one's life in Christ. If Christian faith is lived in relationship with God through Jesus Christ, then prayer is the key to maintaining this relationship. In Colossians, stress falls on the need for believers to grow in the knowledge that reflects genuine spiritual wisdom (1:9–10). This letter contrasts the true source of such wisdom (1:27–28; 2:2–3; 3:10, 16) with the new "philosophy" that had only the appearance of true wisdom (2:23).

The writer to the Hebrews warns believers against being comfortable with a rudimentary understanding of "the elementary truths of God's word" and sets forward the goal of a more mature wisdom that is able to "distinguish good from evil" (Heb. 5:12, 14). Consequently, proper Christian prayer should be listening for knowledge of God's will. Learning comes in two basic ways for believers, according to Paul. Often in his prison letters, including Colossians, he uses the Greek word *epignosis* for the knowledge gained through personal experience, knowledge that truly penetrates and grasps something beyond the surface level. He also uses *gnosis*, the type of knowledge that tends to focus on theory, theological abstraction, and mystical contemplation, even on speculative philosophy. Ideally, the heart and mind are companion avenues to spiritual insight.

If one believes that God's purposes actively determine the ordering of the world and that the Christian life is to be a participation in the fulfillment of these purposes, then every believer is to gain knowledge of God's will to whatever degree possible. This goal is Jewish in character (Ps. 40:8; 143:10) and was shared by Jesus (Matt. 6:10; 7:21) and the first Christians (Acts 21:14; Eph. 5:17, 6:6). Paul stresses knowing through personal transformation (Rom. 12:2) and walking in accord with the Spirit (Rom. 8:4, 13–14; Gal. 5:16, 18, 25).

Wisdom can be an illusive thing. While the Colossians thought that they already had it, Paul begins to lay the groundwork for questioning their supposed attainment—what they thought was deep spiritual wisdom was, in fact, only deceptive speculation. Paul prayed for true spiritual wisdom and understanding. If *wisdom* is the Greek *sophia*, knowledge of fundamental principles, right orientations to reality as a whole, then *understanding* is *sunesis*, knowledge of how to implement *sophia* in the many circumstances that arise in daily life. Being, knowing, and doing are not to be separated.

Understanding the theological foundations of Christian faith is one thing, but equally significant is the will and practical know-how needed to apply the foundations to the facts and demands of life. Knowing God's will must lead to right conduct. Prayer is to be a practical activity and not a mystical escape from some harsh reality. We pray not because we need to escape life, but to be better able to meet it redemptively with the wisdom and power of God.

3. LIVING WORTHY OF THE LORD 1:10A

Jesus declared, "I am the bread of life. He who comes to me will never go hungry, and he who believes in me will never be thirsty" (John 6:35). He also said, "I have come that they may have life, and have it to the full" (John 10:10). Given this wonderful spiritual resource for believers, why is it so rarely reflected in the lives of Christians and their churches? John Wesley tended to believe that it was because believers seldom feast on the bread of life and have not yet given themselves over completely to God in Christ. To live worthy of the Lord requires living *in Christ* by the wisdom and power of Christ's Spirit.

In the Hebrew Scriptures, wisdom frequently focuses on practical knowledge, the crucial ability to choose right conduct. For the Colossians, Paul prays for insight from the Spirit that has obvious ethical content. Knowledge of the divine will is not an end in itself. The intended result of knowing is *doing*, engaging in conduct truly reflective of what comes to be known. The power requested from God is not to be employed for its own sake or for any wonder-working show that enjoys a large television audience and massive income. The power of the Spirit is for the mission of the Spirit.

The essence of living in a way worthy of the Lord was exemplified for the Colossian believers by Epaphras. Central to what is truly worthy is the process of **bearing fruit in every good work** (1:10). Paul prays that the Colossians may

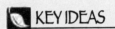

KEY IDEAS

The power requested from God is not to be employed for its own sake or for any wonder-working show that enjoys a large television audience and massive income. The power of the Spirit is for the mission of the Spirit. All spiritual gifts are given by God for the well being of the church. In turn, the multi-gifted church exists in part for the well being of each member. The church is the body of Christ—who is Lord of all!

be **strengthened with all power** (1:11). The God who shares the content of the divine will for our living also is prepared to grant the ability to do what becomes known. The believer's present experience of the Spirit's transforming power is a taste of the world to come and a motivation to do God's will on earth as it is done in heaven. Once the reign of God in Christ is realized in the present, it then comes down to the believer's will, the determination to actually do on earth as God designs in heaven and now enables on earth.

The intense rhetoric of the sixteenth-century Protestant Reformation was focused against any merit for salvation being gained from human "good works." Likewise, Paul's commendatory reference to **bearing fruit in every good work** (1:10) is not a call to gain merit from the work; it is an insistence that salvation grace necessarily should lead to a responsible salvation life. There were those in Colosse who were living worthy of the Lord. The gospel was yielding fruit in and through them (1:3–6). Even the church in that relatively small and insignificant city was experiencing the privilege of participating in the worldwide work of God—with the evidence visible for all to see.

Paul's theology is influenced strongly by the Old Testament concept of a covenant that binds together a gracious God and a grateful people (see Rom. 9–11). Each of the covenant partners has a vital responsibility for the successful maintenance of the agreement. For the Christian, the potential of the new covenant in Christ's blood is the initial, unilateral, unconditioned act of God in Christ. But Paul retains the fullness of the biblical pattern. Ancient Israel's actual participation in the salvation provided by God—the divine side of the covenant—depended on Israel's response to God. There are conditions to be met, "good works" to be done (Rom. 2:5–11; Phil. 1:6; 2 Thess. 2:17). All "works," of course, are the result of divine grace and never substitute for it. When the divine-human covenant is active and effective, salvation is secured by grace and accompanied by the expected fruit of that grace.

Salvation is by faith alone in response to God's grace, but saving faith is never alone. There is the "obedience of faith" issuing in good works. Colossians stresses the bearing of good fruit (1:9–10) that is to include fairness and justice (4:1). Such fruit-bearing will have positive spiritual side effects for the faithful believer. Growth will occur in the ability to endure with patience and joy.

4. BLESSED WITH ENDURANCE, PATIENCE, AND JOY 1:10B–11

Paul already has spoken of faith, hope, and love, the ideal characteristics of true Christianity. Now he identifies a trio of characteristics of Christian maturity that are necessary to overcome the conflicts of spiritual adolescence that stand in the way of realizing the ideal of life worthy of the Lord Jesus. The spiritual life that reflects the working of God's "glorious might" is to be characterized by endurance, patience, and joy. These are fruit of the Spirit's presence and working, evidences that persons have entered the new age of the Spirit (Gal. 5:21–22). Such persons are characterized by their **giving thanks to the Father** (1:12a), an activity likely in short supply among the Colossian believers following the "philosophy" that required them to practice severe ascetic regulations.

Endurance is more than the ability merely to survive. Life brings some severe storms, but those matured in Christ through the Spirit manage to triumph, being aware that in all things God is at work for good alongside those who truly love Him (Rom. 8:28). Positive results may not appear immediately, but God nonetheless is known to be at work and the potential of genuine good is always real. Once a wise pastor laid his hands on a frustrated younger colleague in ministry and prayed, "Lord, deliver him from the sin of immediate results!" When believers learn to see glory being wrenched from negative circumstances, the presence of love, faith, and hope yields the patience necessary to relate redemptively to people who are rude, thoughtless, mean, or worse.

Paul prays that no circumstance will overwhelm a believer's strength to deal redemptively with any situation. No person should be allowed to deflate a believer's preparedness to love. Even more, the goal is that the Christian will love with a sense of joy, salvaging good from evil and singing even while going the extra mile with an enemy. Paul prays that three things ought to be on the lips of every Christian: "Make me, O Lord, victorious over every circumstance; make me patient with every person; and give me the joy which no circumstance and no man will ever take from me."[2]

As this prayer to the Spirit is answered more and more, the humble believer matures spiritually, growing from strength to strength, blessing to blessing. The prayer is for the power needed to endure with patience and joy (1:11). This power is the ability to endure hardship with grace because of the strength gained from divine grace. Paul's prayer for knowledge, wisdom, fruitful good works, and patient fortitude is to be bathed in the experience of thankful joy.

All Christian graces are interdependent and can be sustained only by a joyful honoring of God. Such joy is characteristic of all sound thinking and acting (Rom. 1:21). Christian consciousness is to feature "charismatic" and "eschatological" elements. The first is life filled with awareness of the immediacy of the Spirit's presence and working, providing strength, wisdom, direction, and motivation for Christlike living. The second is life pulsing with the knowledge that God's will is being worked out, divine destiny is being fulfilled, and the renewal of the Spirit anticipated by the prophets of old is truly close at hand. The natural result is grateful joy, as was seen among the first Christians (Acts 2:46; Phil. 4:4–6; 1 Thess. 5:16–18). The outcome of this wonderful maturing process, this advancing Christian consciousness and character, is growing gratitude.

5. GRATITUDE: A CROWNING VIRTUE 1:12–14

As believers find themselves strengthened by God's might to face the dilemmas of life with endurance, patience, and love, they find themselves joyfully giving thanks to the Father who alone has qualified them **to share in the inheritance of the saints in the kingdom of light** (1:12; see 1 Peter 2:9). The deliberate contrast between **dominion of darkness** (1:13) and **kingdom of light** (1:12) announces gratefully that "the sphere over which the Son rules is to be seen as being bathed in the splendor and holiness of the divine radiance."[3] Paul repeats his confession that God is **Father**, thereby reassuring his readers that they are fully understood by God and can be forgiven by the God who reigns supreme, cares deeply for them, and is anxious to cloth them in the light of Christ's gracious reign.

The Father is the God of loving grace, the reaching, relating, redeeming God. Thanksgiving for God's amazing grace is the foundation for prayer and the hope of restoration from whatever failures of thinking and acting were troubling the Colossians and are troubling any of us now. Too often today's "evangelical" Christians are taught that God is "perfect" in the sense that God is unchanging, unaffected by humans, and is directing all events in fully controlled detail. Of course, God is *unchanging* in existence, character, and purposes, but God also grants freedom of choice to us humans, acts responsively as we choose, and is not responsible for all the evil in the world caused by our wrong choices. Rather than standing at a safe distance, God chooses to come close, share our pain, and offer a way out. The cross of Jesus is a prime example of the gracious coming of God.

Well-known theologian Clark H. Pinnock did not grow up in a Wesleyan tradition, but now reports that he was "inexorably drawn to John Wesley." The centerpiece of the attraction was Wesley's vision of God as "loving and personal, relational and triune." Wesley "could not imagine that God as a

278

loving Father would withhold redemptive help from any of his children. His theology was thoroughly relational—to know God is to live in a personal relationship with Him. Since relations cannot be coerced, the grace of God cannot be irresistible. God is wise and loving and not merely powerful."[4] The Bible presents God as actively compassionate, intentionally involved in the historical journey of creation, and specifically reactive to human decisions.

To share in the inheritance of the saints (1:12) is a transition from Paul's earlier prayer and thanksgiving to the heavy theological burden he is about to address. Such sharing and inheriting were both the basis for profound gratitude and part of the arena in which the Colossians were threatened by false thought and practice. On the positive side, readers are encouraged to recall the formative story of the Hebrew bondage in which God called forth an enslaved people from Egypt and gave them entrance into a glorious promised land. To occupy this land was reassurance to them that God makes and keeps great promises. Now, in Christ, Paul is announcing that God has done it again. He has brought the **saints** from the slavery of sin and darkness into the promised **kingdom of light** (see Acts 26:18). God's chosen people again are led to their promised kingdom by divine grace where the Father graciously qualifies them for entrance into the fullness of the promise.

In Christ, the new exodus of the true Israel has occurred and God's people have entered their promised land, receiving the good gifts of their Lord and Savior. What joy! What cause for gratitude! Paul is saying to the Colossians that God already has qualified them for entrance into eternal life both now and hereafter. It is a matter of divine grace through Jesus Christ, not a matter, as some in Colosse were insisting, of fasting, worship of angels, or visionary spiritual experiences. God alone qualifies a believer by the amazing and unmerited grace found in Jesus Christ. Salvation depends fully on the work of Christ, not on our human feelings and works.

In ourselves as humans there is no fitness for entrance into the ranks of God's chosen people. Becoming qualified comes only as a privilege given by a loving Heavenly Father. Gaining the inheritance of full citizens of the **kingdom of light** (1:12) affirms that believers in Jesus Christ, whether Gentile or Jew, are already rescued from the dominion of darkness and even now are dwelling by grace in the kingdom of God's own Son (compare John 3:35). God's saving action (the **has rescued** of 1:13) suggests that the defeat of the demonic powers and the church's entrance into God's kingdom of light have already taken place.

Believers, by divine grace alone, have been brought into the kingdom of God's Son, much like the pattern in the ancient world in which a conquering empire moved the defeated people en masse to the conqueror's land (recall Israel's Northern Kingdom deported to Assyria and then the Southern Kingdom to Babylon). Given this glorious reality of transfer to God's land, being rescued by Christ's victory, and not being penalized for military defeat, gratitude should well up—especially among the non-Jewish Colossians who had no claim to status as God's people prior to the wonderful work of God in Christ.

God has triumphed, and God's people are invited to the victory party that is continuous under the ongoing reign of Christ. Personal sin has found its adequate answer. Its dominion is broken. Conversion into the new age of the Spirit is real and has observable results in the world outside the inner self. An emphasis on this by Paul is intended as a crucial corrective to the false teachers in Colosse who were insisting that the key means of divine grace were heavenly visions (2:18) and earthly asceticism (2:20–23), as though real conversion should shut one off from the present material world rather than sending one into it with really good news.

Sin remains persistent in the world, to be sure. Sinful humanity is easily seduced by

 **LIFE CHANGE**

Asceticism is the discipline employed to deepen one's spiritual life. Jesus said, "If anyone would come after me, he must deny himself and take up his cross daily and follow me" (Luke 9:23). What discipline should you begin that would enhance your own relationship to Jesus and His body, the church? Might it be

- Turning off the television and spending quality time with children?

- Taking better control of your eating and sleeping habits?

- Rethinking long-term financial planning, with the church in mind?

- Opening your Bible and actually reading it regularly and prayerfully?

the fictions of the surrounding secular order. The world routinely promises that good things will result from individual effort, especially when aided by technological advancement and a military superiority that supposedly assures national sovereignty and economic prosperity. But such secular lies have been exposed for the frauds they are. In fact, we humans often feel overwhelmed, thinking we have no real control of our lives that are seemingly determined by heredity and social forces that just wash over us. But Paul says, "No!" In fact, we who believe in Jesus Christ have been delivered into a kingdom of light, a realm of real freedom. We have access to the power of Christ to live against the tides of determinism. As "saints of light," we know that the darkness will never prevail (John 1:4–5).

Relationship with God now can be restored; the slaves of sin can be freed; spiritual sickness unto death can be healed. There is **redemption . . . forgiveness**, and true hope in the Son (1:14). Victory once hung on an old rugged cross and then exited a cold tomb in dramatic resurrection so that even death has now died. Christ reigns supreme. We are to rejoice with overflowing gratitude, praying and living accordingly. We **share in the inheritance of the saints in the kingdom of light** (1:12). Sin is no longer to hold sway in our lives. Even now, Jesus Christ is Lord!

ENDNOTES

1. D. Michael Henderson, *John Wesley's Class Meeting* (Nappanee, Ind.: Evangel, 1997), p. 15.

2. William Barclay, *The Letters to the Philippians, Colossians, and Thessalonians* (Philadelphia: Westminster Press, rev. ed. 1975), p. 110.

3. Andrew T. Lincoln, *The Letter to the Colossians*, The New Interpreter's Bible, vol. 11 (Nashville, Tenn.: Abingdon Press, 2000), p. 596.

4. Clark H. Pinnock, "The Beauty of God: John Wesley's Reform and Its Aftermath," *Wesleyan Theological Journal* (38:2, Fall 2003), pp. 57, 62.

Part Two

The Supremacy of Jesus Christ

COLOSSIANS 1:15–23

3

THE SCOPE OF CHRIST'S SUPREMACY

Colossians 1:15-18

1. RENEWING THE ORIGINAL TEACHING

The Christian gospel is the proclamation of the event of the coming of Jesus Christ. He is the full and final revelation of both God and true humanity. The task of Paul in Galatians and Romans is to insist on the central importance of Jesus Christ for our salvation. Now, in the face of an evolving Colossian heresy, Paul finds it necessary also to affirm vigorously the cosmic status and significance of Christ. He soars in eloquence as he speaks of the all-sufficient Christ.

In Christian belief as biblically defined, Jesus Christ is that lone, unprecedented, and amazing point where the divine and human intersect, where the otherness and wonder of the divine are linked with God's loving and redeeming immediacy. The "ground of existence bears a human face—that of Jesus Christ."[1] Nothing is more central than this confession in identifying the true nature of Christian faith. The Colossians needed to hear this again—and so does the church of today.

"Orthodoxy" is the deposit of truth that the Christian community, in its corporate wisdom and under God's guidance, has determined is accurate, apostolic, and biblical teaching. Deviations from this teaching certainly are tempting and common, but they are unacceptable if one is to be faithful to the authority of divine revelation. Without doubt, at least in Paul's view, the Colossian believers were being confronted with a dangerous and quite unorthodox teaching. It was time for them to realize anew the riches of the apostolic faith.

Although at the writing of the Colossian letter there had not been sufficient time for an orthodox tradition to be established, at least its base—the original proclamation of the first apostles—was clear enough. The Colossian congregation, so it had been reported to Paul, was facing some **fine-sounding arguments** (2:4) concerning a **dominion of darkness** (1:13) from which they needed rescued. This deviant teaching called for a limitation of the scope of Christ's supremacy.

In studying verses 15–18 of chapter 1, it is vital that this divergent teaching be kept in mind. Of primary concern was the fact that the false teachers in Colosse were urging Christians to pay close attention to and maybe even worship certain principalities and powers, "the powers of this dark world" (Eph. 6:12), in order to advance in their Christian faith and life.

The most dangerous aspect of this heresy was its obvious devaluing of the person and role of Jesus Christ in the process of human salvation. Rather than being the triumphant Redeemer who holds all authority in heaven and on earth, Jesus Christ was being presented as only one of many spirit beings bridging the gap between God and humanity. In vigorous response, Paul makes three claims about the expansive scope of the complete and sole supremacy of Christ.

Before examining these three stunning claims about Jesus Christ, note that Colossians 1:15–20 functions as an effective part of Paul's overall strategy for addressing the believers in Colosse. He had begun this letter with thanksgiving and prayer and now continues with praise to Christ in a moving context of worship. Paul seems to quote elements of a previous hymn, evoking cherished memory and instincts of adoration.[2] This approach encourages the readers to be open to accepting the subsequent message founded on the hymn's perspective. The first of Paul's three great claims about Jesus Christ centers in the relation of Jesus to deity.

2. THE RELATION OF JESUS TO DEITY 1:15A

A danger faced by early Christians was the attempt by some to "improve" the faith by observing that it was not adequately rigid, effective, or exciting enough. Maybe more disciplined respect should be shown to the mysterious forces that were thought to have governing roles in relation to human life. Two ways chosen by some teachers to make Christianity more attractive to the religious highbrows of the time were *pagan asceticism*, designed to conquer the flesh, and *Jewish ritual observance*, designed to train the soul in humility and obedience. This was an attempt to blend Christ into a composite religion, a tendency that provoked Paul to his most comprehensive statement of the singular significance of Jesus the Christ.

The cosmic scope of Christ's supremacy is clarified in 1:13–23. Here is painted in broad strokes the spiritual journey of God's redeemed people from their first call from God to the final consummation. Verses 13–15 highlight the beginning of the journey when we repentant humans experience conversion from darkness and death to the kingdom of the Son. Verses 15–20 then focus on Christ's current lordship over creation in general and over the new creation, the church, in particular. Finally, verses 21–23 point to the future and radiate hope about the eventual consequences of our reconciliation to God through Christ.

Colossians 1:15–21 appear to contain elements of an early Christian hymn sung in praise of Christ and couched in language commonly used by many Jews and referring to divine wisdom. The hymn likely was familiar to the Christians in Colosse. Paul subtly reintroduces fragments of the original lyrics. There appear to be two verses (strophes) being used by Paul. Verse 1 focuses on Jesus' relation to God and the creation (1:15–18a); verse 2 deals with Jesus' relation to human salvation (1:18b–20). Here is one reconstruction of the verses:

1. He is *the image* of the invisible God,
   the *firstborn* of all creation;
   for *in him* all things were created . . .
2. He is *the beginning*,
   the *firstborn* from the dead . . .
   for *in him* all the fullness of God
   was pleased to dwell . . .

For Christians at such an early stage of the faith's tradition, to use such elevated language about Jesus Christ suggests an intellectual vitality already being employed in the service of communicating to wider audiences the significance of the Hebrew Christ. Such evangelistic and apologetic mission service was not an intellectual activity created in isolated ivory towers, but was sung in settings of instruction and worship. To feature this hymn so early in the Colossian letter probably means that Paul (and Timothy) judged that the preeminence of Christ in creation and redemption needed to be stressed again for these readers. Such preeminence was an essential "orthodoxy" grounding the integrity of Christian faith.

Some readers in Colosse apparently were inclined toward divergent thinking and religious practices. Paul was clear and unrelenting. Echoing perspectives also seen in John 1:1–14, he insists that Jesus Christ is none other than God now becoming human for our salvation. This Christ is the creative purpose that initially shaped all creation, remains supreme over all its orders of being, and is the unifying principle that underlies the whole cosmos and continues to hold it together. In short, Christ is the visible expression of the invisible God (1:15). To know the heart of God, look at Jesus (John 14:9).

 GREAT THEMES

Who Christ Is

Christ is the creative purpose that initially shaped all creation. Christ is the visible expression of the invisible God. Christ is the Alpha and Omega (Rev. 22:13), the full alphabet of past, present, and future reality. Nothing greater can be conceived and nothing less is adequate Christian belief.

According to Paul, the keynote of the Christian gospel is that Jesus has a unique relationship with God. The strict monotheism of Jewish tradition is not to be violated; even so, a dramatic new reality has come about, one that soon would have Christian theologians talking seriously about the "Trinity" of God—a *multiplicity* in relation to the *one* God. Speaking adequately about God necessarily involves reference to divine revelation in the Son as now illumined for us by the Spirit.

Paul's letters consistently highlight Jesus as the Son of God (Rom. 1:3; Eph. 1:3; Col. 1:3). Our concern with the nature of the Godhead should not be abstract curiosity. The creation now is in turmoil and needs a Savior. Like the classic Christian creeds, John Wesley focused on the second and third Persons of the Trinity in order to address the twofold need of alienated humanity. In Christ we are graciously reconciled to God (justified); by the Spirit of the Christ we are graciously gifted and empowered to become what God intends (sanctified). Anything short of this grand picture is seriously shortsighted.

In Paul's three affirmations concerning the supremacy of Jesus Christ, there are echoes of earlier confessions of faith, and probably hymns of faith familiar to the Colossians. These memories, Paul hoped, would encourage these believers to rethink their current circumstance and reaffirm Paul's perspective as their own. His perspective centered in two grand convictions about the absolute supremacy of the lordship of Jesus Christ. They are each highlighted with the pronoun "he" and the linking verb "is." **He is the image of the invisible God, the firstborn over all creation** (1:15) and *he is* the **beginning and the firstborn from among the dead** (1:18).

The teaching opponents of Paul in Colosse were saying that Jesus was only a partial revelation of God, one among many intermediaries between God and humans. Pauline opposers were saying all matter is evil. If Jesus actually were the Son of God, then surely Jesus could not have dwelled in the filth of human flesh. He must have been an "emanation" from God, one of the gradations of angels, implying that He had not lived as a real man, His suffering on the cross had not been literally real, and there was no point in anyone teaching about a "resurrection" because Jesus had never really lived and died as a material being. But Paul judged such thinking a great threat to the integrity of the Christian gospel.

Since God is **invisible**, how can one gain informed access to this higher world of the Spirit? The answer given by Paul is an image that bridges the large gulf between God and creation and enables human knowing of what is not knowable apart from divine revelation. The power of God was expressed in the metaphor of wisdom, through which creation itself came into being. It now has been seen embodied in Jesus Christ and clarified in the light of his cross and resurrection (1:18, 20). The image (*eikon*) of the invisible God probably reflects a popular philosophic thought of Paul's time. Creation was said to be the visible expression of the invisible, the material realization of the eternal and spiritual.

A present image helps us understand properly what otherwise would be beyond our limited ability. Paul describes Jesus as the incarnated substance of the divine reality. Jesus makes the redemptive heart of God concrete and knowable. There could be two concepts of "imaging," one a mere *representation* of the reality in question and the other a *full manifestation* of it. The image could symbolize its reference point or actually be that point. Jesus is the *perfect manifestation* of God to humans. He is God actually with us, the embodiment of the wisdom anticipated by the Jews and the *Logos* idealized and sought after by the Greeks. Such is said to be the amazing scope of Christ's supremacy over all things.

The man Jesus is the supreme image of God as God is eternally. Put otherwise, Jesus is the perfect portrait of God. In Him we see the distinguishing marks and present intentions of God. If you want to see what God is like, look at Jesus. If you want to know what humans were intended to be like, look at Jesus. To avoid any impression of a lifeless portrait, however, Paul adds the word *pleroma* (fullness, completeness). Jesus is not merely a good sketch or helpful summary of who God is and what God is doing. He is the *full and complete revelation*. God was pleased to have the divine fullness dwell in Jesus the Christ (1:19). There are no rivals to Jesus, no new and fuller revelations of God.

The importance of this biblical language is "to indicate that the completeness of God's self-revelation was focused in Christ, that the wholeness of God's interaction with the universe is summed up in Christ."[3] Jesus shares the divine being; He is its image and visible manifestation. He is "not a copy or likeness of God, but the 'projection' of God on the canvas of our humanity and the embodiment of the divine in the world of men and women."[4]

Although many of the Colossian believers likely were Gentile in origin, Paul's teaching opponents in Colosse were nonetheless drawing heavily on Jewish tradition as known locally (especially the focus on holy days, dietary rules, and ritual observances). Therefore, Paul also draws on biblical traditions as an effective way of reminding his readers that the authentic exodus, once limited to the Jews liberated from Egyptian slavery, now belongs to all people who are initiated into the kingdom of the Son through acceptance of the liberating Christian gospel.

Salvation hinges on the Son, both on who He is by nature and what He has done for us in His earthly life, death, and resurrection. The hinge of redemption and the victory over evil do not rest, as some Colossians were claiming, on what we humans can do through denials of the flesh and claiming to have visions of the heavenly realm. Against the Colossian perversion of the apostolic message that rejected the material in favor of the spiritual, falsely posing these as opposites, Paul affirms that Christ's supremacy is cosmic in scope. He is Lord over both the world of the material creation and the spiritual realm, now and forever. The Christ of God is Lord of all!

3. THE RELATION OF JESUS TO CREATION 1:15B–17

Jesus is more than the **image of the invisible God** and the **firstborn over all creation**; everything was **created by him and for him** (1:15–16). Paul says that God was reconciling to himself all things in Jesus Christ. The Greek is neuter (*panta*), implying all creation, animate and inanimate. Surely Paul was thinking here of the Gnostic false teachers troubling the Colossians with supposed limitations on the scope of Christ's accomplished work.

The false teachers were arguing that the original creation was accomplished by an inferior "god," one more closely aligned with the evilness of the creation. Since matter is presumed to be inherently evil, the true God who is wholly good could not have soiled himself by direct contact with a material creation. Therefore, there must have been levels of divine descent to the sordid human scene, spiritual beings with lessening levels of spiritual purity. Vigorously denying such thinking, Paul takes a traditionally Jewish stance on this significant matter.

God had once acted directly to create from nothing through the agency of His Son (1:16). Originally the creation had been judged "very good" (Gen. 1:31). Consequently, human salvation should not be thought of as rescue from an inherently evil world, but a reclaiming from sin by the one who was the divine agent of the world's origin. Redeemed humans are made more and not less human by their salvation because they are being returned to their original status before God. Once redeemed, believers in Christ increasingly should appreciate God's creation and be ready to work with Christ to transform the world's structures in the direction of their original intention. Believers in Christ should be aware of the natural environment of all creation, appreciating it, preserving it, and seeing God's glory through it.

The Son, Jesus, is said to be the **firstborn over all creation** (1:15), with **firstborn** not to be taken as time sequence. The New English Bible translation is preferred: "His is the primacy over all created things." Christ is not a creature born first in a long line of births, but is **firstborn** in the sense of special honor, like Israel was the firstborn of God (Exod. 4:22). They were the people chosen and especially honored. God has assigned Jesus the first place, the lordship and sovereignty over all creation. By contrast, the Colossian "philosophy" was claiming the existence of angels, principalities, and powers. Paul bypasses such speculation, instead proclaiming Jesus as Creator and controller of all, the one who created angels and the one who remains in charge of their activities. It is in the Son that all creation originated, is sustained, and in whom **all things hold together** (1:17). The laws and processes that order the creation have no independent existence, but are extensions of the mind of the Son.

Paul's claims for Christ's supremacy are stunning. The Son is the beginning, sustainer, and destiny of all that is! Christ has dominion over creation because He was the agent of its beginning. All things are *in* Him, *through* Him, and *for* Him. The **all things** (*ta panta*) is truly comprehensive. Whatever supernatural powers there may be, Christ made them and remains their Lord. Christ, the agent and goal of creation, is the Alpha and Omega (Rev. 22:13). Paul extends the lordship of Christ to cover the present life of the created order. Thus, it is true both that those people who accept God's grace in Christ are themselves re-formed into a *new creation* and that they in turn are to embody the leading edge of God's ultimate intent of reconciling all things to himself (1:20). The religious, social, political, and economic lives of believers are intended to be influenced by spiritual reconciliation to God in Christ so that the Creator's invisible will and ways can be made visible for all to see (Heb. 11:1–2).

Paul's central point is that "dichotomies between the visible and invisible, public and private, external and internal are false. His confession of

Christ's lordship over all things shows his confidence that Christ's death establishes God's grace in every nook and cranny of God's creation."[5] God's will was embodied in the earthly life of the Lord Jesus and now is to be seen again in the lives of those who belong to the community of Christ's present reign, the church.

Horoscopes, astrology, the occult, and the paranormal are still common in the Western world of the early twenty-first century. Modern people commonly experience forces that threaten their feeling of well being, causing a sense of helplessness and fear. These forces include destructive economic, social, political, and religious systems. We are threatened by the serious deterioration of the world's ecological system, the potential of a nuclear nightmare, and the possibility of natural disasters such as a meteor of massive proportion. When so threatened, people hope for and often imagine into existence spiritual worlds and beings that they assume must be recognized, appeased, and even worshiped. Insists Paul, ultimate reality does indeed lie in the spiritual, but spiritual reality lies in Jesus and in none other.

4. THE RELATION OF JESUS TO THE CHURCH 1:18

Verse 1:18 is clearly transitional. The move in Paul's thought is from God's first creation to God's new creation, the church, with the Son the divine agent of the first and Lord of the second. There is rich biblical precedent for this. In Genesis, the first creation (chapters 1–11) became linked to the new creation of a selected people, Israel (Gen. 12–50). Now, having stressed the role of Jesus Christ in relation to the whole created order, Paul comes to the present application of Christ's supremacy among the newly called community of believers. The application centers in affirming the church as "the greenhouse in and by means of which the green shoots of God's purpose in and for creation are brought on."[6] Christ is the second Adam. His coming marked a new start to world history through creation of a new race, the church, over which He is to be preeminent. Christ is the origin of the church, the singular fount of its true being.

This grand theological conviction of the supremacy of the Christ in the church has a practical meaning. Congregations of God's people are to be living demonstrations of the divine grace that reconciles all things to

God's will. In fact, Christ is the principle of cohesion that should inform a society and enable a rising above typical gender, class, and race distinctions. In Christ we humans are to be one. The work of Jesus fully embodied the redeeming work of God in the world. Now the life of God's people is to reflect that embodiment, to be an extension of the Jesus life through the power, wisdom, and gifting of the Spirit of Christ. The point of right theology is to undergird and enable right living. The proper point of beginning is God in Jesus Christ.

The sanctification of believers is central to the completion of God's work. It centers in the process of Christ's resurrection victory *for* us becoming His victory realized *in* us by the indwelling Spirit (Rom. 8:1–11). Christ, through His Spirit, seeks to duplicate His triumph over sin and death in our personal histories and in whole congregations. It is a perfecting of love that dissolves sin, builds redeemed relationships, and opens one to the fruit of the Spirit. One such fruit is the wisdom to understand and the will to accept Christ as the reigning head of the church. The church is to be "a microcosm in which the divine purpose in reclaiming the entire creation is anticipated and through which, as a reconciled and reconciling community, that purpose is furthered."[7]

Christ is said to be the *arche* (beginning), the first in time, first in honor, and first in authority. This conviction arose from awareness in the early churches of the physical resurrection of the murdered Jesus. Because of the resurrection, Christ, **the firstborn from among the dead** (1:18), now has initiated a new age of salvation history (1 Cor. 15:12–28). He is the living presence of God in the church. As such, He is to be granted supremacy and authority in all things. He has conquered every opposing power, even death. Because He lives, we too can live!

Life together in Christ constitutes the true church. Now, in Christ's physical absence, the disciples of the risen Jesus are enabled to form a community in Him, the body of Christ, God's true temple. The vision is vast and the implications major. Here is a vision of the church that is to function as a means toward cosmic reconciliation—the community in which such reconciliation has already begun to take place and whose responsibility it is to live out as well as to proclaim the good news (see 4:2–6).

The core reason for the frequent impotence of the modern church is that congregations are filled with "the nicest, kindest people who have nothing apostolic or missionary, who never knew the soul's despair or its breathless gratitude."[8] Paul tells the Colossians to remember that they were once lost and without hope; but now they were **reconciled . . . by Christ's physical body through death** (1:22). He is the wonder of it all—none other than God in the all-sufficient Jesus Christ!

ENDNOTES

1. Andrew T. Lincoln, *The Letter to the Colossians*, The New Interpreter's Bible, vol. 11 (Nashville, Tenn.: Abingdon Press, 2000), p. 609.

2. For a quality exploration of this apparent hymn and the theme of the lordship of Jesus Christ over against the Roman Empire, see Sylvia Keesmatt and Brian Walsh, *Colossians Remixed: Subverting the Empire* (Downers Grove, Ill.: InterVarsity, 2004).

3. J. D. G. Dunn, *The Epistles to the Colossians and to Philemon* (Grand Rapids, Mich.: William B. Eerdmans, 1996), p. 101.

4. Ralph P. Martin, *Ephesians, Colossians, and Philemon*, Interpretation: A Bible Commentary for Teaching and Preaching (Louisville, Ky.: John Knox Press, 1991), p. 108.

5. Robert W. Wall, *Colossians and Philemon*, The IVP New Testament Commentary Series (Downers Grove, Ill.: InterVarsity Press 1993), p. 63.

6. Dunn, *Epistles*, p. 96.

7. Lincoln, *Colossians*, p. 611.

8. Maxie D. Dunnam, *Galatians, Ephesians, Philippians, Colossians, Philemon*, The Preacher's Commentary (Nashville, Tenn.: Thomas Nelson, 1982), p. 350.

4

THE FRUIT OF
CHRIST'S SUPREMACY

Colossians 1:19–23

The apostle Paul completes his vigorous affirmation of the supremacy of Jesus Christ by explaining that in Christ believers can find all they need. There is no need of relating to other mediators between ourselves and God. There is no need of experiencing something deep and mysterious to gain full salvation. This Pauline stance was nothing other than what originally had been proclaimed to the Colossians. Any recent changes in their thought and practice had come from an alien source and needed to be checked against the original apostolic message.

The burden of Paul's message to Colosse is clear. Jesus Christ is central for faith; the fruit of Christ's redemptive work on the cross is fully adequate for all human need. All spiritual resources are found in Christ (2:3). Alternatives are dangerous intrusions into the church's life. Foundational for church life as it should be is the prime proclamation that it is *through Christ* that we experience forgiveness and redemption; it is *by way of Christ* that we are set free from the bondages of darkness and despair; and it is *in Christ* that we become heirs of God and share in a rich spiritual inheritance with eternal consequences.

1. THE GOSPEL: GOD RECONCILING IN JESUS CHRIST 1:19–22

What is the original and authentic good news, the message first proclaimed to the Colossians? It is the word about God in Jesus. God was pleased to dwell in Christ with the divine fullness (1:19) and through Christ to reconcile all things to himself (1:20). Paul says boldly to the Colossians that they were the ones who once were alienated from God and now are the ones who had been reconciled (1:21–22). The Christian good news is personal; its life-changing effects are assured if one will continue in the authentic faith (1:23). That to which the Colossians should cling (the cosmic Christ identified so expansively in 1:15–18) is the heart of the apostolic gospel.

Excursions into theological abstraction reach beyond the ability of the human mind to comprehend fully. They outrun the ability of human language to express adequately. Thus, believers in Christ's supremacy must remain humble and grounded in concrete reality. With his references to "blood" and "cross," Paul identifies this reality by rooting his theology firmly in a particular history. The gospel of Christ is all about the crucified and risen Jesus of Nazareth. The famous Apostles' Creed that first evolved early in the church's life is structured around Father, Son, and Spirit. It affirms the heart of the faith by narrating the earthly story of the life, death, and resurrection of the man Jesus. God has acted in Christ for the reconciliation of all creation. Christianity is founded firmly on the story of the incarnation—God in flesh for our salvation.

One fact is clear. God stands behind the whole work of Jesus Christ. Christians sometimes think of Christ's work in contrast to God, as though Jesus acted to pacify an angry God who wanted to punish sinners. That is wrong. There is to be no contrast between Jesus the Son who loves, sacrifices, and forgives and God the Father, often falsely pictured as the stern judge poised to punish disobedience if not satisfied. For Paul, the whole plan of redemption originated in the heart of God, proceeded by the direct action of God sending Christ, and was based in the great desire of God that all be saved (1 Tim. 2:4).

Based on the known facts, an event as stunning as the physical resurrection of Jesus and recognized as an actual historical happening must be affirmed. Jesus had been executed at the angry instigation of some of His own people. Something quite dramatic must have happened next to transform this horrible death into what could be avowed joyously and without reserve as Jesus being the one before all things and over all things, nothing short of God with us humans for our redemption! Paul is saying that, in none other than this crucified Jesus, God has brought forgiveness and new life for all of the lost creation. Affirming the absolute supremacy of Jesus Christ is meant to be more than a masterpiece of metaphysics or an exercise in theological finesse. It is the foundational truth that grounds the fruit of God's saving work, the sharing of redeeming love now available for the saving of all lost sinners.

The centerpiece of Paul's counterargument to the Colossian heresy is the affirmation that in Jesus Christ (and not in any other cosmic power) the fullness of Deity dwells bodily. Thus, the classic Christian creeds insist that the incarnation of God in Jesus is neither *adoptionism* (a good man chosen and taken up into deity) nor *charade* (the earthly Jesus being God only playing the role of a man without really being one). Insists Paul, Jesus was the fullness of God living an actual human life.

With this divine-human paradox assumed, three claims are made by Paul that together form the foundation of Christ's supremacy in human salvation. First, the divine "fullness" is said to have been resident in Jesus. Second, through Jesus, God reconciled all things to himself. Finally, the peace resulting from this reconciliation has come through the death of Jesus on the cross. The medium of the reconciliation was **through his blood, shed on the cross** (1:20). It was the death of Jesus that resulted in Paul's teaching that God had not spared His own Son, but had given Him up for us all.

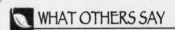 **WHAT OTHERS SAY**

The classic Christian creeds insist that the incarnation of God in Jesus is neither *adoptionism* nor *charade*. The church over the centuries has been very clear here. The Nicene-Constantinopolitan Creed (A.D. 381) reads, "We believe in one Lord, Jesus Christ, the only Son of God, eternally begotten of the Father, Light from Light, true God from true God. . . . For us all and for our salvation he came down from heaven: by [the power of] the Holy Spirit he became incarnate from the Virgin Mary, and was made man." Thus, Jesus was both *truly divine* and *truly human*. This is an amazing paradox, the heart of the glorious gospel of Jesus Christ.

Central to the difference between Judaism and Christianity is their contrasting interpretations of the meaning of the death of Jesus. For the Jews, the death of the coming Messiah was an almost unthinkable thought; accordingly, Jesus could hardly have been the true Messiah. Jesus had suffered the natural end of any captured anarchist against Rome's rule. The fact that Rome had successfully executed Him was proof enough that He was not the powerful and conquering Christ expected from God.

By contrast, Paul taught that God had saved humanity from sin through the death of Jesus, so that what humans saw as tragic for Jesus was actually glorious for all who would believe and thereby be reconciled. It might have been an ugly old cross, but look at what God has made of it—the carpenter's Son fashioned it into an instrument of salvation! A brutal execution has become the means of a loving reconciliation. Christ's shed blood was a sin-atoning death that renewed the church's covenant with God (Heb. 9–10).

The reconciling God had salvation in view, at least potentially, for **every creature under heaven** (1:23). If Christ is Lord of all creation, then surely the salvation made available by Christ is available to every creature. All lost people live in the context of Christ's cosmic lordship and by faith can be beneficiaries of God's saving grace. Christianity was cradled in Judaism, to be sure; it also was destined to be a world religion, informed but not captured by Judaism. Since the saving grace of God is freely offered to all people, no one has to suffer from unforgiven sin, no one has to walk alone, no one has to be a prisoner of fear, and no one has to stay as she or he was. In fact, "all could be redeemed and all could, by God's grace, travel the road to perfection."[1]

Jesus told His disciples to go and make other disciples in all nations (Matt. 28:19). Here is the good news: "God has not left himself without witness anywhere, though he has revealed himself definitively in one particular human life. . . . Jesus is the incarnation of God, but the Spirit also sustains human relationships with God broadly. On this basis, we expect the Spirit to be drawing humanity into the range of Christ's saving work everywhere."[2] None will be saved except through the redemptive work of Jesus Christ, but many may be saved who have never had direct contact with the Christian witness to Christ.[3]

2. FAITHFULNESS MAKES THE GOSPEL PERMANENT 1:23A

Paul also places emphasis on the responsibility of his readers to continue in the faith initially proclaimed to them. Reconciliation with God has ongoing meaning only in the context of moral relationships that are intentionally maintained. Paul's understanding of salvation is Jewish; it is covenantal. The fulfillment of God's promises is conditioned by the proper response of the human partners in the covenant. Reconciliation to God is not an automatic process, not a "once for all" decision for Christ. It must be worked out in the midst of a believer's faith journey.

No doubt this emphasis of faithful responsibility was occasioned by the circumstances in Colosse. Christians must continue to determine to hold closely to the content of the faith itself, especially belief in the full supremacy of the person and work of Jesus Christ. There is a definite article before the word *faith* in verse 23, suggesting that proper Christian believing is more than an attitude of trusting; it also and necessarily includes the teaching of the apostolic gospel as expounded by Paul throughout this letter. Apostasy (breaking away from the faith) always remains an option. In fact, this is exactly what worried Paul about the church in Colosse.

There is a teaching popular among many Christians today that deserves questioning. Sometimes called the "perseverance of the saints" and known commonly as "once in grace, always in grace," it is taught as a means of reassuring believers of the mercy and dependability of God. While few would question the mercy and dependability of God, there is a significant problem with this teaching. The interrelatedness of two sharply contrasting concepts requires careful attention. The two concepts are (1) the both/and synergism of divine grace and (2) the claim of "once in grace, always in grace."

The first of these concepts focuses on the mutuality of giving and receiving. The primacy of divine grace is necessary for salvation, but there also is to be a *mutuality of both partners* in a covenant relationship. Grace is not cheap—it cost Christ His life and it costs ours as we yield to the will and ways of Christ. There is, therefore, a significant flaw in the commonly heard Christian claim that intends to honor God by insisting that what God does cannot be undone by mere humans. Without diminishing the effectiveness of divine grace and the dependability of divine choices, the *synergism of grace* rejects the idea that God ever enters into unconditional covenants with anyone.

There is no such thing as an experience of salvation that is guaranteed as a once-for-all transaction regardless of the conduct of the believer. Covenants are between two parties and failure on the part of the human partner invalidates the relationship. This potential of failure includes the salvation covenant made possible by Jesus Christ. The plain meaning of at least four discourses of Jesus argues directly for the reality of this potential (Luke 8, parable of the sower; Luke 12, parable of the lord and his steward; Matt. 18, parable of the law of forgiveness; and John 15, the vine and branches imagery).

Why does this matter so much? It is because those who have responded to the saving grace of God now have a responsibility to be transformed by it. Believers are responsible to do God's will, nurture the new life given in Christ, grow up into the full stature of Christ, and reflect the fruit of the Spirit to the world. There are real choices to be made, and human choices matter to God. If we choose wrongly, violating the covenant of grace, God responds accordingly, invalidating the salvation relationship. God's grace is fully dependable, and so is God's attitude toward sin. If we abide in God, God will dependably abide in us (John 15:4). If we do not, God does not. God's power should be thought of as a sovereignty that chooses to *empower* rather than *overpower*. John Wesley was fond of saying that God works "strongly and sweetly," meaning that God's will for human salvation can be resisted since the *response-ability* we have by God's grace renders us *responsible* to respond appropriately to the gracious and redeeming overtures of God.[4]

The Colossians needed to hear this sobering reality. The potential loss of salvation roots in the continuing freedom of the human will to sin against God and thus to reject God's dependable grace. Believers must be faithful and fruitful. We deal with

a divine self-sufficiency which overflows its banks and gives the creature room to be. God not only sustains himself and creates, but has willed a world which would not be a mere mechanical expression of his purposes. Creation is the womb in which God would make free spirits, beings who, as pale images of himself, could exist with a degree of creaturely autonomy, decide things with a measure of authentic freedom, and act with real independence of him, themselves being laborers together with God (1 Cor. 3:9).[5]

Reconciliation is enabled by the faithfulness of Jesus unto death; faithfulness is required for the working out of salvation, although not for its provision in the first place. Then comes **peace** (1:20). Our peace with God depends on God's grace and the faithfulness of Jesus; but it also depends on us in the sense that we must respond and follow Christ's way—being downwardly mobile in an upwardly mobile world (Mark 10:43–45). We are to have the mind of Christ (Phil. 2:5), reconciling even as we have been reconciled.

3. THE GOSPEL AS SERVANTHOOD 1:23B

Once Paul has set forth his dramatic, apostolic perspectives on the foundation and scope of Christ's supremacy over all things, including the potentials of salvation of all people and salvation's loss when there is faithlessness, he becomes autobiographical. Paul was personally involved with this good news in Christ. He had become its humble and faithful servant, less a systematic theologian and much more a grateful believer who speaks from the treasures of his own spiritual experience. In effect, he is saying, "I have experienced the Christ myself. Jesus has acted on my behalf, transformed me, and now I am confident of the truth about who Jesus is. I have committed myself to Him and what has followed confirms what I and others have faithfully taught."

Theology is important to the church, as the letter to Colosse seeks to make clear; but theology should never function in isolation from real life and never for its own sake. At the center of the Christian gospel, according to Paul, is not an abstract and speculative theory, but a concrete historical reality, the Christ event, that should yield practical life results. New life for us humans comes from a loving God by way of an atoning death. The physical death of Jesus somehow saves lost people from the penalty of their sins. The heart of Christian theology is a faithful recounting of the acts of God as directed by the biblical narrative. The Bible is inspired by God's Spirit and now is available to us as one of the gracious acts of God for the guidance of believers in all times.

The supremacy and full lordship of Jesus Christ is central to Christian life and provides the distinguishing characteristics of Christian service. Jesus is supreme for understanding Christian ministry because He is its *pattern* (1:24–25), the one being *proclaimed* (1:26–28), and the *enabling power* of ministry itself (1:29). The Christian way is to renounce privilege and commit to a life of service.

Paul identifies himself as a constant companion of **Christ's afflictions** (1:24; compare 2 Cor. 11:23–28). He makes the point that he has suffered, not because he is a foolhardy man who chooses to live dangerously, but because, especially as an apostle to the Gentiles (Eph. 3:1, 13), his servanthood is **for the sake of his** [Christ's] **body, which is the church** (1:24b). The afflictions, however, have not dimmed hope. Christian believers can remain established and firm, **not moved from the hope held out in the gospel** (1:23). The hope is that we all will be reconciled with God through union with the Lord Jesus and then be effective agents of that reconciliation. Heaven is sure for the faithful, but, for Paul's readers whose religion was too much a retreat from the world, he stresses the present possibilities of life in Christ. Following Christ may lead to suffering, but it also should lead to present relevance and future hope, never to self-pity.

In the physical absence of the now-exalted Christ, Paul and Epaphras are appointed agents of God's saving grace among these Colossian readers. The responsibility of such divine agency is heavy to carry. The public's perception of the church and the gospel of Christ always depends largely on the integrity of the messengers who bring it. The highly publicized corruption of prominent Christian ministers is tragic for the Christian cause. Thus, Paul shifts the theological focus from God's provision of salvation (1:13–23) to the resulting church and to himself as an apostle of the good news to the Gentiles. Gospel content is foundational; also critical is the character of the gospel's messengers.

In our time there is considerable hesitation by the public about affirming any one creed, world perspective, or faith tradition as appropriate and necessarily true for all people, times, and places. There is thought to be no common "meta-narrative," no creed, tradition, or person with a legitimate claim to universal truth. This assumption is held at a time of increased awareness of the diversity of religions in the world and the violence against unbelievers that too often has seriously soiled religious history—including Christian church history. What we find in Colossians, nonetheless, is an ultimate faith claim, that of the absolute supremacy of Jesus Christ stretching from the creation to the consummation of all human history. This claim is put forward in an unusual way, however, namely in exceptionally peaceful terms. What holds the world together is the reconciliation brought by the Prince of Peace. Unbelievers are to be loved, not persecuted.

The only violence associated with Christ's reconciliation, **through his blood, shed on the cross** (1:20b), is not perpetrated *by* but *on* Christ. How unlike human ways this is. At the heart of Christian faith is the cosmic ruler, Jesus Christ, who was willing to be the victim of human violence! The rule of God is achieved through suffering; "peacemaking is accomplished through the absorption of violence."[6] The proper fruit of the gospel of Christ is reconciliation and peace, not dominance over and violence against those who do not believe.

There should be no separation between the work of Christ in resolving past human alienation from God and His work of enabling the present discipleship of believers. John Wesley was concerned that Christian ministers instill the pattern of Christ's work in Methodist people. He wanted to insure "that God's grace known in Christ as Priest was never separated from the response of discipleship that Christ modeled as Prophet and calls for from his followers as King."[7] The Christ who died *for* us will also reign *in* us and carry on His present mission in large part *through* us—and in ways consistent with love, peace, and self-sacrifice.

ENDNOTES

1. Rueben P. Job, *A Wesleyan Spiritual Reader* (Nashville, Tenn.: Abingdon Press, 1998), p. 91.

2. Clark H. Pinnock, *Flame of Love: A Theology of the Holy Spirit* (Downers Grove, Ill.: InterVarsity Press, 1996), p. 207.

3. For elaborations of this view as found in the Wesleyan tradition, see Randy L. Maddox, "Wesley and the Question of Truth or Salvation through Other Religions," in *Wesleyan Theological Journal* (Spring/Fall 1992), pp. 7–29, and Philip R. Meadows, "Candidates for Heaven: Wesleyan Resources for a Theology of Religions," *Wesleyan Theological Journal* (Spring 2000), pp. 99–129.

4. Randy L. Maddox, *Responsible Grace: John Wesley's Practical Theology* (Nashville, Tenn.: Kingswood Books, Abingdon Press, 1994), pp. 54–55.

5. Clark H. Pinnock, "The Beauty of God: John Wesley's Reform and its Aftermath," *Wesleyan Theological Journal* (Fall 2003), p. 59.

6. Andrew T. Lincoln, *The Letter to the Colossians*, The New Interpreter's Bible, vol. 11 (Nashville, Tenn.: Abingdon Press, 2000), p. 609.

7. Maddox, *Responsible Grace*, p. 113.

Part Three

Faithfully Following Jesus Christ

COLOSSIANS 1:24–2:23

5

DISCIPLES WHO SUFFER AND SERVE

Colossians 1:24–2:7

Paul identifies himself to the Colossians as a servant of the church. He is a pastor-teacher who is determined to apply the message of the gospel of Jesus Christ to the actual lives of his readers. He understands himself to be a servant of Jesus Christ, functioning on behalf of the church, serving *for* Christ and *like* Christ, all made possible because he is privileged by God's grace to be living *in* Christ. He is anxious that all believers be and do the same.

1. SERVANT STEWARDS IN CHRIST 1:24–29

The servant leadership of the Christian life is the suffering-servant kind (Isaiah 53). It sets aside self-interest and political manipulation of people in favor of submitting to others and sharing their burdens (Gal. 6:1–10; Phil. 2:1–11). Submission and burden bearing, however, come at a price. Note this about the life of Jesus:

When we look for the conquering hero to make his move, to enter into the royal city on his white charger to signal to the people that the time has come to establish his kingdom, we find instead a Jesus who enters into Jerusalem astride a humble donkey. . . . When we look for a deliverer who will crush the opposition by superior force, we find instead a servant-messiah who allows himself to be crushed and bruised for us. What kind of God is this?[1]

How easily human self-perception leads to selfish and distorted God-perception. Dominant social groups often create God in their own image and then make a convenient idol of that image at the expense of others. How different it is supposed to be for Christians! For the servants of Christ, suffering often accompanies faithful discipleship. God freely gave His only Son; disciples of the Son are to give themselves freely in loving service, regardless of consequences.

LIFE CHANGE

For the loyal servants of Jesus Christ, suffering often accompanies faithful discipleship. God freely gave His only Son for the sin of us humans; disciples of the Son are to give themselves freely in loving service, regardless of consequences. Has any discomfort come into your life because of faithfulness to Jesus Christ? If not, why not? If you were more faithful, what consequences might follow? Are you prepared to give yourself more freely to the Christ—whatever the cost?

In Paul's case, the issue of suffering was not theoretical or limited only to threatened bodily harm or imprisonment. He admits he was in the midst of a struggle on behalf of the faith at the time of his writing to the Colossians (2:1). The Colossians' neighbors, the Laodicaeans, also were unknown to Paul face-to-face, but he reports nonetheless that he was deeply engaged with them at the heart level. This engagement was said to be *agon* (2:1), from which developed the English word *agony*. These believers were threatened by false teachings, and Paul was unable physically to go to them and confront the circumstance.

For a man like Paul, the limitations of imprisonment would have been frustrating. Of course, and less admirably, Paul also may have been struggling internally with the threat of a possible death sentence and the temptation to back away from the truth himself, thus saving his life at the expense of his integrity. Such a defection would have been a disastrous scandal for the young Christian movement. Many were watching Paul, and any temptation to take the easy way out of his circumstance would have been agony for him indeed. His choice was clear. The easy way was unthinkable. The broad road of personal comfort usually leads to destruction (Matt. 7:13).

To be *in* Christ is necessarily to live *like* Christ. Paul's typical definition of a Christian is **Christ in you, the hope of glory** (1:27). These words or their equivalent are used often in Paul's writings. Here lies **the**

mystery (1:26), **the hope of glory** (1:27), the good news **now disclosed to the saints** (1:26). His own testimony was that he had been crucified with Christ and now was living because Christ was alive in him (Gal. 2:20). The very Christ who has the primacy over all things and who will stand at time's end as the final judge now lives *in the believer* by the Holy Spirit.

2. COMPLETING THE SUFFERING OF CHRIST 1:24–25

The combination of **rejoice** and **suffered** (1:24) is a strange one, but these are the twin realities to which Paul testifies. In the faithful service of the church, the apostle to the Gentiles informs the Colossians that he is rejoicing even in the midst of necessary suffering. It is clear that Paul had faced considerable opposition in his ministry. Persecution is not too strong a word. In fact, at the time he was writing to the Colossians, he was languishing in a Roman prison. Paul was a pioneer evangelist, a frontline apostle with a dramatic message to be delivered to people often unprepared to hear it. Some of his Jewish-convert friends were reluctant to share it. They had great concerns about the gospel of Christ being offered to new (non-Jewish) people without including tradition-conserving controls. Crossing new frontiers risks new dangers and opens new doors of opportunity.

Whenever one serves the church boldly by trying to establish its faith, save it from errors, and widen its borders, at least there will be friction and usually some sacrifice that will involve suffering of one kind or another. The pain can come from inside or outside the believing community. Even so, to suffer in the service of Christ should be seen as a personal privilege. For Paul, to be persecuted while pouring himself out on behalf of the believers was thought of as sharing in and even to **fill up in my flesh what is still lacking in regard to Christ's afflictions** (1:24). Hearing this thought from Paul is strange indeed in light of Colossians 1:15–20. There Paul stresses the all-sufficiency of Christ's reconciling work on the cross. This present statement appears to imply that something is lacking in Christ's afflictions, something that believers can supply. Clarity is critical here.

The term *hysterema* (deficiency, need) is found nine times in the New Testament, but only here in Colossians in relation to Christ. Paul speaks elsewhere of sharing the sufferings of Christ (Phil. 3:10), but not for other believers and not as though he were filling what is "lacking" in Christ's suffering. What could Paul mean by saying that his own sacrifice and suffering on behalf of the church somehow complete or fill up the sufferings and sacrifice of Jesus Christ? What is yet empty, incomplete, left to be done by those of us who now serve?

Paul was not adding in any way to the redemptive suffering of Jesus Christ as completed on the cross. That sacrifice was full, complete, once for all. Paul's afflictions, subsequent to Christ on the cross, were on behalf of the church and *in the pattern* of the suffering Christ. Paul was continuing the suffering-servant role of Jesus Christ as he functioned as missionary to the Gentiles. He was rejoicing in the suffering that was accompanying his fulfillment of God's plan of carrying the good news of Jesus to the wider non-Jewish world—and he was willingly bearing the burden that was coming with that controversial, dangerous, and wonderful task.

The theme of joy in the face of suffering often appears in the New Testament. Believers may be persecuted, as were the biblical prophets earlier, but there is a sure reward ahead (Matt. 5:12). As the gospel of Christ is faithfully proclaimed, the church will grow and more of the sick will come for healing (Acts 5:14). Faithful members of the church are to stand firm in the face of suffering, even when losing their property, enduring with joy because there are more lasting possessions not subject to human confiscation (Heb. 10:34). G. K. Chesterton said, "The golden age only comes to men when they have, if only for a moment, forgotten gold."[2]

Like Paul, and in every time and place, the church always is to be a living demonstration of the reconciling grace of God, the contemporary embodiment of what it means to live under the reigning lordship of Christ, whatever the cost involved. The church is to be the fellowship of servants who pour themselves out, like the Christ, on behalf of God's saving mission in the world. Paul was living this way and calling the Colossians to do the same. The basic point is this: "We do not suffer as a repetition of Calvary but as an extension of it—as an expression of Christ-life which, like our Master, is a cross-life."[3] This cross-life is to become a cross-shaped people in today's secular world. The intended result is this: "Healing begins in identification with the pain [of others]. . . . With the vision of Christ ever before us, we take our stance beside, not above, those who sin and who suffer. . . . Pride give[s] way to compassion. And only as pride gives way to compassion will we become a cruciform church."[4] To be "cruciform" is to be shaped by a cross-like, sacrificial servanthood.

3. JESUS CHRIST IS FOR ALL PEOPLE 1:26–29

Embodying the good news in Jesus Christ involved a particular task for the apostle Paul in those first years after the earthly sojourn of Jesus. He was to proclaim a marvelous message far beyond the traditional borders of the Jewish community. The glorious hope of the Christian gospel is for everyone! Paul was shattering the old idea that, since God had once chosen a particular people to be His special treasure (Exod. 19:5), that people somehow had a corner on divine grace, an exclusive right to the privileges of being children of the divine Parent. No, says Paul. The love and mercy of God are the property of no one; to the contrary, they are the privilege of all who will believe and receive. All ethnic and national barriers were demolished by Christ's death (Eph. 2:11–22). Paul's own calling was to warn every person, teach every person, and ideally present every person complete in Christ.

Many Jews struggled with Paul, fearing that his work with the Gentile world was a prostitution of a privileged covenant, a throwing of pearls to swine. Since Christianity began as a messianic movement within Judaism, they argued, should being Christian not also mean remaining Jewish? The Gnostic-like thinking now infecting the Colossian congregation also resisted the message of Paul, but for other reasons. It restricted the grace of God by insisting that special knowledge and elevated states of spirituality are necessary for salvation. Since such things were said to emerge from special opportunity and intense discipline, only a small number, the spiritually enlightened and elite, will ever attain the goal of the truly saved. In other words, the wisdom of God is not equally for everyone. But Paul actively argues otherwise. In Christ, he insists, the grace of God has been extended freely to all humanity. Levels of understanding and gifting vary among believers, of course, but the gift of salvation and the hope of glory belong to all. The good news of the gospel of Christ is both that it truly saves and that it truly is for all people.

4. MARKS OF A FAITHFUL CHURCH 2:1–7

As Paul suffered and served, sharing both the good news of the Christ with the Colossians and his concern for the Laodicaeans, he described what might be called the marks of a faithful church. God will provide if the people will be receptive and responsible. Divine provision is adequate for all of the church's needs if the provision is properly honored and nurtured. The divine provision is elaborated in terms of eight marks of church maturity. They are descriptions of a church that is properly rooted in the truth of God's revelation and positioned to be effective in Christ's mission.

MARK 1: COURAGE

For Christian believers pressured by false teachings and existing in cultures unfriendly to Christian faith, Paul prays that they be encouraged. He longs that they will be so settled in the assurance of their faith that comfort and confidence will grow and support them daily. This way of living the faith brings all that is necessary to cope with any situation. It was time for such courage in the Colossian congregation.

MARK 2: UNITY

A key aspect of the encouragement of believers is that their communities of faith be knit together by a special love. Patterns of church government and styles of worship will vary, of course; personal preferences on a range of matters are to be expected in any human gathering, including the church. However, what should be basic, consistent, and so unusual about the church in the world's eyes is how differently the people making up the bodies of Christian believers truly love each other (1 John 4:7). Love makes people one, even when there are differences. This is beyond what the fractured world manages to experience. Jesus prayed that His disciples would be united so that the world may know (John 17).

MARK 3: WISDOM

The mature church is marked by a multifaceted knowing. Paul uses three different words for knowing, suggesting that a full range of wisdom is to be present within healthy bodies of believers. In 2:2 he uses *sunesis*, "understanding," a critical kind of knowing that carefully assesses a situation and determines the best kind of action to take in it. Some believers are strategic visionaries and planners. Then Paul says that in Jesus are hidden the treasures of both **knowledge** (*gnosis*) and **wisdom** (*sophia*) (2:3). *Gnosis* is the ability, almost intuitive in nature, to grasp a truth merely on seeing or hearing it, while *sophia* goes on to the additional ability to probe, confirm, and convey a truth by the use of reasoned argument. The mature church, then, is a body of believers that, functioning together in unity with their various gifts, effectively represents Christ in the world because it properly discerns the truth in Christ, senses in the Spirit what is right, is able to determine the best ways to proceed on mission in given settings, and articulates thoughtfully and persuasively the truth for the understanding of others.

All of this knowing, says Paul, is **hidden** (*apokruphos*, 1:26) in Christ and is **mystery** (1:26) in the sense that it is not available to common view apart from divine revelation. The really good news is that this hiddenness now has been openly revealed so that all who choose may enter in. The obvious implied contrast is with the false teachers at Colosse who were insisting that a range of hidden knowledge is required for salvation and is accessible only by a few. This knowledge is what select teachers were saying they had captured and could be gained only by the spiritually elite. It required following rigid regulations controlling particular religious practices to be engaged in for the purpose of a high level of eventual spiritual insight. Paul says to such misleading teachers, "You Gnostics have your wisdom hidden from ordinary people; we too have our knowledge, but it is not hidden in unintelligible books; it is hidden in Christ and therefore open to all men everywhere."[5]

MARK 4: RESISTANCE

Being in possession of the wide range of knowledge hidden in Christ is crucial for the church, but such possession needs to be protected. The needed safety comes when the church also has the ability to recognize and resist the intrusion of false but nonetheless seductive teaching. Believers must not be beguiled by **fine-sounding arguments** (*pithanologia*, 2:4), those smooth arguments by which a clever lawyer sometimes gets a guilty client freed. Truth must be received, understood, and held tightly in the face of all self-serving and clever arguing to the contrary. The world specializes in marketing designed to draw public attention and serve the ends of the advertiser. But let the buyer beware! The church must not allow itself to be beguiled by "truths" currently on sale by others, however attractive their spiritual packaging.

MARK 5: DISCIPLINE

Paul speaks approvingly of **orderly** and **firm** faith (2:5). These two words are military in origin. *Order* (*taxis*) means a rank or a carefully aligned group of soldiers. Similarly, the church is to be much more than a polite gathering of like-minded people seeking to get their perceived needs met. It is to be more like a trained army, with all members knowing their gifts and assignments, each equipped with the spiritual weapons that the battle will require, and each in place and ready to function together as the Lord may command.

Firm is *stereoma*, a solid front, a mighty bulwark, an immovable phalanx. Enemies may charge the church with volleys of false teaching, but God's army can be enabled to stand firm so that the gates of hell finally will not prevail against it (Matt. 16:18). There should be warmth, joy, and flexibility among believers, of course; but there also should be a corporate strength and an ordered discipline that keeps the body from crumbling when under attack and allows the body to move out on divine mission in ways really useable by the Spirit who is in command.

Paul and Timothy rejoiced about the way many Colossian believers had generated "resistance to the specious arguments and deceptive tactics of those who would entice them away from an exclusive loyalty to Christ. . . . They had taken up battle stations to combat error."[6] Such courage and caution should always mark the Christian community. Says verse 3 of the Christian song titled "Lead On, O King Eternal,"

Lead on, O King eternal, we follow, not with fears,

For gladness breaks like morning, Where e'er Thy face appears.

Thy cross is lifted o'er us, We journey in its light;

The crown awaits the conquest, Lead on, O God of might.

MARK 6: IN CHRIST

The Spirit of God is none other than the Spirit of the Christ, meaning that the true church is Christ's body because it has its life in Christ through the Spirit. The body of the church is to be like a great tree that is deeply rooted in the divine revelation about the supremacy of Christ's being, life, and work. The church regularly draws nourishment from this root. It is like a great house that keeps standing because it sits on a solid foundation, successfully resisting storms because of the strength of its base. Believers should sing with deep conviction, "How firm a foundation, ye saints of the Lord, is laid for your faith in His excellent Word!"

MARK 7: APOSTOLIC

Paul obviously was anxious for the Colossians to hold firmly to the faith originally preached to them. This holding is not to be an inflexible and mindless kind of orthodoxy. Faith always has an element of mystery. God is always beyond the full comprehension of mere humans; no creed is the exact wording of truth that is good for all times, cultures, and languages.

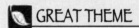 GREAT THEME

In Colosse long ago and in all generations, the church is faced with claims to "new revelations" often not consistent with the Christian gospel's apostolic foundation. These are temptations that must be resisted. God among us in Jesus Christ is the full and final revelation of God to humankind. One problem area involves looking anxiously to the future. Is too much energy being spent by Christians today in fruitless speculation about "final things"—always an open door to claims of fresh revelations that often sound so unlike the Jesus of the New Testament?

Even so, there are a few fundamental beliefs that do not change and are so basic that they define what it means to be Christian. They are the "apostolic" teachings, the heart of the message proclaimed by those nearest to Jesus. Paul understood himself to be one such apostle (1:1) and meant for his letter to be fully in line with such teachings. In Colosse long ago and in all generations, the church is faced with claims to new revelations often not consistent with the gospel's apostolic foundation. They must be resisted.

MARK 8: OVERFLOWING GRATITUDE

When rightly established in the apostolic faith, the obvious result should be a community of faith that overflows with **thankfulness** (2:7). The proper conclusion is clear. Those who have been incorporated into Jesus Christ are to be securely rooted in Him, progressively built up in Him, and live under His lordship. Such anchored and enlivened walking by faith yields an abounding gratitude to God. After all, Christ Jesus is more than adequate to safeguard all of His own against the empty traditions of mere humans. Walking worthy of the Lord is defined by four participles— **rooted**, **built up**, **established**, and **abounding**. The joy of the Lord, when properly founded and matured, brings an overflow of gratitude.

ENDNOTES

1. Philip D. Kenneson, *Life on the Vine* (Downers Grove, Ill.: InterVarsity Press, 1999), p. 206.

2. Quoted in C. Leonard Allen, *The Cruciform Church* (Abilene, Tex.: Abilene Christian University Press, 1990), p. 1.

3. Maxie D. Dunnam, *Galatians, Ephesians, Philippians, Colossians, Philemon*, The Preacher's Commentary (Waco, Tex.: Word, 1982), 358.

4. Allen, *The Cruciform Church*, p. 183.

5. William Barclay, *The Letters to the Philippians, Colossians, and Thessalonians* (Philadelphia: Westminster Press, rev. ed. 1975), pp. 130–131.

6. Thomas L. Trevethan, *Our Joyful Confidence: The Lordship of Jesus in Colossians* (Downers Grove, Ill.: InterVarsity Press, 1981), p. 61.

6

BLIND ALLEYS OF FALSE FAITH

Colossians 2:8–23

Paul writes to Colosse as a concerned elder and loving shepherd caring for an endangered flock of young Christians. He already has explained his view of the supremacy of God in Jesus Christ and how this ought to be considered absolute for Christian thought and life. Now it is time for him to address forthrightly a major challenge to this view.

The Colossian church was in danger of being taken **captive** (2:8) by false teachers and carried off as a prize of war. The attacker was a **deceptive philosophy** (2:8) that was degrading the Colossians' view of the person and authority of Jesus Christ. While philosophy—the pursuit and love of wisdom—can be a noble thing, in this case it was acting as a deceptive alternative to the Christian faith as preached by Paul and the other original apostles of the Christ.

To participate with Christ in the fullness of God's salvation, insists Paul, one must hold first to two core convictions that the philosophy gaining ground in Colosse did not embrace. These convictions are (1) Christ is the complete revelation of God within human history (2:9–10); and (2) Christ rules over all powers within God's created order (2:10–15). Accordingly, Paul's warnings are rooted in his central assumption that the person and work of Jesus Christ are sufficient for human salvation from sin and for vital growth in spiritual life.

1. BEING CARRIED AWAY BY FALSE TEACHERS 2:8–10

Paul's Colossian letter is filled with allusions to the dangerous teaching in question. While the references to it would have been quite clear to the Colossian readers, they are less so now. The general landscape is visible; some of the details, however, are matters of speculation only. What is clear is that some new teachers were endangering the believers with hollow and deceptive ideas rooted in this world and not in Jesus Christ (2:8). They were saying that Christians have to go through certain "spiritual powers" to reach the Christ. Going this way meant recognizing, appeasing, and maybe even worshiping various powers. In response, Paul argues vigorously that Christ is the head over **every power and authority** (2:10). The false teachers may think that God's rule over the church is mediated by angelic agents; in fact, the Lord himself mediates the divine human relationship, is directly accessible to believers, and alone deserves worship.

In a few generations this doctrinal danger in Colosse would be widespread and formalized into what we now call Gnosticism. By then the Christian movement would have developed three main lines of defense against it not available to Paul. They would be (1) established creedal statements to fight off false doctrine; (2) the official listing of recognized books of the Bible (closed canon), an assured source for identifying apostolic teaching; and (3) the episcopal office, recognized and authoritative leadership to control church life. Lacking these, at least in their later forms, Paul used personal influence and careful reasoning to block the great danger as it was already appearing in his day. Having reminded his readers of the central elements of the gospel (1:12–23) and defended his authority to teach and admonish his readers in light of the gospel (1:24–2:3), he now addresses the problem head on. For him, "the problem with bad ideas is that they result in distorted notions of Christ and what it means to follow him."[1]

The pattern of false teaching in question was removing Jesus Christ as sole occupant of the divine throne. The new thought was that Christ is not sufficient, not unique, only one among many manifestations of God, and that it is necessary to know and to serve other divine powers. How contemporary this sounds! It was a philosophy that was difficult for the average believer to understand. Apparently it included elements of astrology. People were assumed to be under the influence of stars, planets, and angels. Thus, people need a special knowledge beyond that of Jesus to be liberated from these influences. Since some were saying that Jesus is not the only link between the believer and God, it may be necessary to honor and even worship angels (2:18).

Paul rejects this teaching as a fundamental danger to the integrity of Christian faith. For those ancient Asians who were surrounded by a diversity of pagan religions and for we "moderns" who seem little changed in many ways, he insists that Christ is the key to all wisdom and knowledge and the source of all needed spiritual liberation. Only by being fully grounded in Jesus Christ will the Colossians or we be able to resist the allure of futile speculation and humanly devised belief systems. Some of the Colossians, however, were relying on human imagination and the **basic principles of this world** (2:8). The word *principles* (*stoicheia*) likely is better translated *elements*, referring to the classic four (earth, water, air, and fire). These were commonly considered frivolous and profane in Greek thought, misleading Christians into an ascetic lifestyle with strict injunctions against involvement with the material world that was being judged unspiritual.

According to Paul, salvation must not be thought of as something to be gained by

LIFE CHANGE

Only by being fully grounded in Jesus Christ would the Colossians or will we be able to resist the allurement of humanly devised belief systems. Given the numerous allurements surrounding believers today, how can churches better ground their members in Jesus Christ? Is it too much to say that it is as important to encourage *mature discipleship* as it is to get a person saved in the first place? Learning how to be *in* the world without being *of* it is essential for believers who hope to make a difference for Christ in the realities of our time.

what we do, but something that by sheer grace God offers in Jesus Christ. Salvation originates from who God is, not from who we are or what we do. The Jewish tradition apparently tended in the doing direction in Colosse. This tendency was a problem to the Christian community since it was being mixed with a Greek idea to form an unholy alliance. This idea loathed the human body as the seat of sin. Matter was said to be inherently evil and to be distinguished sharply from the purity of God. Many layers or grades of spiritual beings were said to exist between God and our material existence. The material must be disciplined vigorously. Degrading the body and reaching to these heavenly beings were thought essential doings of true faith. Rather than God's free grace having arrived directly in the flesh of Jesus Christ, said the false teachers, we must find our way to God through intense and dematerialized visions of a complex spiritual world.

Why was Paul so concerned about such thinking in Colosse? First, it brought into question the actual incarnation (fleshing) of God in Jesus. John elsewhere identifies as antichrist any thought that Jesus Christ had not come in the flesh (1 John 4:1–3; 2 John 7). Next, assuming that the body is inherently evil usually leads either to immorality (it matters little how one uses what is of no inherent value) or to the opposite, a rigid asceticism that denies normal satisfaction to natural physical desires. Honor is granted to the most restrictive people who think they are gaining by doing. Finally, the usual outcome is a fractured fellowship, a church with many common believers and a few who think they are the spiritually elite. To the contrary, Paul insisted that mature Christian faith is available to all (Col. 1:28) and that divisive differences among Christians have been wiped out in Jesus Christ (3:11).

How often Christians have devalued God's creation, fallen into an arid legalism, and measured spiritual maturity by a lack of "worldliness" as this was judged by the self-righteous ones. This approach usually means an excessively inward spiritual focus that undercuts significant Christian impact on public life. Paul contends that the secret is in a person, not in a philosophy. True faith centers in Jesus Christ and relationship with Him. Believers must resist all those who would **deceive you with fine-sounding arguments** (2:4). True Christian life is not primarily affirming doctrinal propositions, achieving intense spiritual visions, or gaining some specialized religious knowledge. It is knowing Jesus Christ as Lord of all, including oneself, and coming to **fullness in Christ** (2:10). This does not mean that we can "be sloppy in our thinking. . . . Right thinking [however] does not make us righteous, only the cross can do that; but right thinking—right in the sense of being hard, honest, clear, disciplined—is essential if we are going to communicate the gospel effectively to a huge segment of the world."[2]

The Colossian heresy was especially tempting to sensitive believers who wished to go on "to perfection" in their spiritual lives. It presented itself as an advanced opportunity for spiritual maturity, but it actually led to a misguided spiritual elitism. Christian believers were being wrongly urged to reach upward for a progressive "wisdom" (*sophia*) and "knowledge" (*gnosis*), to explore hidden mysteries by successive spiritual initiations until they reached their perfection (*teleiosis*). Christian baptism was said to be

 WHAT OTHERS SAY

True Christian life is not primarily affirming doctrinal propositions, achieving intense spiritual visions, or gaining some specialized religious knowledge. It is knowing and gratefully accepting Jesus Christ as Lord of all, including of oneself, and coming to maturity in Christ. Martin Luther's famous *The Freedom of a Christian* (1520) makes clear that the Christian is justified before God by grace through faith alone. The believer is completely free of any need to establish worthiness before God through ceremonial, legal, or moral works. Christians, of course, are to serve the work of Christ in this world, but without any thought of self-justification by means of such work.

only the beginning of the Christian journey; the rest of the way involved putting off material things by practicing an ascetic regimen that led to the mysterious world of the truly spiritual—attained only by a few.

Paul certainly was committed to a high level of spiritual maturity for believers, but he insisted that those who are in Christ should seek their maturing in Him, not elsewhere. All the necessary wisdom and knowledge for Christians reside in Christ and are readily available to all faithful and seeking people (2:3). Holiness is the goal, and going on to spiritual maturity is not optional. The central concerns are how one defines holiness and how one proposes to achieve the grand goal.

2. THE REAL CIRCUMCISION 2:11–12

Some in Colosse were teaching the necessity and effectiveness of certain religious practices—like the historic practice of physical circumcision—

for the mature spiritual life of Christians. Paul counters this teaching. Just as the fullness of deity dwelled bodily in Jesus, believers are to come to fullness of life **in Christ** (2:10). It is in Jesus Christ that true circumcision comes, a circumcision **done by Christ** (2:11). As one is buried in baptism, so one is raised to new life in Jesus Christ. If someone claims to be super-spiritual because of meticulous adherence to some religious practice, that believer is to be reminded that new life comes in the power of the Spirit and solely on the basis of the work of Jesus Christ on the cross (2:13–15).

For the Jews, circumcision was the traditional symbol of identity with the people covenanted with God for salvation. Paul's word to his non-Jewish readers is that access to this covenant is now open to all people who are in Jesus Christ. The word translated **putting off** in 2:11 has the sense of stripping off one's clothes. In contrast to the Jewish practice of foreskin removal, the Christian rite of passage is done by Christ who cuts off **the sinful nature** of those who are in Him. Jewish opponents to Paul's mission of converting Gentiles to Christ centered in their criticism of his not insisting that the converts become outwardly Jewish as well as inwardly Christian.

According to Paul, circumcision only becomes meaningful for a convert to Christ when that person sheds the unregenerate nature and is enabled by the grace of God to experience something of the death and resurrection of Jesus. By His cross Jesus has freed us from the demands of a law that we could never fulfill; by baptism believers are marked as the covenant people who belong to God and no longer to **the powers and authorities** (2:15). Special Christian rites like baptism have an important role to play in Christian life. Even so, Paul was concerned that in Colosse certain mandated religious practices had been invested with transformational power, thus substituting them for trust in the all-sufficient work of Christ. In fact, insists Paul, the true Jew is the one who experiences the circumcision of the heart accomplished by Christ's Spirit rather than by Judaism's "circumcision of the heart" (Rom. 2:28–29). The true Christian is the one baptized into the redemptive results and transforming power of the work of Jesus Christ.

3. THE "POWERS" ARE DETHRONED 2:13–15

Paul proceeds to show the folly of any course of action based on a wrong theological premise. Failing to hold to the full supremacy of Jesus Christ as the **Head** (2:19) is to base life on some self-made religion. Exposed as powerless are the malign forces that once were believed to control human life. These powers, whatever they are or were, have been disarmed, made a **public spectacle** (2:15), and triumphed over. Through the death, burial, resurrection, and enthronement of Jesus, victory is now achieved over sin and death (2:12–13, 3:1).

Idolatry has been a persistent problem for the people of God. Often an image is created, allowing the worshiper to assume that more direct access to God is thereby gained. One of the Ten Commandments speaks against any such images because they tend to draw worship to themselves and distort the perception of the true God. Idolatry at its core "is a religious disguise for self-centeredness. Idols are projections of the human will. They represent attempts to make God less transcendent, less elusive, less sovereign and free, more at the beck and call of human interests."[3] Paul feared for the Colossians in this regard and warned them to shy away from every alternative to direct access to God, through the Son by the Spirit. All such alternatives are exposed for what they are—nothing but dangerous diversions. The warning of Paul is much like chapter 46 of the prophet Isaiah who ridiculed the helpless "gods" of Babylon and announced on behalf of God, "To whom will you compare me or count me equal? . . . I am God, and there is no other" (Isa. 46:5, 9).

One should not think that belief in mysterious spiritual powers belongs only to the ancient world. We should heed Paul's warning against **fine-sounding** religious words (2:4) that actually are only Christless myths shaped by a secular culture. Religious fads are always alluring to a hurting and gullible public. Christian teaching and preaching should not pander to people's fears and preferences, but be Christ-centered without apology. Believers need to cultivate critical minds that can distinguish between fascinating falsehood and solid biblical teaching. Television therapists of the soul often convey popular psychologies and quasi-religious notions that attract good ratings and sell expensive products. What these people tend to do, however, and all that they can do, is push clever soothings of troubled psyches; they cannot convey the forgiving and recreating grace of God in Jesus Christ.

 KEY IDEAS

Christian teaching and preaching should not pander to people's fears and preferences, but be Christ-centered without apology. Believers need to cultivate critical minds that can distinguish between fascinating falsehood and solid biblical teaching. Here are a few fascinating falsehoods popular among today's Christians:

- Health and wealth always follow faith and faithfulness.

- The nation of one's citizenship is the special apple of God's eye.

- What one "feels" is as crucial as what one believes.

- Participation in church life is optional; "I go only where and when I feel the need and find my personal wants addressed directly."

4. STAY OUT OF REVERSE GEAR 2:16–23

Moving back into legalism is viewed by Paul as a serious reversal of the liberation gained in Jesus Christ. There are no principalities or powers that need to be placated constantly by severe self-denial. Whatever once stood against us with its legal demands has been dethroned, canceled, set aside, and nailed to the cross of Jesus (2:14). The key question posed to those tempted to slip back into reverse gear is "Why?" Why do you choose to live as if the world is still in charge? Why do you submit to mechanical and unnecessary regulations? Why are you fooled into serving things that are unable to solve the problem of self-indulgence, but in fact only give the appearance of promoting deep spirituality? Why do you voluntarily move backward into the old captivity when the forward thrust of the freeing Christ is so graciously available?

For Paul, true Christian faith is not rigorous compliance with religious rules of self-denial, but active faith in Jesus Christ and an embracing of the enabling grace found in life with Christ's Spirit (Rom. 14:13–18). Any brand of believing that features a laundry list of negatives rather than positive paths to personal transformation is as spiritually deluding as it may be attractive. The bottom line, of course, is not a devaluing of discipline in the Christian life, but a deep Pauline concern. The concern is about any kind of religious practice, good as it may be, that promotes self-righteousness and supplants Christ's central importance for human salvation. Christian faith must not bow to any legalism that offers convenient rungs in a ladder said to allow one to climb spiritually and thereby increasingly please God.

Paul is not anti-Jewish; he was himself a well-trained Jew who was rejoicing in the fulfillment of his cherished tradition through the coming of the long-expected Messiah. Even so, he was strongly opposed to any recourse to mandated Jewish practice that replaced the core conviction of Christian faith—the superiority of Jesus Christ in all things. To grow spiritually, a believer is to be constantly open to God, as God is fully revealed in Jesus Christ. Believers are to be constantly instructed, inspired, and established by the Spirit of the Christ.

No human efforts can ever attain what God already has graciously provided in Christ. While focused Christian devotion and discipline are vital indeed, they should not be understood as means of acquiring God's grace, but as means of incorporating and implementing that grace in all of life. There should be a measure of self-denial so that a believer is not shaped by the world. Having said that, it is equally important to realize that success and growth in Christian living are always because of the sheer grace of God. John Wesley taught a proper balance. Faithful attention to baptism and the Lord's Supper, for instance, provides an established means of grace, a means less for the *being* and much more for the *well being* of believers and the church. In other words, "the outward practice is never the bringer of salvation, but it does signify and is able to nourish that salvation."[4]

True Christian spirituality lies in a maturing relationship with Jesus Christ. The idea of a careful stewardship of life is certainly affirmed by Paul. What he is concerned with is the nature of religious motivation. Proper motivation roots in real character renewal in Christ and results in conduct that reaches out in love to the neighbor. Nothing created should be substituted for the Creator. Nothing that is not Christ-centered is finally effective or worthy. A veneer of spirituality is no substitute for the transforming work of Christ on the cross and the ongoing work of the

Spirit in the believer's heart. Holiness is the clear goal of Christian life and can come into being only if freed of false restraints. Mere "religion" is never adequate.[5]

Note that the liberty to which Paul refers is the opposite of license and the miserable individualism whose highest ambition is to do just what it likes. The intent of Paul's comments to the Colossians is on behalf of "the fullest, deepest and most watchful holiness. He wants his Colossian converts above all things to be holy, that is, to live a life yielded all through to their Redeemer, who is also their Master."[6] The reality has come in Christ. Ritual observances designed to "keep the flesh in subjection" may have the appearance of wisdom, but in themselves they are of little value in checking **sensual indulgence** (2:23). The goal is to live *in Christ* and thus to become *like Him*. Herein is true holiness.

ENDNOTES

1. Robert W. Wall, *Colossians and Philemon*, The IVP New Testament Commentary Series (Downers Grove, Ill.: InterVarsity Press, 1993), p. 98.

2. Maxie D. Dunnam, *The Preacher's Commentary: Galatians, Ephesians, Philippians, Colossians, Philemon* (Waco, Tex.: Word, 1982), p. 360.

3. C. Leonard Allen, *The Cruciform Church* (Abilene, Tex.: Abilene Christian University Press, 1990), p. 87.

4. Barry L. Callen, *God as Loving Grace* (Nappanee, Ind.: Evangel, 1996), p. 330.

5. See Barry L. Callen, *Authentic Spirituality: Moving Beyond Mere Religion* (Grand Rapids, Mich.: Baker Academic and Paternoster Press, 2001; Lexington, Ky.: Emeth Press, 2006).

6. Handley C. G. Moule, *Colossian Studies* (New York: Hodder and Stoughton, 1898), p. 204.

Part Four

Living in a Christian Way

COLOSSIANS 3:1–4:18

7

ESSENTIALS OF THE RISEN LIFE

Colossians 3:1–4:6

M oving beyond direct reactions to the false philosophy gaining ground in Colosse, Paul now turns to the positive alternative, a description of the authentic Christian life. He alternates between the indicative and imperative, what God has done for us and what we are to do in response to God's graciousness. Christian faith is to be inseparable from Christian behavior. The nature of the believer's behavior should be a natural, Spirit-assisted outgrowth of the substance of the believer's faith. Believers are to be raised with Christ to new life that reflects the character of God as made known in Jesus Christ.

1. RESULTS OF BEING RISEN WITH CHRIST 3:1A

The Christian way of life as presented by Paul is quite different from how many of the Colossians were viewing it. The real issue is less an insistence on mastering methods for dealing with evil powers in the world and much more actually becoming Christian in character and learning how to live the Christian life individually and corporately. Chapter 3 begins with a crucial "if." If a person is risen with Jesus Christ, then some dramatic life results should follow. The problem is not that the material world is inherently evil and, therefore, must be avoided and fought at all costs; the core problem is that a ruptured relationship with the Creator has been produced by sin, spoiling all of life. The good news is that God has provided reconciliation (1:21–23) in the Son and has made available new resources for right living through the power of Christ's resurrection (3:1–4).

Believers are to be genuinely new people who appropriate the divine resources now available; we are to be cultivating the virtues that transform relationships between husbands and wives, parents and children, employers and slaves. Resurrection with Christ is to bring God's kind of righteousness to our lives. To be newly alive in a holy God brings a holiness to life in all its dimensions. True life is to be one hidden in Christ (3:3). The hiddenness is not to imply a private spirituality lacking public consequences; it is to speak of life with a solid and secure center that is rooted in Christ. John Wesley had a remarkable ability to link personal piety with public justice, translating doctrine into daily living. For decades, he engaged in ministries of caring for the poor and imprisoned, even while he pursued a rigorous life of prayer, study, and reflection.

KEY IDEAS

In accord with the best of the Jewish tradition, wisdom goes beyond right knowledge to *skill in right living*. In the Christian context, rooted as it is in Judaism, wisdom means proper conduct worthy of Jesus Christ. Right belief is basic, but such belief, when not lived out, is virtually meaningless. Right belief must and can be lived out successfully in this world by God's grace and power. God enables us to stand confidently in the face of any circumstance. Paul told the Colossians that God had made them alive together with Christ, who, having "disarmed principalities and powers," made a public spectacle of them, triumphing over them in the cross (Col. 2:13, 15).

Paul earlier had declared that all wisdom is to be found in Christ (2:3). Now he appeals to his readers to walk in this wisdom. In accord with the best of the Jewish tradition, wisdom goes beyond right knowledge to skill in right living. In the new Christian context, wisdom is to mean proper conduct worthy of Jesus Christ (1:9–10). In the interim between the first and final comings of the Christ, the church is to live as a present signpost pointing to and embodying what human life in society is supposed to be (3:11; Gal. 3:28). Accordingly, the church in all times should assert "that God, not nations, rules the world, that the boundaries of God's kingdom transcend those of Caesar, and that the main political task of the church is the formation of people who see clearly the cost of discipleship and are willing to pay the price."[1]

The moral standards laid down by Paul are hardly new in their ethical idealisms. After all, God and the nature of creation are stable and generally recognized. What is new is the focus on moral competency. Believers actually can be "made capable by God's grace to do God's will."[2] A cardinal principle of New Testament ethics is that *being precedes doing*. A constant temptation for Christians is the subtle tendency to works righteousness. Believers too often act like they can and must earn their way into God's favor by many good deeds of Christian devotion and service. We seek to create a long record of worthy works done for Christ's sake, as though a trail of faithfulness by itself will cause God to say "well done" on the day of judgment.

According to Paul, God's grace enables a new way of being in this world that necessarily yields a new way of acting. In line with this Pauline exhortation to holiness of life, the Wesleyan tradition champions an "optimism of grace." Wayward humans can be made new creations in Christ. Through the ministry of the Spirit, the love of Christ can mature in us. The Bible calls believers to be holy even as God is holy (Lev. 11:44).

The essentials of the Christian life are laid out by Paul in three parts. First comes the foundation or root principles of the Christian way (3:1–4). Then there is an explanation of what life in Christ is *not* (3:5–11). Finally, Paul presents what Christian life *should be* within the congregation (3:12–17) and in the home (3:18–4:1).

2. ROOT PRINCIPLES OF THE CHRISTIAN WAY 3:1B–4

Christian life is based on the unrivaled supremacy of the person and work of Jesus Christ. Therefore, Paul stresses the theme of union with Christ. Jesus Christ has been raised from the dead; Christian life, therefore, is essentially being raised by Christ's Spirit to new life in the Son. Because Christ lives, we too can live! Believers are told that they should set their minds **on things above** (3:2) where the new-creation life is **hidden with Christ in God** (3:3). The "old self" is identified with the fallen humanity living under the present evil age and its powers. The "new self" made possible by God's grace is the new humanity living in the new order inaugurated by Christ's death and resurrection (3:9–10).

This most basic principle (in Christ) of Christian life has obvious association with Christian baptism. Believers have died with Christ (2:12b, 20) and now are raised with Christ (3:1). This conversion process includes entrance into the community of faith, the fellowship of those being grafted into the new order inaugurated by Christ's life, death, and resurrection.

Spiritually resurrected lives are presently hidden in heaven with Christ, but one day will be revealed in glory with Christ. We have been rescued from **the dominion of darkness** and brought into **the kingdom of the Son** (1:13). The negative reality is that there is a dominion of darkness; the good news is that light has blazed forth to disperse the darkness—and this light is the cosmic radiance of Jesus Christ. Christian life is necessarily "Christological," based on and centered in Christ, who is mentioned four times in 3:1–4. His lordship is foundational for the church's obedient response to God's will. New life in Christ, a product of God's redeeming grace, "constitutes hard evidence that the new creation that God promised through the prophets is now being fulfilled in the life and history of God's people."[3]

The phrase **in whom are hidden** (2:3) probably is prompted by the idea of secret knowledge stressed by the Colossian heresy. The false teachers were compiling their presumed wisdom in books that they called *apokruphoi*—books hidden except from especially initiated people. By using a form of this same word, Paul is saying that, for Christians, wisdom is hidden in Christ and not in any human books. The truth of the wisdom of Christ is not available to those not buried and raised with Him. It is spiritually discerned, a byproduct of life in the Spirit. The day is coming when Christ will return in glory. Then the divine wisdom will be fully known to those who **will appear with him in glory** (3:4). Human wisdom seems to make some sense now, but "some day the verdicts of eternity will reverse the verdicts of time and the judgments of God will overturn the judgments of men."[4]

Paul invites a continual seeking (Greek present tense) of the "above" things and the exercise of faith that is focused on more than the passing trivialities of this world. Believers are to pursue actively the values and lifestyle of heaven itself. All is to be judged in light of the gracious God who gave His Son for the sake of the reconciliation of all things to himself and to each other. The great questions of life in this world will not be fully answered this side of heaven. Believers are on a faith journey and much more lies ahead. We can be sure of at least this, however. What finally comes to pass will be in Christ and like Christ. One day we will know as we now are known (1 Cor. 13:12). The Christ who was Alpha will also be Omega (Rev. 22:13).

The crucial question now is *how* one gains access to the heavenly realm above. In the face of an insistence on ascetic observances as the required doorway to heaven, Paul asserts that "through God's gracious initiative the readers have already been brought into such life. It is on the basis of their union with Christ in his resurrection that they are the ones—all of them, not a special group of initiates—who can be exhorted to further their relationship to the heavenly realm."[5] The contemporary interest in the transcendent (reality beyond the present and merely material) should be directed to the distinctively Christian fostering of a relationship with the transcendent person, the risen and exalted Christ.

In focus here is the related question of how seeking the things "above" should relate to life in this present world. Focusing on gospel proclamation of the good news in Christ has key significance for the church. The point of the gospel is to shape the believing community into a functioning embodiment of Christ in the world of today. There are Christian virtues that are to be prominent and function well in order that the community of believers will be a healthy and effective witness. The list of such virtues found in 3:12–14 are those Paul considers required for harmonious community living in Christ.

The teaching in the Colossian letter does not support limiting the Christian hope to something merely individualistic and futuristic—a focus restricted to "my getting to heaven when I die." To be heavenly minded should not equate to being neglectful of earthly relationships and responsibilities. The "above" reference is intended to give Christians a divine perspective that drives them to pursue divine life and social justice here and now. In all arenas of life, God inclines one to seek what is **right**

and fair (4:1). According to Paul, when spiritual devotion is focused properly on the reigning Lord Jesus and His unique relationship to God, it becomes possible to view "earthly things" from God's compassionate perspective.

When the things above are truly seen and embraced by faith, committed believers are thereby transformed into new persons who, by Christ's Spirit, can know and do God's will in this world. To do everything **in the name of the Lord Jesus** (3:17) is to accept His lordship claims to every part of a believer's life and to accept the gift of divine love, that is the distinctive nature of the new age come in Christ. Being Christian necessarily involves being **called to peace** and allowing **the peace of Christ** [to] **rule in your hearts** (3:15). Conflict may remain in our human lives, but so does the confidence of knowing that, in the new humanity, Jesus Christ is the ever-present model, pioneer, enabler, and judge.

3. SINS ABANDONED, VIRTUES CULTIVATED 3:5–17

When God has rescued people from the kingdom of darkness and transferred them into the reign of God's triumphant Son, it is natural for them to put off vice (what contrasts with Christ) and put on virtues that reflect the mind of Christ. To embrace the truth of God in Christ is to receive God's enabling grace and be empowered to live out God's will (1:9–10). The proper response to participation in Christ's triumph and grace is to exchange the earthly for the heavenly values and norms of life. The work of divine grace is from the inside out; the privacy of the transformed heart is to be fleshed out in the public actions of the body and in the life of the church.

This logic echoes that of the Lord's Prayer: "Our Father in heaven, . . . your will be done *on earth* as it is *in heaven*" (Matt. 6:9–10, emphasis added). Typical of Paul's writings, the theological base moves to its ethical implications. The language of taking **off your old self** in 3:9 picks up the ascetic terminology of the Colossian "philosophy" (see 2:11, 15), but gives it theological roots and ethical substance. Paul calls for an end to the sinful way of life, not an end to bodily life itself by means of severe acts of self-abasement. It is not the material body itself that is the problem; it is the corrupted relationship with God that fails to use the body in the context of the Christ reality.

Following the thinking of Jesus (Matt. 5:29–30) and that of himself expressed elsewhere (Rom. 8:13), Paul here insists that a believer put to death whatever opposes the doing of God's will. The goal is true holiness of life. He gets specific by listing several actions, attitudes, and speech patterns that are idolatrous and self-serving, therefore, unholy. The Colossians are to strip themselves of all such contamination, putting off the old clothes of sin and receiving the white robes of righteousness—as Christians traditionally have done symbolically at the time of baptism and actually in the new life that follows. The "earthly" is to be put to death in the face of the arriving resurrection life in Christ.

Sexuality, for instance, is to be used for God's glory, not as a self-debasing instrument for dominating others. Today we see the tragic results of sexual perversion on a massive social scale. Paul's message remains so important. Conversion to the new age of Jesus Christ is to be obvious in a changed lifestyle flowing from God's character-creating grace. Flowery Christian words must be accompanied by corresponding changes in attitudes and actions if the world is to believe that God truly was in Jesus Christ.

Being fully Christian, however, is not to be reduced to following a detailed moral code. After all, Christ has **canceled the written code, with its regulations** (2:14). Rather, Paul lists moral virtues and immoral vices "in order to describe the effective yield of God's transforming grace in the believer's lifestyle."[6] Believers must not be enslaved to some rigid plan of self-denial in place of true devotion to Jesus Christ. Instead, love for Christ should be central and lead naturally to the proper social life of the new age of God's salvation. Life must be rooted in a relationship with Him. As was the case with many of the Colossians, too often "religion" is based mostly on human traditions that feature a wide range of spiritual beings, experiences, and regulations that are powerless to renew people in Christ's image.

Abandoned sins are to be replaced by the cultivation of Christian virtues. If 3:10 focuses primarily on individuals and the new humanity, 3:11 highlights the corporate aspect of new life in Christ. Social barriers basic to the old humanity are to be abolished. A key Christian virtue is the dropping of destructive barriers among humans, barriers that breed discrimination and hatred. Paul addresses the Colossians as **God's chosen people** (3:12), a phrase traditionally coveted by the Jews as referring to themselves alone. No longer is this form of arrogance to be tolerated. All those who are in Christ—be they Jew or Gentile, cultured or uncultured, slave or free, male or female—are truly one! It is Christ who is **in all** (3:11).

Human relationships that are guided by the mind of Christ will be humble, kind, compassionate, and patient. The destiny of God's chosen ones is to mirror the divine life (the "fruit of the Spirit"). Spiritual elitism is a misguided church sickness—a false spirituality rooted in arrogance. True holiness is the heart of the church's intended life. So is unity among believers, a natural byproduct of holiness. Denominational pride and theological labeling frequently have disrupted church fellowship and undermined the credibility of the church's witness in the world. Such human-based divisiveness should end. The Wesleyan revival of eighteenth-century England evidenced a disdaining of human distinctions that divide believers and distort mission. Within the societies formed by John Wesley, the people who were the least in the eyes of polite and established society had full dignity and an equal say. The Holiness Movement of the nineteenth century birthed fresh hope that God's people, once they were deeply rooted in the Spirit, could again be united with each other. Christ is in all and for all equally (3:11).

What, then, is the Christian way to live? Be ruled by the peace of Christ; be committed to the community of Christ where love is the way of life; be thankful, singing praise to God and doing all things in light of the Lord Jesus. Peace, love, gratitude, and singing hardly reflect dour and moralistic people whose religious convictions have narrowed them into a restrictive life that appears most unhappy. To the contrary, believers **sing psalms, hymns, and spiritual songs with gratitude in** [their] **hearts to God** (3:16). Paul says that there is to be no self-promoting piety that masquerades as faithfulness when it actually is still chained to the world. There must be genuinely new life that relates to and rejoices in the re-creating and uniting power of the risen Christ.

4. RELATIONSHIPS STRENGTHENED, DUTIES PERFORMED 3:18–4:6

The flow of the Colossian letter moves from general principles of Christian living to a discussion of how these principles are to be worked out in specific social situations. For Christians, proper behavior is to be motivated by what is **fitting in the Lord** (3:18) and what is anticipated— **you will receive an inheritance from the Lord as a reward** (3:24). What is fitting is quite different from the severe hierarchy and patriarchy of the Jewish and Roman worlds of Paul's day—although Paul's comments are conditioned to a degree by these existing structures of first-century society in which the early church first found itself.

Controlling concerns of Paul included making Christian faith relevant to all of life and countering the tendency to lax morality that some believers wrongly assumed was justified by Paul's "charter of freedom" (see Gal. 3:27–29). Now that the new age had dawned in Christ, Paul insists that all believers are equally valued regardless of social status or role. For instance, under ancient Jewish law, a woman was the possession of her husband and had few legal rights. Children and slaves faced similar situations. This is not to be so among Christians.

The Christian ethic Paul announces, by considerable contrast with the typical social practice of his time, emphasizes reciprocal obligations. The focus is on what grateful believers owe others, not what is owed to them. Christian life is not to be driven by any need to do good works in an effort to repay God for past sin. It is not an effort to keep God pleased or a way to gain an insurance policy to avoid eternal disaster after death. What should drive the life of faith is gratitude to God for the many divine gifts, including salvation itself. In 3:16 Paul calls for a life of song in the heart. Jesus came less to provide a ticket to heaven for a select number of rugged individuals and more to create a body—the church—that in peace, love, and joy will reveal in its own life in the world the redeeming God graciously active in Christ.

The emphasis of Paul on **submit** (3:18) and **obey** (3:20, 22) may reflect in part the social standards of his world. Even so, marriage for Christians is portrayed as a true *partnership*, not a relationship of control and certainly not abuse. In view is how each partner is related to the Lord and thus to each other. Human notions of submission and love must be replaced by how Jesus Christ submitted himself to God and loved sacrificially. A married man and woman are to relate to each other in ways that show forth the loving wonder of the new creation that has begun in Christ. It is significant that in 4:15 a house church in nearby Laodicea is mentioned under the name of a woman, Nympha. How like Jesus this is; how unlike the world it is.

GREAT THEME

Jesus came less to provide a ticket to heaven for a select number of rugged individuals and more to create a body—the church—that in peace, love, and joy will reveal the redeeming God who is graciously active in Christ. Richard B. Hayes (*The Moral Vision of the New Testament*, 1996) identifies the three "root metaphors" of the Christian life as found in the New Testament. Emphasizing the centrality of the distinctive life and mission of the church, they are

1. **Community:** being an alternative model of group life, a witness to the world
2. **Cross:** living the sacrificial way of Jesus through the community's life
3. **New Creation:** exhibiting the first fruits of the coming of God's future

Paul gives special attention to the master-slave relationship, possibly because of the runaway Onesimus, a circumstance so well known in the Colossian setting. Slaves are told to be conscientious in their work even as they share in the inheritance provided by God. Under Roman law, slaves could possess little or nothing, but the eternal riches brought by Jesus Christ belong to all people equally. Anyone who is a master in this life must remember that Christ is Master of all (4:1). God gives hope to all people and in Christ conveys the good news that all people have great value and will be rewarded properly.

Even as acting lovingly and justly is a Christian duty, so is prayer. Paul calls for believers to **devote yourselves to prayer** (4:2). Literally, he says to be wakeful, not to fall asleep as often happens with disciples fatigued at crucial times (Luke 9:32; Matt. 26:40). Paul asks prayer for himself, not necessarily that his imprisonment would end, but that he may have opportunity to complete his missionary calling of sharing Christ with the world. He also instructs readers about how best to share the good word of God in Christ. Often the "how" of Christian witnessing is nearly as crucial as the "what."

Opportunities for witness are to be sought. Once found, Paul counsels, it is time for wisdom, respect, and even charm. The good news about divine grace is to be shared gracefully, even with a touch of wit, and always in the context of a gratitude to God that can be infectious. Overt "evangelism," in the sense of marching for Jesus and passing out tracts on street corners, is not pressed on most believers as a primary duty. Christian disciples usually witness best by living wisely as they function responsibly in the world. Transformed lives will be observed by the public and opportunities for Christian witness will arise naturally when the witness is **seasoned with salt** (4:6). Rather than trampling on the sensibilities of nonbelievers by aggressive insistence on their attention to a message for which they may not be ready, reliance should be placed on the work of the Spirit in opening doors of conversation and loving relationships that mediate hope and faith. The goal of the Christian life is to **make the most of every opportunity** (4:5) to proclaim **the mystery of Christ** (4:3).

ENDNOTES

1. Stanley Hauerwas and William H. Willimon, *Resident Aliens: Life in the Christian Colony* (Nashville, Tenn.: Abingdon Press, 1989), pp. 28, 48.

2. Robert W. Wall, *Colossians and Philemon*, The IVP New Testament Commentary Series (Downers Grove, Ill.: InterVarsity Press, 1993), p. 128.

3. Ibid., p. 133.

4. William Barclay, *The Letters to the Philippians, Colossians, and Thessalonians*, rev. ed. (Philadelphia: Westminster Press, 1975), p. 148.

5. Andrew T. Lincoln, *The Letter to the Colossians*, The New Interpreter's Bible, vol. 11, (Nashville, Tenn.: Abingdon Press, 2000), p. 637.

6. Wall, *Colossians*, 139.

JOYS ON THE JOURNEY OF FAITH

Colossians 4:7–18

The Christian life is a journey and the trip is not meant to be taken alone. Reflecting its Hebrew heritage, Christianity centers in Jesus Christ and a called community—the people chosen by God to be faithful to God's purposes and standards. God's people, now chosen in Christ, are a special treasure of God and are intended to be a redemptive witness to the good news of Christ. There are both wonderful joys and distracting dangers as the people of God journey together by faith.

In the Colossian letter, Paul is prominent as an exemplary Christian witness. Made clear, however, in 1:5–8 is that many witnesses were already carrying the gospel of Christ effectively to widening circles of people. Paul was the called apostle, the special one being sent by God, but he also was only one faithful brother among numerous others. His apostleship was on behalf of the whole people of God and was reliant on the faithfulness of others. The success of the gospel of Jesus depends on far more than "superstars" like Paul; the church sky must be full of lights, the majority of which appear to most eyes as only little dots in the big sky. In fact, there are no little dots, only disciples called to be faithful to their own particular missions.

The Colossian believers had learned about the gospel of Jesus Christ from Epaphras and likely from other teachers whose names remain unrecorded. All were crucial, whether or not they became well known. The vitality of the first Christian churches was nurtured by a network of personal friendships that knit people closely together. Sometimes these relationships were loving, sometimes stormy, but always they were infused by the uniting love and grace of God in Christ. Many of the teachers were reliable. Paul has insisted, however, that some of them were not. The faith journey of the church is sometimes marked by dangerous detours and, unfortunately, undependable leaders.

Paul capitalizes on the power of personal witness and experience. Personal testimony is encouraging to the larger body of believers and is an especially effective means of witness to God's life-changing grace. For instance, for many years I have taught college courses in Christian theology in a way that emphasizes the actual life circumstances of prominent theologians. The point is that one can learn much about complex theological writings if the actual life and faith experience of their authors are known. Such has been the case from the beginning of church history. The good vine is known best by its good fruit.

According to Paul, Tychicus was acting as a personal envoy of his and would tell the Colossians many things about Paul that were not contained in the relatively short letter itself. Much necessarily was left to word of mouth and the modeling of actual life reported and observed. So it always is. Believers on the faith journey must tell about their life-changing experiences of the amazing grace of God and exhibit actively the fruit of those experiences.

1. COMPANIONS ON THE JOURNEY 4:7–17

In Paul's several letters now found in the New Testament, he mentions at least fourteen fellow workers, four fellow prisoners, two fellow slaves, two soldiers, and one yokefellow. It was clear to Paul that, regardless of its special prominence, his was no solo ministry. The journey of Christian life and ministry is to be a team effort. Valued companions on the faith journey are indispensable. The heroes of the faith, mostly unsung and now unknown, are celebrated appropriately by Paul. The fact is that "on the ship of the church there are no passengers; all are members of the crew. The church is not a trumpet corps, but an orchestra."[1]

The final greeting to the Colossians includes brief notes about a small list of names, unheralded examples of Christian faith. Note this summary of the circumstances of the composition of the Colossian letter: "Paul was in prison awaiting trial and it is always dangerous to be a prisoner's friend, for it is so easy to become involved in the same fate as the prisoner himself. It took courage to visit Paul in his imprisonment and to show that one was on the same side."[2] Nonetheless, a cluster of colleagues in the ministry of Christ was in Rome with Paul and he identifies them briefly for the Colossian readers. He proceeds to name six, three of Jewish and three of Gentile birth, a balanced picture of Paul's own mission as a serious Jew called particularly to proclaim the good news of the Jewish Messiah to the larger Gentile world.

The list of recognitions begins with **Tychicus . . . a dear brother** (4:7) who would be carrying more news about Paul. Then there was **Onesimus**, the slave who now was **our faithful and dear brother who is one of you** (4:9). Next came **my fellow prisoner Aristarchus** (4:10). This reference to imprisonment probably was to be taken literally—he was a slave of Christ now paying the public penalty. **Jesus . . . Justus** also is named, with Paul noting that Aristarchus, Mark, and Jesus (Justus) were **the only Jews among my fellow workers** (4:11). Mark's name is highlighted especially. The Colossians are instructed to **welcome him**, but there is the accompanying caution, **if he comes to you** (4:10).

Mark's relationship with Paul had been troubled years earlier by his defection from a missionary tour of Paul's (Acts 13:5, 13). Thus, there still was the possibility that Mark would fail again in following through as intended. While confidence in him had been restored in Paul's eyes, Mark still needed support in facing some believers in Colosse who may have remained suspicious and doubtful about him. Later, as a good sign of full restoration, Mark is connected warmly with Paul (2 Tim. 4:11). Like those in Colosse who had been misled by false teaching, grace redeems and the glory of Christ can return anyone to usefulness in the life of the church.

Others mentioned by Paul include **Epaphras, who is one of you** (4:12), someone well known to the Colossians and especially commended at length by Paul—presumably because the circumstance in Colosse required such emphasis. Epaphras knew best the destructive nature of the false teaching then spreading in Colosse. This good brother had prayed earnestly that the believers there **may stand firm in all the will of God** (4:12).

The reference in 4:12 to the goal of Christian endurance and maturity touched on a key issue in Colosse. The false teachers were encouraging a path to spiritual growth other than through Christ alone. This unacceptable alternative was judged by Paul to be a dangerous path through their **deceptive philosophy** (2:8) with its ascetic practices, visionary experiences, and special revelations. The details vary over time, of course, but this kind of dangerous distraction persists in the church to this day.

Next to be identified by Paul is **Luke, the doctor** (4:14), likely Paul's personal physician in prison and author of the Luke-Acts narrative so central in the New Testament. Finally named is **Demas**, who is honored by Paul without comment, although someone later falling from the faith or at least leaving Paul's service for other interests at an inopportune time (2 Tim. 4:10).

How interesting it would be to listen in on a meeting of Christian mission strategy called by prisoner Paul and including all his valued companions in one room at the same time! The church is always made up of a wide range of people, each with differing gifts and on an individual faith journey with its occasional failures and frequent joys. These disciples from long ago and those we know personally today are precious companions on the journey of faith—despite their inevitable limitations.

Verses 15–17 focus on the individuals who were sending greetings to the Colossians from Rome and note briefly some messages intended for recipients beyond Colosse. The believers in neighboring Laodicea are to be saluted, especially **Nympha** in whose home the church there apparently met. **Archippus** is to be reminded to fulfill his ministry—some well-meaning disciples are not necessarily self-starters. Letters of Paul to these two churches are to be exchanged for mutual edification (the letter to Laodicea has not survived).

Paul was surrounded by key colleagues, a circumstance highlighting the diverse and interactive nature of the church. In fact, in a letter that features teaching about the church as the body of Christ, deals with the cosmic scope of Christ's person and work, and explores the crucial implications of the resurrected Christ for the present lives of believers, the ending of Colossians provides an appropriate reminder. The church is always made up of particular individuals and dependent on supportive social networks of people who are being changed by the grace of God and carrying the good news of this grace into the world. This view of church life reinforces a central thrust of the Colossian letter. A right relationship to the exalted Christ actively resists a spurious otherworldliness and features engagement in and through human relationships and structures of life in the world. What believers need is grace for the ordinariness of life, for their relationships with each other, and for their witness in the midst of the realities of the world.

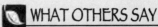 **WHAT OTHERS SAY**

What believers need is grace for the ordinariness of life, for their relationships with each other, and for their witness in the midst of the realities of the world as it is. Recognizing the need for the Spirit of Jesus Christ, Barry L. Callen suggests that we should pray this prayer:

> Come, Holy Spirit of God!
> Come: To consume all sin that may exist among us.
> Come: To convert us to the will and way of Christ.
> Come: To gift us with yourself and whatever gifts of service we need.
> Come: To consecrate us to the mission of God's church in this needy world.

2. SYNAGOGUE AND CHURCH

A significant part of the problem in Colosse was the inappropriate use of Jewish tradition in relation to Christian life. Therefore, it is significant that three of the faithful believers who sent their greetings along with Paul's are identified as Jewish Christians. Paul speaks of these three with great appreciation (4:11). Although feeling keenly about his own growing alienation from the traditional Jewish community, elsewhere he speaks harshly about "Judaizers" who in fact come in a different spirit and preach a different Jesus (2 Cor. 11:4). If now-outmoded aspects of the Hebrew tradition are to be insisted upon for all believers in Christ, Paul realized that the growing church was in real trouble as it spread across the largely non-Jewish world. On the other hand, for the new faith to foster a sharp separation from its Hebrew roots and adopt Gentile attitudes toward truth would be an equal tragedy, one that actually happened and for centuries has led to doctrinal debate and unintentionally even encouraged brutal anti-Semitism.[3]

The three Jewish-Christian men with Paul, however, had been a wonderful support to him. The original word for comfort is an unusual Greek medical term from which English derives *paregoric* for relief of pain. We should not be surprised at Paul's use of this word since Doctor Luke was with him in Rome. Christian service in this troubled world can bring pain; brothers and sisters in the faith are to serve side by side and bring relief to each other.

There certainly was pain being experienced in the Colossian congregation. There was a growing rift between synagogue and church and among members in the church who had contrasting Gentile and Jewish backgrounds (Acts 15:1–4; 21:17–26; Gal. 2:1–3:5). Unfortunately, this pain would increase over the centuries as these two faith communities, both rooted so deeply in the Abraham-Moses-David tradition, would clash often. In fact, in the twentieth century, a "Christian" nation, Nazi Germany, would seek to exterminate the Jewish community altogether! Christians must rediscover their Jewish roots in order to fully understand and properly celebrate their Jewish Messiah.

Paul was well aware that the Hebrew Scriptures were read openly in synagogue services, signifying to Jewish worshipers their enduring authority for the gathered people of God. In a similar way in the earliest Christian congregations, only material highly revered was read in public (4:16). It is noteworthy, then, that Paul directs that his own letter to the Colossian believers be read in public. He is claiming for the letter a divine inspiration and authority (compare 1 Cor. 2:12–13). There would be much more health in the Christian community today if the biblical material, so revered over the centuries, were read more and honored with seriousness as truly from the heart of God. Since the facts are that our lives are busy and many believers read so little, it is especially crucial that church leaders feature the public reading of the Bible in worship services. Honoring the Word of God is basic to being the people of God.

3. BLESSINGS FOR THE ROAD 4:18

Only a few things remained to be said to the Colossians. Paul wanted it to be clear that he wrote the final greeting **in my own hand** (4:18). To take the stylus from Timothy (the likely scribe) and sign his own name was a way for Paul to authenticate the letter and make a final appeal for his teaching and warnings to be taken seriously by the readers. Paul had to reckon with potential forgeries of his letters (2 Thess. 2:2) and may have worried that his teaching opponents in Colosse would discredit this letter by claiming it was not really from him. The fact is that the early Christian community soon came to know and treasure this Colossian letter as having continuing significance for instructing in Christian faith and practice—a sure mark of assumed divine inspiration of its writing.

It is quite possible that Paul was chained to a guarding soldier and literally had to pull his chains across the table to write these last words. The deliberate mention of his chains (4:18) is not mere sentiment and dramatics on his part, not merely a subtle play for sympathy. Paul "holds up his manacled wrists to impress the readers with his authority as a suffering apostle."[4] As his readers think of him enduring the hardship of prison, however, he did not want them to think of a pathetic and lonely man, but of a bold and faithful man of God "who makes good his calling to lead the church into the truth of the Lord Jesus through obedient imitation of the suffering Lord of glory."[5]

Paul had chained himself to Jesus Christ (Eph. 6:20). Quite apart from whether or not he actually wore hand chains as he signed this present letter, reference to chains was an effective rhetorical flourish, like in Galatians 6:17 where he mentions carrying the marks of Jesus branded in his body. Christian discipleship is serious business; obedience to the truth can be a costly thing. Those who pay the price thereby earn the right to speak—and speak they must, both to share the good news of Christ and to protect the integrity of this grand message from doctrinal perversion.

To be well heard, advises Paul, the Christian evangelist must **be wise** in relating to those outside the faith (4:5–6). The *medium* of communication must not overwhelm and even change the *message*. It is the sad fact that immature Christians often hurt the message of Jesus Christ by their own poor manner of communication and their inconsistent modeling of the life called for by Christ. While style must be chosen carefully and be compatible with the message, it also is true that substance without style usually fails to convince non-Christians. Unbelievers frequently justify their unbelief by reference to the faults of the Christians they know.

Lifeless words, tired slogans, and witnesses not themselves obviously made new by God's grace can be highly ineffective in their evangelistic efforts. Paul points proudly to Tychicus and Epaphras as good models of wise and effective Christian communication. The pathos of an evangelist in chains for Christ certainly models a man prepared to live convincingly the message he sends in writing. His communication was both significant and influential.

This Colossian letter concludes with heartfelt praise of the God who is faithful in all circumstances. Thus, typical of Paul, the final note is one of celebrating divine grace. What was proving sufficient for Paul's needs, even in prison, is surely adequate for all who truly believe in the all-sufficient Christ! The letter ends much as it began—**grace be with you** (4:18). Paul's deep desire is that the Colossians apprehend more fully the wonderful grace of God in which they stand. He finishes his letter tenderly, with words about God's unmerited love, the love by which the church in Colosse lived and by which all people can live if they will receive God's grace in faith, gratitude, and obedience.

 LIFE CHANGE

While the letter to the Colossians has specific reference to concerns at that time, the relevance of the issues addressed and teaching offered extends beyond any one locality or time. The work of God offers the potential of immediate application today. As you listen to the Spirit's voice, what in the Colossian letter requires change in your present life? Are you prepared for this change to be made? How can you come to know what the Spirit is saying? Refer to the graphic, often called the Wesleyan Quadrilateral. Note that the Bible is foundational and the work of God's Spirit seeks to infuse the whole process of believers interpreting Scripture with their reason, experience, and traditions.

Paul directs that this letter to Colosse be passed along and also read to the assembled congregation in Laodicea (4:16). While the letter has specific reference to concerns about the Colossian church, the relevance of the issues addressed and teaching offered

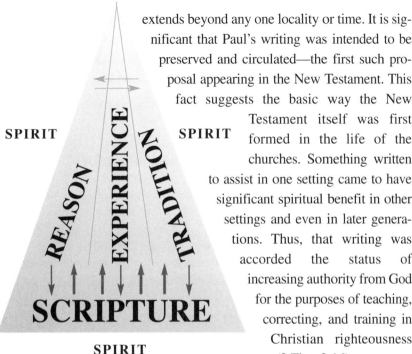

SPIRIT   **SPIRIT**

REASON   EXPERIENCE   TRADITION

SCRIPTURE

SPIRIT

**The Wesleyan "Quadrilateral:"
An Interactive Pattern of Authority
in Christian Faith**

extends beyond any one locality or time. It is significant that Paul's writing was intended to be preserved and circulated—the first such proposal appearing in the New Testament. This fact suggests the basic way the New Testament itself was first formed in the life of the churches. Something written to assist in one setting came to have significant spiritual benefit in other settings and even in later generations. Thus, that writing was accorded the status of increasing authority from God for the purposes of teaching, correcting, and training in Christian righteousness (2 Tim. 3:16).

The letter to the Colossians is an enduring word from the Spirit of God about the Christ and His central and unrivaled position in Christian thought and practice. As such, this letter is universal and timeless for believers in Jesus Christ. It resists vigorously any false alternatives to the good news of God in Jesus. All wisdom is to be found in the Christ; all sufficiency for spiritual life lies in the rich resources of Christ that now are available through the ministry of Christ's Spirit.

The letter closes as it began, celebrating God's grace. The grace of God in Christ has opened a new possibility for human life. It is not what *we do* to earn divine approval; it is what *God has done* in loving grace in the person and work of the Son. Charles Wesley has expressed so well the joy, salvation, and spiritual liberation to be found only in Jesus Christ:

> Long my imprisoned spirit lay,
> Fast bound in sin and nature's night;

> Thine eye diffused a quickening ray,
> I woke, the dungeon flamed with light:
> My chains fell off, my heart was free,
> I rose, went forth, and followed thee.

ENDNOTES

What Others Say Sidebar: Barry L. Callen, *Authentic Spirituality* (Grand Rapids, Mich.: Baker Academic, 2001; Lexington, Ky.: Emeth Press, 2006), p. 52.

1. Maxie D. Dunnam, *The Preacher's Commentary: Galatians, Ephesians, Philippians, Colossians, Philemon* (Waco, Tex.: Word, 1982), p. 396.

2. William Barclay, *The Letters to the Philippians, Colossians, and Thessalonians*, rev. ed. (Philadelphia: Westminster Press, 1975), p. 168.

3. For good perspective, consult Marvin R. Wilson, *Our Father Abraham: Jewish Roots of the Christian Faith* (Grand Rapids, Mich.: William B. Eerdmans, 1989).

4. Ralph P. Martin, *Ephesians, Colossians, and Philemon*, Interpretation: A Bible Commentary for Teaching and Preaching (Louisville, Ky.: John Knox Press, 1991), p. 132.

5. Thomas L. Trevethan, *Our Joyful Confidence: The Lordship of Jesus in Colossians* (Downers Grove, Ill. : InterVarsity Press, 1981), p. 162.

6. This is verse 3 of Charles Wesley's hymn, "And Can It Be" as in *Hymns of Faith and Life* (Marion, Ind.: The Wesley Press), no. 273.